Fernando Jiménez Cavieres

Chilean Housing Policy

HABITAT – INTERNATIONAL

Schriften der Habitat Unit
Fakultät VI Planen Bauen Umwelt
Technische Universität Berlin

herausgegeben von

Prof. Dr. Peter Herrle

Band 8

LIT

Fernando Jiménez Cavieres

Chilean Housing Policy

A Case of Social and Spatial Exclusion

LIT

Gestaltung des Covers: www.fumagi.de

Der Druck dieser Arbeit wurde durch die finanzielle Unterstützung des KAAD ermöglicht.

D 83

Bibliographic information published by the Deutsche Nationalbibliothek
The Deutsche Nationalbibliothek lists this publication in the Deutsche Nationalbibliografie; detailed bibliographic data are available in the Internet at http://dnb.d-nb.de.

ISBN 978-3-8258-9874-8
Zugl.: Berlin, TU, Diss., 2005

A catalogue record for this book is available from the British Library

Auslieferung/Verlagskontakt:
Fresnostr. 2 48159 Münster
Tel. +49 (0)251–62 03 20 Fax +49 (0)251–23 19 72
e-Mail: lit@lit-verlag.de http://www.lit-verlag.de

Distributed in the UK by: Global Book Marketing, 99B Wallis Rd, London, E9 5LN
Phone: +44 (0) 20 8533 5800 – Fax: +44 (0) 1600 775 663
http://www.centralbooks.co.uk/acatalog/search.html

Distributed in North America by:

Transaction Publishers
New Brunswick (U.S.A.) and London (U.K.)

Transaction Publishers
Rutgers University
35 Berrue Circle
Piscataway, NJ 08854

Phone: +1 (732) 445 - 2280
Fax: + 1 (732) 445 - 3138
for orders (U. S. only):
toll free (888) 999 - 6778
e-mail:
orders@transactionspub.com

Acknowledgements

This work is the result of a long process that I could not have gone through without the support of many people and institutions. Therefore, at this moment, I would like to thank everyone who in one way or another has helped to make this work possible. However, a complete account for it would be endless. I would also emphasise that I alone am responsible for the results. Friends and colleagues in Santiago, Stuttgart, Wuppertal and Berlin encouraged me in the beginning and throughout the entire process. I am incommensurably grateful to all of them. I particularly want to thank my colleagues Ana Sugranyes and Maria Elena Ducci who were not only a source of information but also a reference for important discussions.

I owe special gratitude to my main intellectual creditor during this four-year period, Professor Dr. Peter Herrle at the Technische Universität Berlin, who not only believed in my research project and helped me to organise my, usually, chaotic ideas, but also because his "humane" support encouraged me to continue and conclude this work. I am really thankful also to my second adviser, Professor Dr. Adrian Atkinson who enthusiastically accepted to support me and to evaluate my work.

I also owe thanks to various institutions. I have not forgotten any one of the people behind them, and wish to thank them all. I am particularly grateful to the Katholischer Akademischer Ausländer-Dienst, KAAD, which not only provided me with financial means through a scholarship, but also with the moral support to reach my aims. I would like to pronounce my particular recognition and thanks toward Thomas Krüggeler and Renate Flügel who were my main "visible" KAAD supporters.

I would also like to thank Martin Romünder of the Katholische Studenten Gemeinde, KSG, "Thomas Morus", in Berlin, who also believed in my project and not only helped me to receive a scholarship from the KAAD, but also became a friend who accompanied me throughout this long process. I also owe recognition to many other institutions that made my research possible such as the MINVU, the municipalities of Puente Alto, La Pintana and Macul, among others.

Last but not least, I would like to dedicate this work to my family who, in spite of our physical distance, accompanied and supported me constantly. I am particularly grateful to my parents. Sadly, my father died two years ago and will not be able to share this moment.

Berlin, August 2004

Table of Contents

List of Figures

Maps

Boxes

Allegados: 'Drop-ins' or people who have to share a home, usually with their relatives, under overcrowded conditions.

Barrios: Neighbourhoods

Blocks: Estates or flat-buildings

Caja de la Habitación Popular: "Savings Bank for popular housing"

Callampas: Shantytowns were called *Callampas*, which is the Spanish word for mushroom, because they used to appear overnight.

Camino de Cintura: First ring-road

CASEN: Acronym for *"caracterización económica y social"*. A socio-economic characterisation survey periodically implemented by the Ministry for Planning MIDEPLAN

Comuna: Districts or boroughs

Consejo de la Habitacion Popular: Workers' Housing Council

Consejo Superior del Bienestar: Welfare's Superior Council

Conventillos: Is derived from the word *"convento"* which means "convent" and it is used to describe a type of dwelling that is usually small and overcrowded.

CORHABIT: Habitat Corporation

CORMU: Urban Improvement Corporation

Corporación de Auxilio y Reconstrucción: Aid and reconstruction corporation

Corporación de Fomento de la Producción: Development and Production Corporation

CORVI: Housing Corporation

Enclaves: Residential areas where people choose to live apart from others

Estates: block of flats or apartment buildings

Exclusion "through" housing: A phenomenon that combines spatial and social aspects. It occurs when people are housed in inadequate dwellings -overcrowded and sub-standard-, and they are involuntarily concentrated in locales that not only prevent access to goods and services, but also concentrate more people with the same problems -unskilled, unemployed, etc. -. Exclusion through housing also highlights the role of housing and the neighbourhood in shaping outcomes such as health problems, low education attainment, and delinquency, as well as other "intangibles" such as depreciated identity, low self-esteem and lack of a sense of belonging.

Ficha CAS: Is administered by the municipalities and consists of a concise questionnaire that provides detailed information on the socio-economic situation of the household and their living conditions (type of dwelling, number of people in the house, assets held by the family, etc.).

Fondo Concursable Para Proyectos Habitacionales Solidarios: Contestable fund for solidary housing projects

Ghettos: Residential areas that people did not choose to live in and are apart from others

Indios: offensive word to name native indigenous
INVI: Housing Institute for Research in affiliation with the University of Chile (*Instituto de La Vivienda de la Universidad de Chile*)

Ley de copropiedad horizontal: Estates cohabitation law -the legal instrument that regulates this type of housing.

MIDEPLAN: Ministry for National Planning (*Ministerio de Planificación Nacional*)

Ministerio de Educación: Ministry of Education

Ministerio del Trabajo: Ministry of Employment

MINVU: Ministry of Housing and Urban Affairs (*Ministerio de la Vivienda y Urbanismo*)

OGUC: General Ordinance for Urbanisation and Construction (*Ordenanza General de Urbanización y Construcción*)

Operación Sitio: Plot or site operation -a system to provide an urbanised plot of land for low-income families

Operación Tiza: Chalk Operation. Similar to the *Operación Sitio* but less urbanised

Partitioned city: Marcuse and van Kempen (2002) use the word "partition" to explain the current fragmentation of urban spaces which seems -for these authors- more adequate than dualization or polarisation because cities usually are not divided just into two parts.

Plan Regulador: Regulatory plan -the planning instrument for districts and cities

Poblaciones: *"Población"* is the name that Chileans assign to every housing development that contains a repetitive typology and has been built either directly or indirectly by the government. Some authors also use this term as a synonym for "slum". Residents prefer the term *"Villa"*

PRIS: Inter-Borough Regulatory plan for Santiago's metropolitan area

Programa Chile Barrio: Chile Neighbourhood Programme -a holistic programme for slum or shantytown upgrading

Programa de autoconstrucción y ayuda mutua: Self-help for Construction and Mutual aid Programme.

Programa de equipamiento comunitario: Community "equipment" programme: the governmental programme that finances social infrastructure and social facilities to low-income neighbourhoods

Programa de Parques Urbanos: Urban parks programme -implements parks and green areas throughout the whole city

Programa de Pavimentación Participativa: Participatory pavement programmes -finances road paving in low-income districts

Programa de Subsidio General Unificado, SGU: General unified subsidy programme. It provides housing subsidies for middle and middle-low income families

Programa de Subsidio Rural, PSR: Rural housing subsidy -provides housing subsidies for families living in rural or isolated settlements.

Programa de Vivienda Básica, PVB: Basic housing programme -provides housing subsidies for low income families usually to acquire a flat or single-housing

Programa de Vivienda Progresiva, PVP: Progressive housing programme -provides housing subsidies for low income families and is a site-and-service scheme (land, urbanisation and a sanitary unit -bathroom and kitchen-)

Abstract

The main hypotheses underlying this work are that current Chilean housing policy has contributed to processes of social and spatial exclusion, and that the phenomenon of "exclusion through housing" can also take place in Chile. Current Chilean housing policy is widely known for its success in providing affordable dwellings for most of the population, and therefore, even promoted by international agencies such as the World Bank as a system to be copied by other countries in the "south". Nevertheless, its quantitative approach has disregarded its hand in creating social outcomes such as health problems, low education attainment, and delinquency, as well as other "intangibles" such as depreciated identity, low-self-esteem and lack of sense of belonging, among others.

The principal assumption is that urban inequalities hamper social integration because they prevent the equal access to urban opportunities for all citizens. In other words, part of the population is "excluded" from having equal access to economic, cultural or institutional privileges and benefits, goods and rights that are supposed to be recognised as "universal" in a society. This exclusion, on the other hand, is represented in the housing arena by the concept of "exclusion through housing".

Yet, The main aim of this work is to explore the extent to which current Chilean housing policy affects urban spatial and social inequalities and, in particular, to find out whether the phenomenon of exclusion through housing has also taken place in the Chilean case. The main problems addressed by this study are the early physical and social decay of complete neighbourhoods, as well as the lack of policies aiming to upgrade these areas; with particular emphasis on neighbourhoods with three to four-storey estates that have been a result of the *"Programa de Vivienda Básica"* in the city of Santiago.

To tackle these problems interpretative and analytical approaches are used. While the interpretative approach aims to understand which factors have determined the structure of the Chilean housing model, the analytical approach pursues to closely observe its impacts, results and its prospects of improvement. Therefore, besides the revision of relevant literature and the development of a conceptual framework, this work confers special attention to both the interpretation of historical policies and the analysis of a concrete case study carried out in the city of Santiago, in three compounds of estates.

The theoretical framework aims at developing parameters to interpret and analyse social and spatial exclusion in Chile, which can be applied methodologically through combined approaches. A first approach aims at reviewing the historical patterns of public interventions through housing policies in the city of Santiago in order to interpret the shifts in paradigms and the roots of social and spatial exclusion. A second approach is to analyse current housing policy and its implementation in the city of Santiago through the development and use of diverse indicators such access to infrastructure, distribution of poverty and physical aspects, among others. The third and final approach aims at closely observing and comparing three case studies located in districts that should present both differences and similarities. The analysis of these cases studies aims at evaluating both the factors that creates social and spatial exclusion as well as the possible main outcomes. As a result of this discussion and analysis, the main conclusions are presented as well as some interpretations and new insights.

PART I

Chapter 1: Introduction

1.1 Genesis and Motivation of the Research

> *"Una ciudad quiero tener para todos construida y que alimente a quien la quiera habitar"* [(1)].

Cities evolve towards social and spatial inequality. Everywhere the winners of globalisation build their protected *enclaves* as far away as possible from the *ghettos* to which the losers are confined. The extent of these generalisations seems, at least, incomplete. Are governments powerless before global changes?

This work assumes that tendencies of globalisation are not the only factors that affect social and spatial inequalities; particular socio-historical processes and their translation into determined governmental policies also have a major role. Moreover, some policies aimed at reducing poverty can also generate new inequalities, and this work intends to prove that this is the case of current Chilean housing policy.

Nowadays, inequality and segregation seem to be global problems. As a matter of fact, in the last decade several studies have shown evidences that in cities across the world the globalisation phenomenon has sharpened former degrees of social inequality and spatial segregation (Sassen, 1994; Borja and Castells, 1997; Wacquant, 2002).

Economic restructuring, deindustrialisation, income polarisation, and tertiarisation processes are usually identified as *"global"* causal factors behind what some authors have called *"polarised"* or *"dual cities"* (Häußermann, et al., 2001; Musterd and Murie, 2001). As a result of this tendency, cities are showing spatial contrasts.

While some parts of the cities are fully "connected" to the world and show a "cosmopolitan" face, other areas are either left to decay and/or have begun to concentrate ghettos of low-income families whose multiple social problems restrict their chances to "enjoy" the benefits of "modernisation". These families are *"socially excluded"*.

Nevertheless, it has become apparent that the urban problems mentioned above are neither exclusively caused by tendencies of globalisation nor exclusively related to governmental neglect (Marcuse and van Kempen, 2002). For example, many European countries such as

---

(1) From the song "A mi Ciudad", Santiago del Nuevo Extremo early 1980`s - Author translation: "the city I want to have, is a city built for all, and that feeds who wants to inhabit it".

Germany, Britain, The Netherlands and France are showing a renewed interest in policies to combat *"social exclusion"* and to promote *"social integration"* including direct actions on deprived areas and neighbourhoods that are concentrating the *"socially excluded"* (Madanipour, et al 1998).

However, not all the European cities present the same level of social exclusion; depending on different historical, cultural, and political processes, deprived neighbourhoods differ qualitatively in Europe (Musterd and Murie, 2001). Therefore, the role of governments, the particular socio-historical patterns of development and the type of policies applied in every country are also relevant factors to understand processes of social exclusion in cities.

But the role of governmental policies in social exclusion or in inclusion and its relation to urban transformation has been scarcely studied in Chile and Latin America (Schteingart, 2000; Rodriguez, 2001) . One exception to this pattern of research are studies about land policies and their relation to social and spatial segregation (Sabatini, 1999). In spite of a renewed interest in socio-spatial problems, most of the Latin American urban research has been concentrated on the socio-economic diagnosis of problems and on the lack of governmental policies devoted to combat urban inequalities (Valladares and Prates, 1994; Ziccardi, 2000; Stren, 2001).

While the main preoccupation in European countries is the augmenting contrast between regions, as well as increasing social inequalities within cities, and social policies pursue to counteract this tendency, countries like Chile are still trying to cope with poverty and basic needs through quantitative approaches, sometimes disregarding the qualitative social and spatial effects of the responses. The latter is, therefore, one of the main allegations of this work: some policies aimed at reducing inequalities can produce new inequalities. What this work wishes to focus on is one national policy in particular and its role in creating social and spatial inequalities: the current Chilean housing policy.

1.2 Framing the Problem

For almost three decades now, Chilean government has been implementing an "effective" housing policy aimed at supplying its population with the basic needs of shelter and infrastructure. This policy is widely known for its success in providing affordable dwellings for most of the Chilean population, and therefore, even promoted by international agencies such as the World Bank as a system to be copied by other countries in the "south" (Gilbert, 2001:10).

The fact that today most of the urban poor have access to basic infrastructure and services is evidence of its success (Ducci, 1997). Moreover, land tenure has been almost completely regularised, and new constructions have exceeded the required level as a result of household growth and replacement of obsolete structures (Sabatini, 1999; Rojas, 1999:3) [(2)]. Furthermore, the number of illegal land invasions in the last decades is almost negligible when compared with the past.

However, Chilean housing policies have a "dark side" (Ducci,1997), and many signals show that this "successful" housing policy is also reinforcing "social exclusion" and the partitioning of the city according to social class. Santiago de Chile, and increasingly also other cities in the country, is showing an expansion of residential segregation and spatial disintegration (Sabatini, 1999; Rodriguez and Winchester, 2001; Fischer, 2003).

Even though these facts could appear to be normal historical features of Latin American cities, one of the objectives of this work is to find evidence of the role played by current Chilean housing policies in exacerbating these urban problems.

Thus, the main hypothesis underlying this work is that current Chilean housing policy has contributed to processes of social and spatial exclusion, and therefore, it leads to the formalisation of new inequalities. This concern is accompanied by the assumption that urban inequalities hamper social integration because they prevent the equal access to urban opportunities for all citizens, and bringing people the opportunity to upgrade their environments could play an important role in the construction of a more inclusive society.

The main question that guides this work is, therefore: has current Chilean housing policy actually produced social and spatial inequalities? Or more specifically: does it lead current housing policies to a process of *social exclusion 'through' housing?* The particular problems this study deals with, are the early decay of complete neighbourhoods of social housing and its relation to the phenomenon of social exclusion, as well as the lack of policies aiming at upgrading these areas. Furthermore, this work focuses on specific case studies: compounds with three to four-storey estates erected through the *"Programa de Vivienda Básica"* built in the city of Santiago.

---

(2) *"Government estimates suggest that by 1994, 82,000 dwellings were required each year to accommodate new families and to account for the obsolescence of the housing stock (McDonald, 1994). The target level of 100,000 new units per year has been surpassed during the last six years. Recent estimates indicate that in 1998, the nation's 14.8 million inhabitants occupied 4.05 million dwellings, a ratio of about 3.7 people per dwelling, a significant improvement over 1992 Census figures of 4.1 persons per dwelling"* (Rojas, 1999:12).

Even though the main focus is on current Chilean housing policy, only in one city and on one particular type of housing, it also takes stance within the global discussion about increasing inequalities in cities. This aim is based on the assumption that in our "globalised" world, national and local experiences are usually references for other contexts: we can learn from others and others can learn from us. However, these references might give not only examples of "best" practices -such as those spread worldwide by international agencies- but also should serve to highlight failures and, therefore, be used to prevent misconceptions in other contexts. In other words: the "wrongs" of Chilean housing policy should also be divulged.

The second hypothesis of this work is that social exclusion -in particular exclusion *'through'* housing- is not only an emergent phenomenon in "developed" countries in the "north" but can also be the "unexpected" result of certain housing schemes used in the "south" such as current Chilean housing policy. Therefore, this work also pursues to include a revision of the current experiences in some "developed" countries, especially regarding the development of concepts and the operation of upgrading policies focused on social integration.

This work pursues the following objectives:

- A discussion of the relationship between housing and social exclusion through the analysis of current international academic debates and concrete programmes applied to "regenerate" and integrate deprived neighbourhoods.
- The definition of parameters or "yardsticks" to analyse social and spatial exclusion in the Chilean case.
- The analysis of the role of social housing policies in sharpening existing (historical) inequalities in Chile, both in physical and social terms.
- The development and use of quantitative and qualitative indicators to "measure" the phenomenon of exclusion through housing in selected case studies in Santiago.

Besides the interest in analysing this concrete situation, there lies a social concern that can be summarised in a simple question: are housing policies exacerbating social and spatial exclusion? can they facilitate people's access to more opportunities? In other words: can social integration be promoted through housing and urban policies?

Some of the reasons for focusing on existing social housing, rather than on inadequate self-help housing or slums are as follow:

- First, there is already a huge body of research that focuses on questions of slums and self-help housing,
- Second, in reaction to slums and housing scarcity many governments have been creating a type of shelter, which goes by the word "social", and yet can create new kinds of exclusions,
- Third, there is evidence that slum communities have stronger internal networks, while people living in social housing projects have mostly lost these type of relations.
- Fourth, housing policies in Chile do not include possibilities to improve standards or increase housing area after a flat is delivered (3)

The case studies especially focus on housing estates provided through the *Programa de Vivienda Básica* not only because they represent most of the social housing stock built in recent decades, but also because their collective character, social estates seem to be much harder to transform than single-family housing.

In order to approach the solution of the abovementioned challenges, this research also expects to answer the following questions: How can socio-spatial concerns such as integration be incorporated into housing policies? Which policy reforms need to be introduced in order to solve current and future problems? How can this housing policy be consistent with the political demands and desires of a society that is growing economically and reaching better opportunities in other aspects of life?

1.3 Organisation of the Dissertation

The aim of combining conceptual inquiries with a concrete case study and the search for proposals requires this work to be divided into three parts or seven chapters:

The first Part covers the introduction in its first chapter, which is devoted to presenting a basic background, the research problem and basic conceptual definitions used in this study. A second chapter is dedicated to the discussion about current academic debate about housing policies and social exclusion. This conceptual framework also includes the definition of a theoretical model of exclusion through housing in Chile, which forms part of the methodology used throughout the entire work. The third chapter includes a general description of the methodological orientation of the work including the main sources and instruments to be used with a particular focus in the case studies.

---

(3) Just some "cosmetic make-up" such as painting or fixing estate fences are part of the current programme of improvement. (see chapter four, 4.6.1)

The second Part is also subdivided into two chapters. The first chapter describes the historical patterns of Chilean housing policies and their urban impacts with a particular focus on the roots of social and spatial segregation. It also includes an explanation of the current policy and a description of its main programmes. With this as a background, the second chapter is devoted to the presentation of the case study, which includes two levels, as follows:

First, the impacts of social housing at the city level are analysed. A mapping of all of Santiago's districts, the tendencies of housing location, the demographic trends, as well as socio-economic tendencies, show how segregation is manifested. This study at the city level permitted the selection of districts suitable for a deeper analysis and the selection of analytical criteria. Further clarification of the criteria for analysis follows with the explanation of the methodology.

The second level of analysis, the neighbourhood and the dwellings, focuses on the specific characteristics of three selected "*barrios*" or districts, their infrastructure, accessibility to urban opportunities and main spatial configuration. It also includes exploratory interviews with a small sample of estates beneficiaries. Here, special attention is devoted to people's interventions and perceptions.

The third part includes the main conclusions of the study, as well as some interpretations and new insights. Besides the discussion of the main patterns of Chilean housing policy founded through history, the main results of the work are discussed, and the phenomenon of exclusion through housing is evaluated and reasserted. Finally, some new insights and suggestions for further research are presented.

1.4 Theoretical Approach and Basic Definitions

> *"Social change arises from politics, not philosophy. Ideals are a crucial step in emancipatory politics, however, because they dislodge our assumption that what is given is necessary. They offer the standpoints from which to criticize the given and inspiration for imagining alternatives"* (I. M. Young, 1990: 256).

The main "conceptual construct" that organises this study, namely what is behind the title of this work and the idea of "Social Housing in Chile: A Case of Social and spatial exclusion", is based on current academic research concerning social exclusion, in particular exclusion through housing, as well as on studies that analyse the role of the state in housing provision. But, what is meant by social exclusion? Is there exclusion through housing? How are social policies and the role of the state understood? Which is the role of housing?. Finally, what is expected from upgrading and reintegration?

Any approach to answering these questions supposes an explicit or implicit set of principles, conceptions or normative values which define the orientation of the study. Here, concepts such as social exclusion and integration are methodologically understood as distinctive normative ideals or, in Weber's words: as *"ideal types"*. Ideal types are mental constructs that aim to visualise and classify typical motives and patterns of action of determined phenomena through generalisations (Saunders,1993:29). *"an ideal type is a concept* (a formed mental representation) *of several relatively similar, complex phenomena"* (Burger, 1987:154).

They also might assist the process of comparison; *"they offer a baseline for identifying significant variations and their possible causes"* (Wacquant, 2002: 224). The reasons for using a Weberian concept are manifold. First, it considers both categorisation and generalisation of a determined social phenomenon. Second, it helps to organise certain types of actions, and processes taking into consideration both conceptual and socio-historical aspects. Third, it facilitates comparative analysis of singular phenomena by framing them in one-sided aspects.

Nevertheless, the theoretical framework of this work is much closer to *"critical theory"* rather than to exclusively assuming a "value-free" Weberian approach. Critical theory also aims at building ideals that *"allow thinkers and actors to take distance from reality in order to criticize it and imagine possibilities for something better"* (Young, 2000:10). Critical theory includes the use of moral arguments and normative ideals which are present in the discussion around particular societal paradigms such as social justice and democracy. Although it is not based on philosophical premises, critical theory uses *"socially and historically situated normative analysis and argument"* (2000:10).

Therefore, the following normative ideal definitions are not only the result of a personal approach, but they are also based on the theoretical framework and moral arguments that are further discussed in chapter two.

1.4.1 Social Policies and the Role of the State

In a normative ideal definition, social policies should represent societal statements of aims, instruments and regulations aimed at bridging the possible gaps between people that have different access to basic opportunities such as health, education and shelter, and the state, as the main societal authority, should assure the "fair" distribution of goods and rights among society. This possibly debatable normative definition aims to recognise that, in spite of differences in emphasis and approaches, the "social question" has been increasingly accepted and incorporated in most western "democratic" countries since the late 1800's (Ziccardi, 2000). The fact that these policies have changed from "universalistic" rights to particularly targeting at the poorest segments of societies -with the crisis of the Welfare system- does not mean that states have lost their role in balancing social inequalities.

1.4.2 Housing and Housing Policies

"Housing addresses basic human needs... Usually it is a place that people want to make into a home" (Vliet, 1998:xix). Housing is a shelter, a crucial asset, a process. Housing is a verb: housing does (Turner, 1976; Haramoto, 2000). Yet, housing is a process that focuses on the fulfilment of people's residential needs. Here, residential needs are understood as all the aspects that individuals could basically expect from a dwelling: security of occupancy (tenure or lease), physical quality and adequacy, rights to modify, to sell or to rent, and accessibility to social, cultural and economical resources.

As other social policies, housing policy may be unable to ensure the satisfaction of all these expectations, in particular for people who already suffer other deprivations. Nevertheless, it can be used as a political instrument to confront social inequalities, as well as a means for social integration and the enhancement of citizens' rights. That could be possible if they bring people the opportunity to take control over their material resources by making them part of a housing process which includes the chance to modify their living conditions over time.

In other words, housing policies should not only provide affordable, valuable and accessible housing -close to the wider set of urban opportunities- but also facilitate people's participation and the adaptation of the housing stock over time.

1.4.3 Social Exclusion and Exclusion through Housing

Broadly, here is suggested that to be socially excluded means to be prevented from being part of the society and its commonly shared values. To be socially excluded is not having equal access to economic, cultural or institutional privileges and benefits, goods and rights that are supposed to be recognised as "universal" in a society; *"It is not simply lack of income and the productive resources necessary to guarantee sustainable levels of existence for a person, but also the societal and cultural constraints and discrimination that prevent individuals from reaching their potential"* (IADB, 2003:2)

Exclusion through housing is a phenomenon that combines spatial and social aspects. It occurs when people are housed in inadequate dwellings -overcrowded and sub-standard-, and they are involuntarily concentrated in locations that do not only prevent access to goods and services, but also concentrate more people with the same problems -unskilled, unemployed, etc. Exclusion through housing also highlights the role of housing and the neighbourhood in shaping outcomes such as health problems, low education attainment, and delinquency, as well as other "intangibles" such as depreciated identity, low self-esteem and lack of a sense of belonging.

1.4.4 Upgrading and Reintegration

Upgrading is to raise a former grade; to improve existing conditions. The idea of *"upgrading existing social housing"* speaks of the aim to bring people opportunities to progressively raise the physical and social living standards where they live with consideration of their needs and expectations. In this sense, it is understood more as a participative process that should be framed in an integral and long-term strategy rather than a one-time activity.

Upgrading is seen as a flexible instrument that should also include diverse stakeholders and alternative means to elaborate and finance neighbourhood improvements. Therefore, a concept such as upgrading should be viewed as an element of a broader plan for reaching an equitable society, and not just be focused on solving immediate area based problems.

Reintegration is an aspiration of reducing inequalities. Reintegration aims at including. Reintegration is assumed as a societal value both in social and spatial terms. In social terms, its aim is to equalise rights rather than to homogenise people, which means to balance the access to decision-making processes in urban affairs by giving people more control over their resources.

In spatial terms, reintegration aims at preventing the isolation of neighbourhoods from their immediate surroundings and the rest of the city, which means to make them part of the city by, for example, improving the access to urban opportunities such as work, health and education. It also aims at balancing the physical value or "built-capital" of districts, which means that every district should have certain distinctive attractiveness for people with different income levels.

Thus, *"Upgrading and Reintegrating existing social housing"* is understood as the process of addressing social and spatial disparities that affect certain areas and parts of the population for whom not only the access to material resources is denied but also the right to use the city and to "flourish"[4]. A city can metaphorically be described as a patchwork, but this does not mean that the fabric is not a consistent and suitable tissue. Giving each part a distinctive character according to inhabitant's desires and strengthening the ties with other parts would lead to an integrative whole.

[4] Understood as the manifestation, expression or exteriorisation of all potentialities human beings have. In other words, "flourish" implies to have the opportunity to endure a life according to people's expectations and the chance to use all their potentialities.

Chapter 2: Theoretical Framework

2.1 Introduction

In the first chapter, two hypotheses were presented, (a) that current Chilean housing policy has contributed to processes of social and spatial exclusion, and (b) that exclusion through housing is a phenomenon which can also be found in Chile. Basic normative concepts were also advanced, but they included only a brief reference to the academic discussion.

Therefore, this second chapter is advocated to elaborate the theoretical framework that supports these definitions, which is mainly based on current academic debate about housing and social exclusion in Europe, Latin America and the United States. It also includes the identification of "typical" patterns to be found within the literature about housing policies and exclusion through housing in order to classify and categorise its main causes and effects. This classification and categorisation has led to the proposal of a theoretical model to be used for the analysis of exclusion through housing in Chile. In spite of the fact that this model represent part of the methodology of this study, it will be presented and explained within this chapter as a conclusion of this theoretical framework.

2.2 The "Social Question" and the Role of the State

The "social question" is particularly linked to urbanisation processes and to the concentration of people with diverse origins, backgrounds and status in what we call cities, in particular since the industrial revolution in the nineteenth century (Ziccardi, 2000:1). As a matter of fact, the industrial revolution provoked massive migration from the countryside to the cities and one of the results was the concentration of low-income people in slum conditions, as Friedrich Engels (2000:55) exemplarily described: *"the dwellings of workers everywhere are poorly planned, poorly built, and kept in the worst condition.... the working class of the great cities offers a graduated scale of conditions in life.... reaching even homeless and death by starvation"*. In Chile, a similar description of deprivation of the "urban-poor" was already pointed out in 1895 by medical doctor Puga Borne (Gross, 1988:12), who made public the overcrowded and unhealthy habitat conditions of *"less-favoured individuals"*.

One of the results of these problems was that much legislation about workers' housing was enacted, for example in the United States and Chile, and they were mainly *"motivated by concerns about the growing maladies of urban life, the diseases and social pathologies"* [(5)] (Davis, 1995:7; Romero,1997:155).

For scholar Alicia Ziccardi (2000:1), the configuration of states and their respective bureaucracy, as well as the differentiation of social classes results in the fact that governments were assuming increasing responsibilities in the provision of goods and services for their citizens, arriving to the "higher" point with the creation and consolidation of the "welfare" state in most capitalist countries after the second World War. These welfare states differ, however, in terms of the type and amount of services and goods to be provided as well as in the ideals behind them.

According to Professor Ali Madanipour (1998: 39-46), Esping-Andersen distinguishes three types of welfare states: the liberal, the conservative and the social democratic, which for Zeylmans (2002:5) represent just ideal types because even within each category there are differences in terms of policy outcomes. For Zeylmans, the Chilean welfare state changed from a "rudimentary" one, which never could meet its "universalistic" aims, to a neo-liberal one which tries to combine economic growth with equality of opportunity, and relies on means tested subsidies targeted to the poorest sectors (see chapter 4, 4.6).

Among the goods and services that governments have been providing or aiming to assure, within the frame of their particular welfare systems, is the provision of housing. As a matter of fact, from these earlier housing legislations based on public health to the current worries about ghettoization and social exclusion, different policies using diverse justifications have been developed to tackle housing problems (Hidalgo, 2002; Marcuse, 2002). In a paper that analyses housing policies in Western Europe and the United States, American Professor Peter Marcuse (2002:3) asserted that social control, fear of social unrest, economic necessity, the Cold War, neo-liberalism and social cohesion have been among the most important justifications behind public interventions throughout the last century.

In general, the main problem with social policies lies in the fact that they are highly debatable moral and philosophical concepts such as social justice, equity, and human rights. Geographer David Harvey (2000:206-207) said that even though *"justice and rationality take on different meanings across space and time and persons, and their political character cannot be denied; policies will always represent the ideas of those in power"*.

---

(5) It refers to the first regulations of physical quality and sanitary conditions that were enforced in Europe and the United States in the early 19th century. This kind of hygienical urbanism was also promoted in Latin America in the early 1900s. Examples of this type of legislation can be found in Chile (1906), Argentina (1915) and Colombia (1918) (Hidalgo, 2002:90)

In the lack of consensus, Harvey sees also the opportunity to develop alternative political approaches because, as he says: neither paternalistic welfare approaches nor market rhetoric are solving the problems of the majority of the human population.

In urban sociology, most of the so-called neo-Marxists such as David Harvey and Manuel Castells, see the state in capitalist countries as a *"mere agent of private capital intervening in conflict over the built environment"* (Basset and Short, 1980:224), and therefore, its role is restricted to facilitate the domination of labour *"not simply in the work process, but with respect to the very definition of the quality of life in the consumption sphere"* (1980:222).

On the other hand, the so-called neo-Weberians such as John Rex and Richard Moore, Ray Pahl, and Peter Saunders, accepted Weber's approach: they see the state as *"an apparatus controlled by individuals with definite aims and motivations; a view of the state's mode of operation in which officials and technical experts are deemed to prevail against elected political leaders"* (Saunders, 1993:118). In addition, they also assumed Weber's analysis of class and class conflict where *"class is a sociological construct which is imposed upon reality in order to clarify analysis -in reality there are only individuals, not classes who act"* (Saunders:1993: 140).

Here, the Weberian approach seems suitable to the present study for various reasons. First, it helps to "reduce" the scope of the research according to a particular topic: housing policy and its role in sharpening social and spatial inequalities. Yet, this study focuses on a "one-sided" aspect: the actions and effects of a determined policy and not on all the aspects included in it such as, for example, the implications derived from its financial mechanisms in the Chilean economy, which can certainly also impact the distribution of resources and affect inequality.

Second, a Weberian approach facilitates the categorisation of actions and effects from a theoretical ideal type. Third, this approach assumes that not all actions and effects are guided by a single ideological position but rather includes contradictory forces within the state and society. Finally, although the approach can undermine an "integral perspective", it still permits the identification of patterns of action and their possible "hidden" mechanisms and aims. Here, the term government is sometimes equated with the term state, and that is so in order to refer to the whole apparatus and not to one specific "regime".

2.3 New Inequalities? The Rise of Social Exclusion

The term social exclusion suggests, literally, that there are people who are excluded from society or from social aspects of life. However, the term means different things for different people (Murie, 2001). Thus, a review of its origins and uses become important.

Since the late 1970s, social exclusion in Europe has basically been associated with the reduction of benefits from the welfare state, increasing and long-term unemployment, and the deployment of social networks. These changes have affected family incomes and have resulted in a considerable gap between those *"included"* and those *"excluded"* from common societal standards of living. That means that there are people who cannot assure basic standards of life without welfare assistance (Murie, 2001:2).

As a result, the contemporary discussion about poverty and housing problems is filled with a variety of apparently synonymous concepts such as marginalisation, disintegration, inequality, ghettoization, segregation and social exclusion which seems to represent, sometimes, all of them. Concepts in response to these problems are usually termed inclusion, cohesion and integration.

Recently though, there is an increasing acceptance of the term social exclusion even at the level of international organisations such the International Labour Organisation (ILO) (Baker, 2001). Indeed, jointly with "integration", social exclusion has occupied an important part of international debates both in social science and in the world of policy and politics during the last decades (Levitas, 1998;Vranken, 2000; Sen, 2000).

Nevertheless, social exclusion is still a contested concept. According to Alan Murie (2001:2), the term social exclusion is not only usually ill-defined but also it continues to mean different things to different interpreters. As a matter of fact, scholar Ruth Levitas (1998:7-29) asserts that most of the divergences among perspectives lie in distinct societal paradigms. She identifies the following main three different discourses:

a) the redistributionist discourse, which understands social exclusion as lack of citizenship and focuses on the processes that cause inequalities, recognising poverty as the main cause of social exclusion. This approach aims to go *"beyond a minimalist model of inclusion"* and to reduce inequalities by a process of redistribution of resources and power.

b) the moral underclass discourse, which avoids the discussion about societal inequalities and includes a kind of moral condemnation of the poor, presenting *"the socially excluded as culturally distinct from the 'mainstream'* ". This approach blames the poor's behaviour for their dependency on social benefits.

c) the social integrationist discourse, which suggests that integration can be only achieved through paid work, reduces the problem of exclusion to an economical problem. Therefore, it *"obscures the inequalities between paid workers"* such as gender and class-related wage divergences in the labour market.

Accepting the limitations of the term social exclusion, Murie (2001:4) suggests a positive and operative approach which considers the multidimensionality and changing faces of poverty. He asserts that social exclusion could be understood as, *"a dynamic concept of poverty: that means to acknowledge that subsistence minima or other poverty levels established at one period of time need to be adjusted in light of changing expectations and opportunities in society".*

Economist and Nobel Prize Laureate Amartya Sen also recognises social exclusion as an operative concept to understand deprivation. In a report for the Asian Development Bank he asserts that *"the helpfulness of the social exclusion approach does not lie, I would argue, in its conceptual newness, but in its practical influence in forcefully emphasizing -and focusing attention on the role of relational features in deprivation"* (2000:14). For him, the concept of social exclusion helps not only to understand -epistemologically- the diverse "faces" of poverty and deprivation considering relational obstacles, but could also help operatively by orienting policies.

Other authors such as political scientist Iris Young (2000:13), criticise the concept of social exclusion in Europe because focusing in a myriad of problems may obscure the presence of misfits such as possible discrimination against immigrants and unemployed youth. *"The concepts of social exclusion and inclusion lose meaning if they are used to label all problems of social conflict and justice. Where the problems are racism, cultural intolerance, economic exploitation, or a refusal to help needy people, they should be so named".*

In Latin America, social exclusion seems to be a chronic historical situation rather than the result of recent global trends. Indeed, inequalities in terms of access to goods, assets and services, poverty and deprivation have been subjects of research and policies for more than three decades (Faria, 1994; Valladares and Prates, 1995). Nowadays, many scholars and politicians in Latin America have begun to accept and to use the concept of social exclusion, but they are still divided into those that favour a "redistributive" perspective and those that emphasise an "integrationist" point of view (Faria, 1994; Ziccardi, 2000).

According to a report from the Inter-American Bank for Development, there is, however, some agreement in the fact that social exclusion facilitates a multidimensional approach to poverty. The report states that *"in the regional context, social exclusion is broadly seen as the impossibility of an individual or social group to participate actively in the economic, cultural or institutional spheres of society"*, and it is also *"an objective and subjective condition that changes over time and space and is shaped by historical and social processes"* (IBD, 2003:30).

In summary, the concept of social exclusion is useful for the present study for various reasons. First, it serves to analyse housing policies in the light of a certain assumed paradigm namely the redistributive discourse. This discourse is preferred because it assumes a broader perspective than the abovementioned integrationist and the underclass approaches. Second, within the framework of a redistributive discourse, social exclusion has to do with the role of governments and social policies in reducing social inequalities and promoting citizenship. Third, it highlights the relational, dynamic and multidimensional aspects of poverty that should not only change over time but should also consider people's objective and subjective needs. Fourth, it permits the identification of tangible and non-tangible factors that have led to inequalities, for example access to goods and services -housing included- on the one hand, and feelings of discrimination and stigmatisation on the other hand.

2.4 The Role of Housing Policies: General Issues

The long road of housing as a social policy has been marked by successive changes in approaches to the "housing problem" under different societal paradigms. Indeed, the question of improving low-income people's housing situation and providing them with urban services and infrastructure is not new. In spite of successive changes of views and emphasis, urbanisation processes have always been challenged by the need to improve urban functioning and social conditions (Hall and Pfeiffer, 2000). Nowadays, most social policies aim at bridging the possible gaps between people that have different access to basic opportunities such as health, education and shelter. However, the question is still whether, and to which extent, society as a whole can be made responsible for the people who cannot meet the widely accepted standards of living. (Ziccardi, 2000)

As a matter of fact, policies have changed over time from "universalistic" rights to particularly targeting the poorest segments of societies -with the crisis of the Welfare system. Within this shift, scholars such as Marcuse (2001:5), for example, points out that much of the current discussion about housing and social exclusion contains similarities to the original focus on public health: ghettos represent a danger for the society because they are the possible source of riots, delinquency and social stress, among others. In the same paper, Marcuse concludes that *"housing policy, it seems to me, will be determined in the future, as in the past, more by struggles around these larger issues* [globalisation, sustainability, neo-liberalism] *than by any benevolent attempt by states to solve the housing problem"* (2002:5).

Housing scholars such as Sam Davis (1995) also identified diverse paradigms underlying the implementation of housing policies. He breaks down the type of policies applied in the United States into two basic types: housing as *"social policy"* and housing as *"public utility"*. The first type aims at integrating people into common standards of living, and sees housing projects as an integral part of urban development, whereas the latter focuses on the supply of a minimum for shelter, disregarding urban and social impacts such as social and spatial segregation.

Other scholars related to architecture and urban planning also criticise the approach of some governmental housing policies, for example, in terms of their excessively deficit-driven interventions that disregard qualitative aspects of housing (Turner, 1976; Davis, 1995; Ducci, 1997; Sugranyes et al, 2000). Indeed, most critics agree on the fact that such a disregard is sooner or later neither feasible in economical terms, nor environmentally sound, or socially desirable. Economically, the most visible problems are that the price of land tends to increase over time and that building on cheaper peripheral areas leads to higher urbanisation costs (Sabatini, 1999).

Environmental problems, are usually connected both to material standards and location issues. Many massive constructions in the world have been built with polluting materials or unsuitable technologies and located in places that force people to commute over long distances - increasing transport costs, and leading to air pollution- or in places that are often not even suitable for urbanisation, for example, rural areas with valuable soil, zones with risks of erosion or flooding, etc. (Knorr-Siedow, 1999).

The social problems lie, in Davis words, in the fact that *"this* [governmental] *patronising attitude has led to the construction of* [social] *housing that stigmatises and penalises its residents, that denies their dignity and their humanity. It has doomed publicly assisted housing"* (Davis, 1995:15). Moreover, Davis (1995:3) also highlights the social importance of architectural aspects. He believes that through "properly" designed households, money in lighting, heating and maintenance, among others, could be saved. This aspect has an undeniable relevance since it could help to reduce the economic burden over low-income families.

In the same vein as other studies about housing (Turner, 1976; Sugranyes et al., 2000) Davis asserts that *"housing is a key ingredient in community building. Islands of low-income projects that are socially, economically and architecturally cut off from the surrounding communities compel their inhabitants to be dettached and alienated"* (1995:3). Furthermore, discussion about this aspect is presented in 2.6.

2.5 Housing Policies and Inequality: Research Issues

Many commentators identify the book *"Race, Community and Conflict"* written by sociologists John Rex and Robert Moore in 1967, as a seminal work on the relation between housing and inequalities (Basset and Short, 1980; Saunders, 1993; Savage and Warde, 1993).

According to Saunders, the main contribution of Rex and Moore was to recover the essential role of urban sociological studies: *"to study the distributional patterns of urban inequalities as these are affected by both market and bureaucratic processes"* (Saunders, 1993:119). In addition, Rex and Moore's study is particularly important for housing studies because (a) it highlighted the importance of taking housing as a distinct subject in its own, and (b) it pointed out the role of housing in shaping life chances.

Rex and Moore carried out empirical research about housing allocation in the city of Birmingham, Great Britain, and one of their main assumptions was that suburban housing was widely desired but not widely available. Thus, it was a scarce resource, and it was unequally distributed among people because its access was mainly dependent on people's income. (Saunders, 1993:116).

Nevertheless, they also considered the role of governmental policies for allocation and concluded that people who either could not afford a house or to be allocated in the public housing stock -in particular immigrants- were forced to live in the most undesirable housing existing in the city. As a result, Rex and Moore coined the concept of "housing classes". The concept of housing classes relates *"the allocation of scarce and desirable housing, both through the market and by the bureaucratic means, and to the resulting struggle over housing by different groups located at different points in the housing hierarchy"*(1993:116).

Rex and Moore also used Weber's methodology by making a classification of types of housing according to an ideal type. Their concerns were related to how different agents and actions play a role in allocation and expressed diverse forms of discrimination that resulted in the concentration of disadvantaged people such as migrants just in certain areas of the city (inner-city deteriorated housing in Birmingham) Therefore, they promoted the idea that income was neither the sole nor the most important reason to explain the type of housing, tenure or location of housing (Savage and Warde, 1993:68).

Basset and Short (1980: 50) considered that Rex and Moore were wrong by assuming housing as a cause of inequalities. From their point of view, housing consumption is a reflection of social stratification itself. However, they also valued the analytical shift towards the analysis of institutions and constrains in the housing market because the allocation issue was highlighted.

Nevertheless, the work of Rex and Moore stimulated other neo-Weberians such as the sociologist Ray Pahl, who also developed a new approach that was labelled *"urban managerialism"*. The main thesis of urban managerialists was that the access to diverse services and goods was mediated by "gatekeepers" represented by key managers in bureaucratic institutions, who controlled and defined the allocation of resources and, thus, they could determine the differential degrees of access that different people could reach (Saunders, 1993:121).

According to Pahl, previous research, in particular this one based on the principles of the Chicago School [(6)] , was too much focused on choice and very little on constraints, and therefore, for him the main questions were *"Who gets the resources and facilities? Who decides how to distribute or allocate these resources and who decides who decides?"* (Basset and Short,1980: 50).

Similar question were posed by John Turner (1976) in his book *"Housing by people"*, where he remarked the need to identify the limits of heteronomy and autonomy. Heteronomy, for him, is the opposite of autonomy, and it is represented in the housing sphere in the fact that citizens are subject to the rule of governmental powers, policy makers and the market, rather than having the right to decide where and how they would live having certain grades of autonomy.

The other mainstream of research about housing and inequality is represented by neo-Marxists such as Castells and Harvey who accentuate the economical role of housing in terms of helping in the reproduction of the labour force. According to Basset and Short (1980), the neo-Marxist approaches permit the realisation that state intervention not only may be reflected in the process of housing production but also in the reproduction of social relations because *"residential differentiation in space is interwoven with class divisions, different modes of consumption and the broad field of the reproduction of social relations"*

[(6)] The Chicago School is represented by scholars such as Robert Park, Ernest Burgess and Roderik D. McKenzie. They began in the early 1920's to develop a theory, based also in empirical research, which aimed to understand the physical form of cities and also included the study of differential location of housing in terms of an "ecological" or "Darwinian" approach.

(1980:180). In addition, neo-Marxist approaches accentuate the broader economical system within which the housing question is placed and attempt to perform an "integral" analysis of society.

In spite of the fact that the neo-Marxist approach proposes an interesting approach to analysing housing inequality, the present study "fits" better with these Weberian approaches that understand the role of the state -through a determined housing policy in this case- as the independent variable. Yet, the dependent variables are represented by the effects and outcomes derived from this "independent" variable, i.e.: exclusion through housing.

2.6 Housing and Social Exclusion: a Close Relation

After the second World War, socialist and capitalist countries in the "north" began to promote and to build social housing estates on a massive scale -mostly to be rented-out - in order to tend to the deficits left by war damage and necessities resulting from increasing population and growing urbanisation (Knorr-Siedow, 1999).

The estates model could be suitable to be built with new technologies -mainly prefabrication- in a "Fordist" way, and also brought the opportunity to apply architectural concepts that modernist architects had long been waiting for. The basic idea was to build modern, clean and well-ventilated flats, and to separate residential areas from other land uses, in order to fulfill both social needs and middle-income families' expectations. In addition, many social housing or public estates were built outside cities and surrounded by big parks and green areas (Knorr-Siedow, 1999). However, according to the same author (1999:2) this was one of the weaker strategies for providing housing, and most of the western countries ceased to implement them in the early 1980s.

Nowadays, considerable research (Morris & Winn, 1990; Madanipour, 1998; Atkinson and Kintrea 2001; Murie, 2001) asserts that neighbourhoods with public housing estates tend to concentrate the "excluded" or people who have no other option but to live there. A great percentage of them receives welfare aid, is unskilled, unemployed and consists of tenants who do not usually have money to invest in maintenance, and their neighbourhoods are, therefore, prone to decay which renders these housing areas undesirable and triggers processes of ghettoization and stigmatisation. Yet, a spiral of decay takes over: welfare-dependent tenants cannot afford maintenance, the concentration of poverty induces bad behaviour and criminality, and private and public services begin to disappear. As a consequence, these neighbourhoods begin to be stigmatised by their dereliction and bad reputation, and only those without alternative accept to live there (Atkinson and Kintrea 2001).

This characterisation allows Australian scholars Arthurson and Jacobs (2003:19), to assert that housing has proven to be a key contributor to social exclusion. After a review of European literature, they identified a clear differentiation between exclusion "from" housing and exclusion *"through"* housing: people who cannot afford a place to live (homeless, squatters) are excluded from housing and people who live in inadequate housing are excluded from society through housing. While the first category points out inequalities in terms of access to affordable housing, the second emphasises the role of housing in shaping negative outcomes such as limited access to employment, health problems and low education attainment, among others.

Authors such as Häußermann (2001) and Musterd and Murie (2001) explored the causes behind these processes. These and other scholars tend to mention economical restructuring - and even globalisation- as a major factor responsible for the decay of public housing or estates. They argue that since income polarisation, deindustrialisation and tertiarisation processes have left many low-skilled employees out of work and dependent on welfare benefits, they have no other chance than to live in social estates or other housing types of "last resort".

However, for some scholars such as Skifter (2001), economical restructuring and global changes are not the sole reasons behind these processes. He understands that changes in patterns of consumption and the attributes of the housing stock in itself are also partly responsible. Therefore, he defines urban decay as "the result of the interaction between social, economic and physical changes in the cities" (2001:3).

Skifter's approach recognises the existence of intertwined factors that affect deprived neighbourhoods, including their own role in perpetuating social exclusion. According to Skifter (2001:4) "...[deprived] *areas differ not only by virtue of different physical qualities, like housing stock, architecture, natural beauties, and access to transport facilities and service supply, but also by more indefinite qualities like social image and status and security"*.

Authors such as Alice Coleman and Oscar Newman (O´Leary, 1998:130-131) draw attention to the association between poor design and social malaise. In spite of the fact that Coleman's methodology has been criticised by some authors such as Morris (1990) and Murie (2002), the consideration of morphological aspects reveals the intertwined factors that affected "estates problems" in Britain. Basically, her approach aims to identify particular estate features that could be responsible for anti-social behaviour like number of dwellings per block, the number of dwellings served by each entrance, and spatial organisation, etc.

Newman investigated the relationship between crime, vandalism and housing projects in the United States. He defined the concept of *"defensible space"* in terms of the existence of clear demarcations of ownership and belonging of space that allow social or individual control over private and/or community space. One example is the existence, or lack thereof, of windows that look out onto external space and bring a sense of surveillance, yet "there is the potential for any wrong-doing to be observed, reported or possibly challenged" (O´Leary, 1998:131).

In the same vein, Knorr-Siedow (1999:2), classifies estate problems into three categories, (a) physical and ecological problems, that are mainly related to their monotonous appearance, the use of polluting materials and their premature decay; (b) economic and housing finance problems connected with high maintenance costs, the departure of middle classes and their replacement by many welfare dependent families and ethnic minorities, (c) social problems related to the loss of social networks, and the concentration of low-income families and (d) image problems: "concentration of social problems in these areas often resulted in a very negative image [bad reputation] among the general population".

The resident's point-of-view is acknowledged by, for example, Loïc Wacquant (2002). Taking as a reference a study done by Pètenot in 1982, Wacquant (2002:225) asserts that *"Living in the (sub)proletarian housing projects of the periphery of Paris creates a 'muted' sentiment of guilt and shame whose unacknowledged weight wraps human relations".*

As a result, people usually avoid to mention where they live at work and isolate themselves by not receiving visitors at home, and even feel compelled to excuse themselves for living in areas with a bad reputation, i.e.: *"I am here just for a while"*. Another result is the emergence of prejudices among neighbours, as the same authors reveals: *"All too often, the sense of social indignity can be defeated only by thrusting the stigma onto a faceless, diabolized, Other - the downstairs neighbours, the foreign family dwelling in an adjacent building, the youth from across the street who 'do drugs', or residents over on the next block that one suspects of illegally drawing unemployment or welfare benefits"*. (2000:226)

As a result of this brief analysis, the concept of exclusion through housing basically applies in Chile, and will be used as a reference point in the following analysis of the Chilean housing policy. It pays attention to the concentration of low-income families in certain neighbourhoods and in a certain types of housing of "last resort". It also considers the role of housing itself in shaping negative outcomes that contribute to social exclusion.

2.7 Upgrading: a Holistic Approach for Housing Improvement

According to the Cambridge International Online Dictionary (2001), the term upgrading represents the idea of *"improving the quality of something through actions of desired characteristics"; or "the raising to a higher grade or standard"*.

Upgrading, as a concept, has been used both in "developed" and "developing" countries. In recent years this concept has usually been associated with integral plans for slums that include both the improvement of physical and sanitary conditions, as well as capacity-building, empowerment and employment programmes (Vliet 1998). The same concept was used for neighbourhood improvement in the United States throughout the 1970's. (Vliet 1998; Broudehoux, 1999).

In those years local governments and professionals in the United States became increasingly concerned with the decadence of some neighbourhoods, especially those located in central areas and with some architectural value or attractiveness. Rehabilitation as well as renewal and redevelopment projects were proposed and implemented that usually resulted in the expulsion of former poor inhabitants and their replacement by upper classes. Thus, the well-known processes of gentrification took place.

In an effort to avoid gentrification social activists and architects raised the concept of *"Incumbent Upgrading"* in less architecturally "interesting" neighbourhoods, (Davis, 1995; Vliet, 1998). The main idea was to implement rehabilitation projects without driving away former inhabitants and to include them in the upgrading process of their neighbourhood (Broudehoux, 1999). This kind of approach has some similarities with the idea of *"Regeneration"* largely used in Great Britain.

However, the concept of regeneration allows certain criticism. A revision of the experiences in the United Kingdom, show that under different administrations the idea of regeneration has stood for very different programmes (Kemeny, 1992; Smith, 2001). While in the 1980s regeneration projects were mainly market-oriented, and physical renewal, as well as tenure policies -privatisation of public stock- usually caused gentrification, in recent years integral programmes which pursued an image-change in stigmatised neighbourhoods have considered inhabitants' concerns.(Altermann and Cars, 1991; Withehead, 2003).

The need of governmental intervention and other stakeholders in programmes of upgrading is based in the fact that the market has no interest in areas that are running down and do not provide lucre. This assertion is confirmed by Morris and Winn (1990: 17) who refer to the problems of carrying out upgrading projects by quoting a statement form a British senior civil servant in charge of such projects: *"In run-down areas, individuals developers or companies will not go in by themselves because the risk is too high. It has to be a coordinated effort"*.

As a result of this short discussion, the term upgrading will be used here rather than regeneration, because it seems to be less controversial, and its meaning more appropriate for this work. Upgrading suggests the idea of improvement based on determined reference points: from a worse to a better. In addition, improvement in this case means "development", rather than the erasure of the former situation. In contrast, most terms with the prefix "re" such as renewal, rehabilitation and regeneration tend to suggest an idea of "doing again but better". Their meaning can further be reduced to the action of returning to a previous situation, as in "renewal", which does not necessarily include a progress.

2.8 Integration and Social Housing

The term integration has been used both in urban planning and in the fields of social science. In urban planning, it has usually been mentioned as part of neighbourhood improvement programmes, such as the German *"Social City"* programme, and the British regeneration approach, as well as in housing policies applied in Singapore and Hong Kong (Borja and Castelles, 1997; Häußermann, 2001)

Within the framework of urban projects, the concept of integration has spatial as well as social connotations. It either describes the idea of combining valuable existing buildings with new constructions or the plan of mixing residents of different income or ethnical origins in "redeveloped" areas (Vliet, 1998; Borja and Castells, 1997:233).

The latter includes policies of relocation of low-income families, which understands integration or inclusion simply as allocating low-income family subsidies to reside in better-off districts rather than attracting the better-off to low-income neighbourhoods. This perspective is starkly criticised by Young because it obscures the problem of segregated areas (2000:197). For Young, the very processes of segregation are an *"obvious form of social, economical and political exclusion"*. She defines segregation as a process of social exclusion.

In the social sciences, the term integration is rooted in the work of Durkheim whose study of suicide motivations first mentioned the importance of social integration for maintaining certain social order (Levitas, 1998). Today, social integration is normally understood as the opposite of social exclusion, though this still is a matter of controversy.

Some scholars and politicians see integration as a positive process of including everyone, especially vulnerable groups, in the development process while others see it as an unwarranted imposition of uniformity or external ideals and values and a disrespect of socio-cultural differences among people (UNRISD, 1994). According to UNRISD (1994, 10), instead of focusing on its moral implications, social scientists held the view that *"the terms invite analyses of the concrete networks and institutions which support the livelihood of people in given times and places"*.

Regarding the discussion about the moral value of integration, the dichotomy could also be understood in the context of the public and the private spheres, which are different but not necessarily contradictory. While every person or group should have the right to control their own private sphere, and to exclude "intruders", the public space should give everybody the same opportunities.

Drawing upon some arguments made by Iris Young in her books *"Justice and the Politics of difference"* (1990) and *"Inclusion and democracy"* (2000), it is possible to suggest that segregation and the lack of public space undermine democracy and justice because, as Young asserts, class segregation endangers democracy in at least three ways a) it discourages public spaces and public encounters, b) it impedes communication between groups and c) privileged people do not need to see how others live, and thus, can abandon a sense of social responsibility and cooperation with them to produce public goods (1990:211-213). Thus, integration measures should be meant to counteract these processes.

For her, equal opportunity and freedom are basic values that *"highlight the need to remove remaining discriminatory barriers in contemporary urbanised democracies"* (Young 2000:197). The problem is not the existence of groups clusters -if people decided them- but the lack of freedom and equal opportunity to choose where individuals and groups desire to live; the problem is lack of choice and involuntary segregation. However, many cities are becoming fragmented and public space is losing its former encounter and integrative function. As a matter of fact, nowadays many public spaces are subject to control and usually used as a means to exclude "undesirable" people (Davis, 1990:243). This situation can be seen in the private enclosure of communities, and in semi-public spaces that are increasingly taking over our urban environment.

In the words of Chilean scholar Carlos de Mattos, shopping centres, malls and other *"urban artefacts"* (1999:41), with symbolic barriers and surveillance, have become more used than squares and streets. As say Peter Marcuse and Ronald van Kempen in their book

"Of states and cities: the partitioning of Urban Space" (2002: 8) the partitioned [7] city is separating the enclaves where the better-off decide to live and the ghettos where the poor are involuntarily confined .

Young (2000, 224) claims that strangers with diverse backgrounds, ways of life, local affinities and goals dwell together in a complex causal relationship in metropolitan regions, and because they dwell together in this way, they have obligations of justice to one another. "It is not a question of tolerance but a question of inclusion, inclusive political institutions do not require that all the members of the polity mutually identify" (2000:225). For Young, (2000:13) inclusion in decision-making is a core of the democratic ideal; then, to the extent that such political exclusion exists, democratic societies do not live up their promise (2000:13) She is suspicious of an ideal of integration that expects people to conform to hegemonic norms and propose to focus on the need to bring people the right to truly influence policy-making processes and outcomes. The importance of Young's approach is that she bases her moral arguments on a theoretical description and interpretation of the structure and processes of contemporary societies that claim to follow democratic values".

Here, it is important to say that the last three Chilean governments have clearly expressed their desire to enhance democracy and to focus on *"growth with equity"*.
Therefore, reintegration should be meant to promote people's freedom of choice and opportunity to decide their locales and the type of housing they want. Justice or integration is not a question of redistribution of goods and services but, even more important, the distribution of rights, and in particular, the access to decision-making processes [8]. But as Young asserts, rights are relationships and not material resources which can be clearly quantified. Rights are *"institutionally defined rules specifying what people can do in relation to one another. Rights refer to doing more than having, to social relationships that enable or constrains actions"* (Young, 1990:25).

Consequently, upgrading and reintegrating existing social housing is understood as the process of addressing social and spatial disparities that affect certain areas and parts of the population for whom not only the access to material resources is denied but also the right to use the city and to "flourish". While the idea of reintegrating existing social housing is focused, predominately, on enabling people to act through establishing the right of upgrading, the latter (upgrading) is the result of such a process of enabling.

---

[7] Marcuse and van Kempen use the word "partition" to explain the current disintegration of urban spaces, which seems -for these authors- more adequate than dualization or polarisation because the cities are usually not only divided into two parts.

[8] It is important to notice that since the return to democracy in 1990, every Chilean government has declared their political commitment not only to the reduction of poverty, but also to "growth with equity".

"Egalitarians should not give up constructive engagement in the debate over what constitutes inclusion [integration], how it may be measured and how it may be fostered. Inclusion can be used to advance the cause of equality" (Levitas, 1998:186).

2.9 Social Exclusion through Housing in Chile: a Theoretical Model

The following model (page 48) represents and *"ideal-type"* of exclusion through housing in Chile and aims at summarising the theoretical framework discussed above. This model brings together a series of assumptions that are both related to this discussion and to the hypotheses as well as to the main question of this work: has current Chilean housing policy actually sharpened existing social and spatial inequalities? Or more specifically: does it lead current housing policies to a process of social exclusion through housing?

The model assumes a causative structure that goes from the definition of housing policy to the need for upgrading and reintegration. That means that every action may direct to an effect. In its first level, it is suggested that housing policies are not merely the result of national politics and socio-historical aspects, but they are also influenced by international trends.

International trends are defined as all possibly identifiable external factors that affect the definition of housing policy, i.e.: international cooperation agreements, conditions imposed by external agencies to give loans (IMF), national advisers (with studies abroad) or international advisers, and even fashionable trends could be considered. National politics has a major connotation. It aims at revealing the different forces that influence the shaping of housing policy, namely political parties, research institutions, grassroots movements, ideological approaches and economical constrains, etc.

The third aspect, the socio-historical aspects, attempts to identify societal paradigms and their shifts throughout history. Paradigms here are understood as predominant models or "leitbilder" that guide action. Once housing policy is already defined, it may play a role in at least three directions: allocation, location and "shaping" the "product" through the definition of standards for social housing. As the implementation of housing policy involves different governmental agencies, departments, and people, the role of this policy in determining these directions is here expressed as "the role of government".

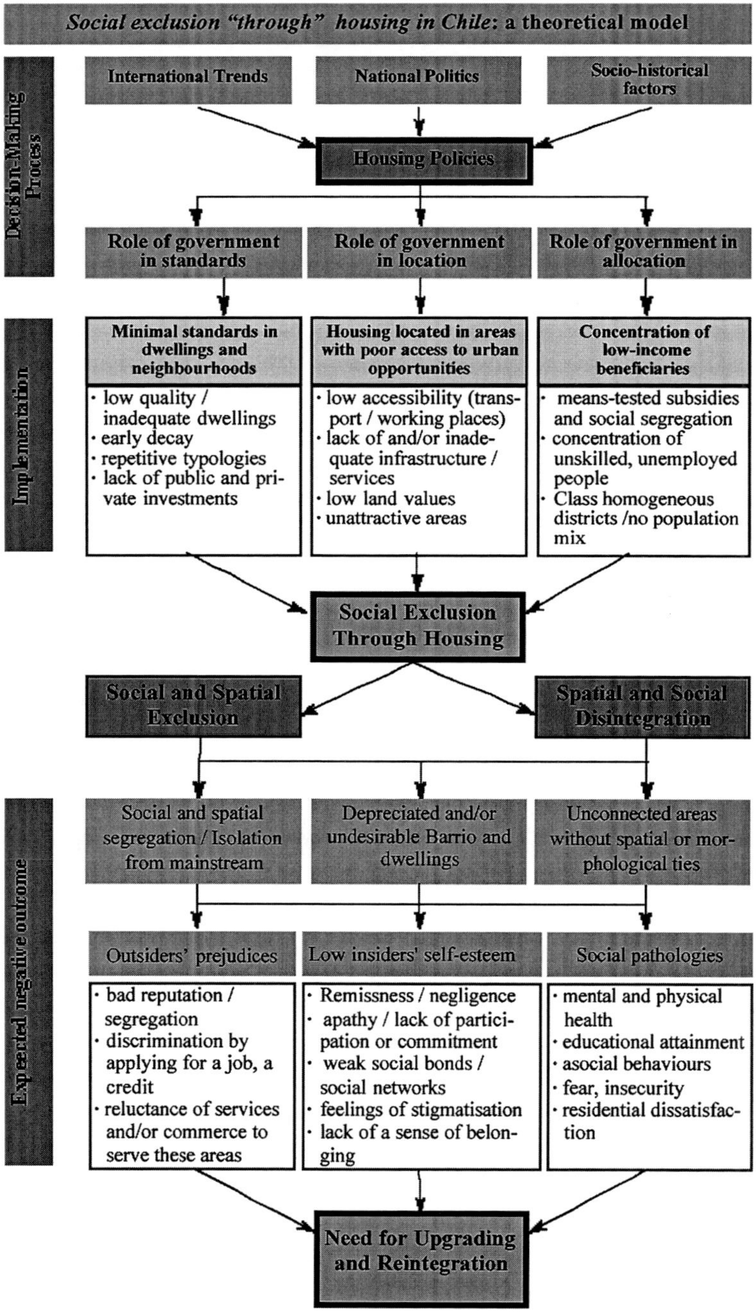
Social exclusion "through" housing in Chile: a theoretical model
Decision-Making Process
International Trends
National Politics
Socio-historical factors
Housing Policies
Role of government in standards
Role of government in location
Role of government in allocation
Implementation
Minimal standards in dwellings and neighbourhoods
· low quality / inadequate dwellings
· early decay
· repetitive typologies
· lack of public and private investments
Housing located in areas with poor access to urban opportunities
· low accessibility (transport / working places)
· lack of and/or inadequate infrastructure / services
· low land values
· unattractive areas
Concentration of low-income beneficiaries
· means-tested subsidies and social segregation
· concentration of unskilled, unemployed people
· Class homogeneous districts /no population mix
Social Exclusion Through Housing
Social and Spatial Exclusion
Spatial and Social Disintegration
Expected negative outcome
Social and spatial segregation / Isolation from mainstream
Depreciated and/or undesirable Barrio and dwellings
Unconnected areas without spatial or morphological ties
Outsiders' prejudices
· bad reputation / segregation
· discrimination by applying for a job, a credit
· reluctance of services and/or commerce to serve these areas
Low insiders' self-esteem
· Remissness / negligence
· apathy / lack of participation or commitment
· weak social bonds / social networks
· feelings of stigmatisation
· lack of a sense of belonging
Social pathologies
· mental and physical health
· educational attainment
· asocial behaviours
· fear, insecurity
· residential dissatisfaction
Need for Upgrading and Reintegration

The role of the government in allocation may basically cause exclusion through housing when it concentrates people with the same income level and, thus, prevents the mix of populations with diverse backgrounds. Allocation may involve not only the creation of class homogeneous districts but also the detaching of people from their original locales and social networks.

The second direction, location, brings attention to the role of the government in determining where social housing is located. The model assumes that social housing is mainly located not only in areas with low land value, but also in districts that lack infrastructure, that are poorly served and that have low accessibility to main urban opportunities such as working places, transportation, leisure, etc. In relation to the third direction, here it is assumed that the government is the main actor responsible in the defining of standards, which are usually "minimal" and lead to inadequate dwellings with low quality and that present evidences of early decay. Adequate housing is basically understood as a type of dwelling that satisfies people's needs in terms of the provision of enough and "appropriate" space to develop their home activities and to avoid overcrowding.

Based on the theoretical framework, the model suggests that the combination of the last three directions (allocation, location and standards) causes social exclusion through housing. Yet, exclusion through housing may have spatial and social outcomes, which are also intertwined, and that affect each other. While the category "social and spatial exclusion" emphasises social aspects without disregarding the spatial connection, the second one emphasises the spatial ones. Therefore, the model organises "more social" aspects on the left side and "more spatial" aspects on the right side of the model. Nevertheless, it is assumed that the boundaries between aspects are far from clear without empirical analysis.

These two abovementioned categories may originate (a) social and spatial segregation, or isolation from the "mainstream", (b) a depreciated and/or undesirable "*barrio*" or neighbourhood as well as the dwellings themselves, and (c) unconnected areas that have no spatial or morphological links with the rest of the city. The category (a) aims at representing the phenomenon of social exclusion in terms of the isolation of certain parts of the population from the rest of the population; they are not "visible" for many and they "feel" a sort of discrimination. The category (b) recognises that some neighbourhoods and properties are less desirable than others, and many people will not move there by choice. Finally, the category (c) attempts to prove the physical and morphological disparities among districts and the quality of dwellings. Yet, it assumes that place and dwellings affect people's integration.

These last three categories may have as outcomes (d) outsiders' prejudices, (e) insiders' low self-esteem, and (f) the triggering of other social pathologies. Outsiders' prejudices may be reflected in different sorts of discrimination such as lack of access to credits or loans, unsuccessful job applications, as well as the reluctance of public and private services and commerce to be located there.

The low self-esteem of insiders may be reflected in several aspects such as remissness, apathy, lack of participation and commitment with their surrounding neighbours, which could be the result of weak bonds or may produce them. In addition, feelings of stigmatisation or shame may be present and their sense of belonging reduced. In the end, social pathologies are expressed in typical aspects presented in most "ghettos" of low-income people: asocial behaviours, fear and insecurity, as well as other undesired outcomes such as early pregnancy, low educational attainment and residential dissatisfaction. Many of these aspects may, in addition, be related to the type of dwelling, i.e.: the lack of internal space in flats may push youth outside, and the lack of adequate social infrastructure in the surroundings may facilitate the formation of gangs.

This model has influenced the methodology for the case studies, and additionally, has influnced the basis of the indicators developed -as well as forming part of them- to measure the needs for upgrading and reintegration.

Chapter 3: Methodology

3.1 General Orientation

In chapter two, the basic framework was delineated and a theoretical model to analyse exclusion through housing in Chile proposed. In this chapter, the main methodological orientation of the study is exposed with a particular emphasis on the case studies.

As was mentioned in chapter one, this work pursues to combine a perspective that intertwines housing policies and their socio-spatial manifestations. It is based on the assumption that housing policies have reinforced social exclusion, but they could, however, be used to help in changing this situation -through upgrading policies- and assembling a reintegrated city. Therefore, the main goals are to prove that *exclusion through housing* is an existing phenomenon in Santiago de Chile and that there is a need for relevant policy changes.

In order to reach these aims, interpretative and analytical approaches have been chosen. While the interpretative approach aims to reveal what has determined the structure of the Chilean housing model, the analytical approach pursues a close observation of its impacts, results and the prospects for its improvement.

The linkages between socio-economic and historical processes, the normative framework that regulates urban and housing programmes, and the socio-spatial characteristics of the city have been examined, with a particular focus on the type of social housing that has been created.

These aspects aim at revealing the first questions posed by the theoretical model presented in chapter two: how was Chilean housing policy shaped? And which relevant factors determined its origins and features? In addition, the analysis of housing policies throughout history aims at setting the "yardsticks" to compare current policy and its effects in relation to former interventions. Once this basic background about current housing policy is established, it arrives to a question derived from the first hypothesis: has current housing policy sharpened existing inequalities?

Therefore, besides the revision of relevant literature and the development of a conceptual model, this work confers special attention to the interpretation of historical policies and the analysis of a concrete case study which includes the analyisis of the impacts of current housing policy.

3.2 The Case Study

The case study focuses on the compounds of estates built through the governmental housing programme *"Vivienda Básica"*(PVB) in the city of Santiago, particularly those located within the urban area that is composed of 34 districts. Besides their quantitative importance[9], the estates completed by the PVB exhibit several pathologies such as substandard construction, inadequacy in terms of internal area -overcrowding- and early decay. In addition, various social problems including delinquency, drug abuse and juvenile unemployment are becoming typical features of these areas.

The fact that the social housing estates are collective structures -with various shared spaces- offers both constraints as well as opportunities for possible improvements. Accordingly, the aims of this study are twofold: first, to visualise the prototypical needs prior to upgrading and the possible requirements to tackle them, and, second, to identify both spatial and social levels of integration. The study also discerns general societal tendencies and the orientation of social policies and identifies the stakeholders involved in such a process.

The case study is carried out at two levels: Macro (the city) and Meso-micro (the neighbourhood and the dwellings). Although every level of analysis has its own objectives, the main objectives of the complete case study are the following:

- To identify and classify the distribution of social housing, in particular the estates of *Vivienda Básica*, in the city as well as at the neighbourhood level,
- To identify both spatial and social interactions between the projects and urban functions such as accessibility to infrastructure, working places and services, among others,
- To analyse and categorise the current state of different estates according to their location, the type of inhabitants and their access to opportunities,
- To categorise the levels of social and spatial exclusion

3.2.1 The City Level

At the city level, the study examines the main spatial features of the city of Santiago as they relate to social housing location and accessibility of infrastructure, services and working places. This analysis leads to a categorisation or clustering of districts with social

[9] The PVB represents more than 16% of the total number of dwellings built-up between 1990 and 1970, and around 70% of the government produced housing for the same period (Rojas, 1999).

housing estates but with different patterns of growth, diverse levels of accessibility and diverse physical surroundings. Three districts and three specific compounds of estates were selected for analysis according to the following additional criteria:

- Age: existence of *Vivienda Básica* estates with similar constructive typology but different periods of construction
- Image and architecture: conglomerates which show different designs of both dwellings and estate configuration and diverse communitary interventions
- State of maintenance : developments that present diverse states of maintenance both of buildings and their surroundings.

3.2.2 Neighbourhood and Dwellings Level

The analysis at the neighbourhood level identifies the main characteristics of the districts and the relationships between housing distribution and its specific location in the neighbourhood such as morphological connections, accessibility to local centre and transport.

The analysis at the dwellings level focuses on the estates' spatial configuration, their state of maintenance, and the type of interventions implemented by the beneficiaries. In addition, it includes exploratory interviews with a small sample of beneficiaries in order to classify resident perceptions in determined groups of estates.

As a result of this analysis, it is expected to find out relevant factors that influence both the physical state of the estates and their level of integration into their closest environment as well as to evaluate their need for upgrading.

3.3. Methodological Tools and Sources

The case study has included three non-linear phases: Data Collection, Field Inquiry and Exploration.

Data collection included basic and general information acquired through the revision of statistical information and a mapping of the city, the neighbourhood and the specific estates to be studied. The City level analysis and the selection of three case study areas are the first results derived from this information.

Data was collected from various sources. Statistics about housing distribution by district and year are from the Ministry of Housing and Urban Affairs' (MINVU) yearly report and were gathered by the Centro de Estudios Sociales SUR. General data about population, housing construction, infrastructure, and poverty come from the last four censuses (1970, 1982, 1992 and 2002) and from the last two CASEN(10) surveys (1996, 1998). In addition, reports and studies coming from different ministries (Ministry of Planning, Ministry of Transportation) as well as basic data from the three selected municipalities were used. Maps and aerial photos are from MINVU.

The field inquiry focused on the direct examination of three particular neighbourhoods and included personal contact with some inhabitants and other onsite observations. Semi-structured interviews were held and a set of spreadsheets and checklists were implemented. In addition, local authorities and community groups relating to the specific neighbourhood were interviewed. The exploratory interviews were conducted in eight randomly selected households per compound, according to a pre-designed questionnaire that is included in the appendix.

Sources of information not directly related with the specific case study area were explored. Interviews with academic, institutional and governmental specialist were held, and information about new programmes and studies were collected. These contacts helped in finding other sources of information and studies recently published, for example, the study about residential satisfaction carried out by the Universidad de Chile and the study about estate pathologies carried out by the MINVU.

3.4 Instruments and Procedure for the Case Studies

Every level of study required a distinct procedure and the use of different tools. Multiple sources of information also needed to be processed using various instruments.

At the city level, the study was based on a digitalised map of the whole city with its main infrastructure which was overlayed with a set of socio-economic indicators previously selected through data collection and which were "performed" in order to make them comparable (11).

The process of overlaying databases and maps was done through a GIS (Geographical Information System) programme, which facilitated the visualisation of the general spatial situation of the city, for example its main transportation nets, location of working areas, as

(10) The CASEN Survey is a socio-economical characterisation of households periodically implemented by the Ministry of Planning (Mideplan)

(11) Sometimes the indicator does not allow comparison, due to they are express in different units such as percentage, number, proportions, and so on. Therefore a process of normalisation should be done.

well as numerical data in the form of indicators. The indicators are managed in a database, for clear registration and better comparability. A sample of these data is included in the appendix.

Most of the data was accessible only in form of crude statistics containing diverse indicators such as access to health, illiteracy and unemployment that are not necessarily comparable to one another. In order to overcome this problem, the indicators had to be normalised using the following formula:

$$0 \leq = \frac{Xij - Xi\ min,\ j}{Xi\ max,\ j - Xi\ min,\ j} \leq 1$$

A value of 1 represents the best situation and a value of 0 the worst. If a value of an indicator is close to or equals 0,5, this represents a mediocre situation. The process of normalisation was performed to compare groups of diverse indicators and, thereby, to facilitate a clustering of districts or "*comunas*" into four categories. These categories are: Social, Infrastructural, Demographic, and Physical aspects.

The first category includes indicators of poverty, unemployment, years of study, food subsidies, quality of health and income. The infrastructural aspects combines indicators of school deficits, working places as well as accessibility to green areas, to health centres and to transportation. The third category basically includes indicators of overcrowding, population and densities. The fourth category includes a selection of indicators of housing quality, land value, average square meters per dwelling and of the location of social housing estates.

In the end, these four categories were combined through an experimental cluster analysis using average values. This resulted in four types of districts which facilitates the selection of three case studies with the help of additional empirical criteria. Further explanation about the selection of case studies is to be found in Chapter 5.

The four categories were selected because they represent some of the main aspects of exclusion through housing and integration discussed in the theoretical framework, namely location of social housing, concentration of low-income families, and access to urban opportunities, among others.

As opposed to the city level analysis, the neighbourhood analysis considers only a general level of data, and mainly relies on direct observations, data checks and semi-structured interviews. A sample of interviews is to be found in the appendix (Page 179).

Different upgrading necessities were analysed and classified into three categories: low quality of the dwelling, inadequacy and image. First, the low quality of the dwelling is already determined by the low construction standards and confirmed by the MINVU's study about pathologies. However, a checklist helped to identify the state of every compound. Second, the inadequacy of the dwellings is basically measured by the levels of overcrowding and the type of interventions carried out by the beneficiaries. On the other hand, the need for improving housing image relies mainly in resident perceptions obtained through the interviews.

The necessity for social reintegration are also the product of the semi-qualitative interviews. Integration was measured through direct observation and according to "felt" integration or belonging with respect to the city, the neighbourhood and the dwelling itself. "Felt" integration was interpreted based on the answers obtained to questions such as: How often do you go to other neighbourhoods? Why do you like this neighbourhood? Do you have friends here? Do you want to move?

The spatial integration of the *blocks* with their immediate surroundings can be measured with the following indicators: type of district (social and architectural features), connectivity to main roads; relation with the urban tissue; typology of surrounding dwellings; type of housing in the surroundings; access to services, social infrastructure; availability of commerce and recreational areas.

As a result, this level of analysis includes a general description of the main characteristics of every district and its situation within the city. This included not only its main features, but also the type of housing interventions carried out there. Besides clarifying the reasons behind the selection of every compound, a general analysis of the spatial configuration of every compound is presented. This analysis goes from the spatial relationship between the compound and its surrounding environment to the dwellings themselves. In addition, both resident interventions and perceptions are briefly discussed. These elements are used to compare the three cases and permitted the identification of similarities and differences among cases.

PART II

Chapter 4. Social Housing Policies in Chile

4.1 Introduction

Unlike other Latin American countries, where the "informal" city is clearly visible, in Chile the government shows a historically active role in arranging housing developments. As a matter of fact, since the early "hygienical" interventions in the second half of the nineteenth century to today's organised subsidiary system, most Chilean governments of the last century have not only tried to cope with housing needs, but have also pursued to institutionalise these efforts.

The results of these interventions are both observable in the large quantity of "*poblaciones*"[12] existing throughout the country, as well as in the consolidated public apparatus that was created to operate housing policies. During this historical process, many different housing schemes were developed; they do not only represent diverse political and technical approaches to housing, but also divergent societal aims that emerged over time.

The following chapter pursues, therefore, not only to describe current housing problems, but also to examine the main patterns of public interventions implemented throughout the history of the city of Santiago. Its main objectives are to capture the roots of urban segregation and the turning points in housing policy and practice that have influenced the current situation and to describe the main features of current plans and programmes that make Chile a particular case in the Latin American context.

4.2 The Origins of the "Social Question" (1875-1925)

Santiago, as many other Latin America cities, has been a hierarchically-divided city since its foundation in 1541. While Spaniards settled within the gridiron[13] -prominent people usually lived near or around the plaza native *"indios"* remained in the outskirts in isolated settlements (de Ramón, 2000). However, in the words of the historian Luis Alberto Romero it was *"a patrician society where decent and plebeian* [people],

---

(12) "Población" is the name that Chileans assign to every housing development that contains a repetitive typology and has been built either directly or indirectly by the government. Some authors also use this term as a synonym for "slum". Residents prefer the term "Villa".

(13) A gridiron of streets from north to south and east to west with a central square or "plaza" at the core, was part of the urban guidelines set up by the Spaniards through the "Ley de Indias" (Indias' Law). The Plaza was both a meeting- and marketplace and the most representative buildings of the city such as the Cathedral, administrative offices, and the most powerful families' houses surrounded it.

[in spite *of being] perfectly separated for a clear and impassable breach* [they] *shared not just a physical space, but also ways of life, attitudes and values"* (Romero, 1997:167-author translation).

Things changed dramatically after independence in 1810, especially within the second half of the nineteenth century when the city started to grow explosively. As the recently born republic preserved the centralist pattern inherited from the Spaniards, Santiago not only began to concentrate most of the investments -represented by a massive urban transformation- but also to consolidate its position as the main political and administrative centre.

The city started to receive massive migration both composed of rural unemployed people and well-off families from southern provinces that were taking positions in the new bureaucracy. In addition, the opening of the new republic to more external markets was also attracting an important stream of migration from abroad (Romero, 1997:168-170; de Ramón, 2000:184-188)

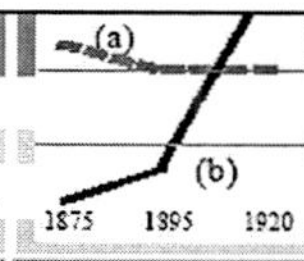

Year	Hectares (a)	Variation Period (%)	Average Increase (%)	
1810	No data	-----	-----	
1875	1.490	-----	-----	
1895	1.836	23.22	1.04	
1920	4.876	165.22	3.62	
Year	**Hectares (a)**	**Variation Period (%)**	**Average Increase (%)**	**Ratio increase (a/b)**
1810	60.000	-----	-----	-----
1875	129.000	115.00	1.12	-----
1895	256.000	98.45	3.30	0.32
1920	516.000	101.52	2.69	1.34

Fig. 01: Urban Growth in the ninteenth century

Source: de Ramón, 2000 and author self-calculation

These were times of affluence, and the city strove to reflect its republican values through the construction of many public buildings, a sewerage system, public lights and parks, which were completed according to "imported" European plans and/or architects. Some of these public investments favoured the first outward migration of wealthier families toward the southwest and west of the city. Indeed, the opening of new boulevards and a big park -the Campo de Marte- located in the southwest, attracted other private investment such as a riding club and the construction of mansions and "palaces" for the most prominent families (de Ramón, 2000). While the first "palaces" close to downtown still used a continuous façade (Fig.2), the new more distant mansions began to use the "garden city" model already "en vogue" (Fig.3).

Fig. 02: "Palace" in Midtown

Fig. 03: Mansion near to the Campo de Marte

Source: CA, 1988. Separata Revista Ciudad y Arquitectura

On the other hand, four types of situations describe the "plebeian" habitat of those times: shanties or *"ranchos"* built outside of the formal gridiron, shacks built on rented land -both outside and within the formal city-, rented rooms in formerly better-off large houses, and privately developed *"conventillos"*.[14]

These various forms of habitats presented different problems. The *"ranchos"* that were mostly located in the northern part of the city, and included a smaller number in the south, were too far away to be a problem, particularly because they were separated from the "official" city by the Mapocho River and the San Miguel Channel respectively (Hidalgo, 2002:93;Romero, 1997:27).

On the other hand, most of the shacks existing on private rented land and *conventillos* were not only located within the gridiron, but they were also much more overcrowded and unhealthy than the ranchos located at the periphery (Gross, 1988:12) (Fig. 4-5).

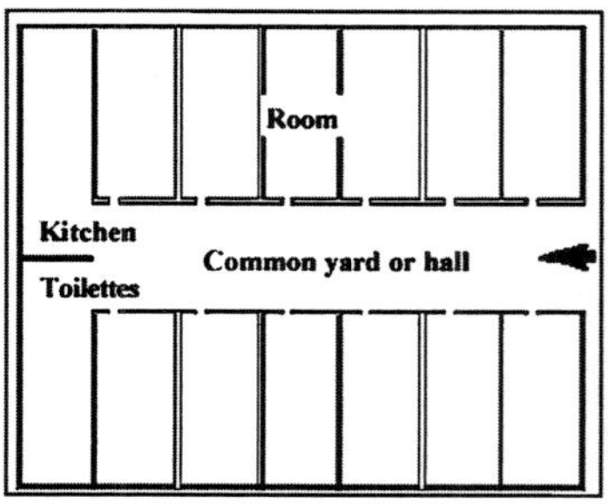

Fig. 04: A Conventillo by the early 1900s

Fig. 05: Scheme of a typical plan of a Conventillo

Source: Archivo Chilectra

[14] There were different types of *"conventillos"*, which included both small dwellings in a common passage (known as *Cités*), and single rooms in a passage with common services at the end of the plot. Overcrowding was one of the main problems in *conventillos*, reaching up to 1100 inhabitants per hectare in some of them.

As a matter of fact, the hygienical conditions of these settlements were seen as the source of many epidemics that affected the city in this period. They were also held responsible for other social problems such as increasing delinquency and alcoholism (Romero, 1997:169).

The "illustrated own city" that was making its own image according to European parameters of what a city should be, started to look with horror at the development of a "barbarian" city just at its side (Romero, 1997: 152)[(15)].

One of the consequences of this pattern of development was that the former kind of social equilibrium, in *"a breached but integrated society"* in Romero's words, began to be lost in the second half of the century when unregulated growth, diseases and initial social distress started to disquiet the ruling élite.

Therefore, the "social question" became the centre of public debate (Gross, 1988:12). This was accompanied by a kind of hygienist urbanism, which pursued not only the prevention of diseases, but also -from a paternalistic and moralist perspective- the "redemption of the indecent classes" (Romero, 1997:155). As a result, several ordinances regulated the minimal requirements for "low born" housing, and restricted the location of ranchos outside of the recently created *"camino de cintura"*. This was also at a time when concerns about public infrastructure requirements arose, especially regarding the delineation of streets, water supply and the removal of garbage (de Ramón, 2000: 151-155).

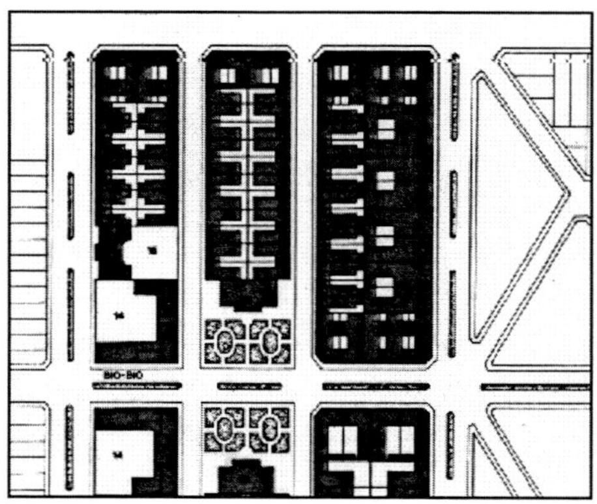

Fig. 06: Población Huemul built in 1914

Source: CA, 1988.
Separata Revista Ciudad y Arquitectura

[(15)] These assertions were pointed out by the intendant Vicuña who distinguished between the "own civilised city" and the "barbarian one" that was "the herdsman of the death" for him. (Romero, 1997:152)

The influence of social trends coming from Europe also played an important role. Indeed, according to Hidalgo (2002), the first international congress of low-income housing held in Paris in 1889 and a number of congresses that followed promoted values such as the cooperative system and property rights for workers as a way to obtain harmonic, sustainable and peaceful societies (Hidalgo, 2002:84).

Within this context, in 1906 the *"Ley de Habitaciones Obreras"*, or Workers' Housing Law Council, was created in Chile based on Belgian and French laws. The operative "arm" of this Law was the *"Consejo de Higiene"* or Council for Hygiene. This Council was in charge of supervising basic sanitary conditions, rehabilitating existing housing, and promoting the involvement of private and charity organisations in the construction of social housing (Hidalgo, 2002:88).

According to the same author, the Council played an important role in the sanitation of dwellings because it actually demolished or improved worker's dwellings that did not fulfill the already established minimal standards of hygiene and habitability. However, the council only built few *"poblaciones"* directly, and most of the initiatives to build social housing arose from philantrophy and Catholic charity (Hidalgo, 2002:89-92) which produced many *"cités"* and *"higienical conventillos"*.

One important property of these developments was that they respected the urban tissue and used the extension of the gridiron as a main pattern. They also pursued to implement a kind of "ideal housing" according to paradigms coming from Europe for workers' dwellings. As a matter of fact, the idea was to build self-sufficient neighbourhoods with complete social infrastructure including health services, a post office, schools and a church, among others (Fig. 6). The typical architectural solution were one-storey houses with a continuous façade, a small yard, and services at the end of the plot.

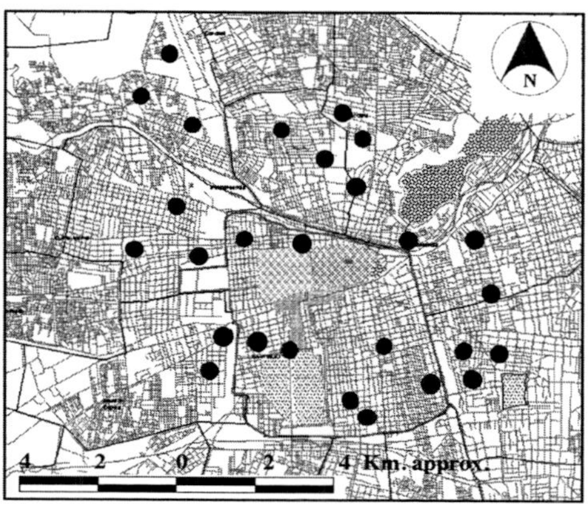

Map 01: Social housing before 1925

Source: Data location from Hidalgo, 2002

Between the late 1890s and the early 1900s, many new districts were created in the outskirts of downtown that attracted middle and high-income families under the promise of better air and a rural atmosphere (de Ramón, 2000:205-210). The tendency to move out of the city centre was reinforced by increasing rents caused by landlord speculation, which also induced social distress and popular demonstrations against landlords.

4.3 The Early Intents of Institutionalisation (1925-1950)

By the early 1920s, the collapse of the Saltpetre industry and the worldwide economical crisis triggered a process of import substitution through industrialisation, and once more Santiago concentrated most of the new manufacturing.

It was also the time of political and social transformation resulting in the creation of new political parties, which represented the whole spectrum of ideas; a new Constitution was enacted in 1925 and modern Unions replaced former artisan organisations. In the same vein, liberal and social democratic governments started to rule the country replacing the former elitist governments (de Ramón, 2000).

At that time, the housing rental market was unable to cope with a steadily increasing demand, and unregulated rents were arbitrarily controlled by speculators (Hidalgo, 2002:103). As a consequence, the first social movement of politically organised tenants began to pressure the government for effective housing policies.

Year	Hectares (a)	Variation Period in %	Average Increase %	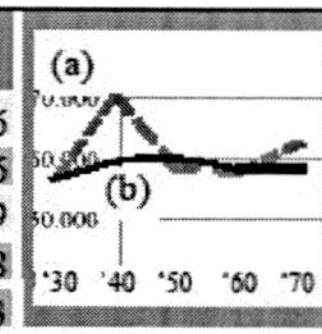
1930	6.500	33.33	2.86	
1940	11.017	69.49	5.16	
1950	15.351	39.34	3.29	
1960	21.165	37.87	3.18	
1970	31.841	50.44	4.03	
Year	**Population (b)**	**Variation Period in %**	**Average Increase %**	**Ratio Increase (a/b)**
1930	696.200	34.92	2.97	0.96
1940	995.600	43.00	3.54	1.46
1950	1.440.000	44.64	3.65	0.90
1960	2.006.000	39.31	3.28	0.97
1970	2.821.000	40.63	3.38	1.19

Fig. 07: Urban Growth between 1920-1970

Source: de Ramón, 2000 and author self-calculation

Fig. 08: Población Manuel Montt built in 1925

Source: CA, 1988. Separata Revista Ciudad y Arquitectura

By 1925, the government had reacted with the generation of "tribunales de vivienda" -housing courts- that were supposed to regulate the rental market and by creating the *"Consejo superior del Bienestar"* or Superior Council for Welfare that encouraged the construction of workers' dwellings both by promoting the creation of workers' associations and by giving incentives to employers to build dwellings for their employees (Hidalgo, 2002).

The *Consejo* also intervened in the land market by buying plots of land and reserving them for future housing and infrastructure developments of public interest. It was also in charge of building social infrastructure such as schools, post offices, public restaurants, and theatres as well as the rehabilitation of unhealthy dwellings. According to Silva, (Silva, 1997: 266), this governmental measure was the first to achieve concrete results: 29 *Poblaciones* were constructed in Santiago and another 19 in the provinces, many of them built through housing cooperatives. However, according to the Association of Chilean Architects, by 1930 almost 50% of the population lived in *conventillos* (Gross, 1988:12), because most of the Consejo's activities only reached moderate low-income families, especially those organised through unions and cooperatives.

In addition, the growth rate of the city was very high (see Fig. 07), and pockets of shanties in the periphery continued to appear. Therefore, between 1930 and 1940, many legislations aimed at controlling urban growth, in particular, regarding the increasing emergence of shantytowns or *"callampas"*[16]. In the late 1920s, the *"Caja de la Habitación Popular"* or

[16] Shantytowns were called Callampas which is the Spanish word for mushroom because they used to appear overnight.

Fig. 09: Población Pedro Montt built in 1938

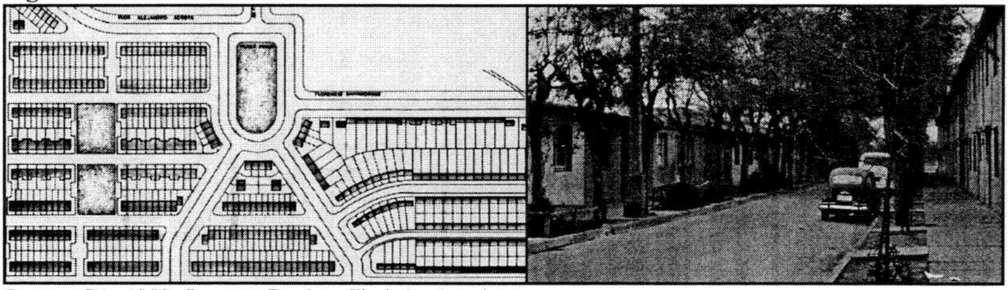

Source: CA, 1988. Separata Revista Ciudad y Arquitectura

"Savings Bank for popular housing" replaced the former *"Consejo Superior del Bienestar"*. This institution gave credits for the construction of social housing, subsidising households with many children and forcing private real estate to build at least 20% of social housing (Silva, 1997).

The first Ordinance for Construction and Urbanisation (OGUC) was enacted in 1931 in order to regulate urban development and housing quality, an important undertaking in a country continuously threatened by earthquakes. The corporation for aid and reconstruction (CORA) and the corporation to promote economic development (CORFO) were also created in this period in order to deal both with emergencies such as earthquakes and floods as well as to promote economic development, (Silva, 1997: 267).

The *Caja de la Habitación* was involved in the construction of more than 43.000 dwellings between 1936 and 1952. Although most of these developments still respected the gridiron (Silva, 1997), other innovations were introduced.

Fig. 10: Población Huemul 2 built in 1943

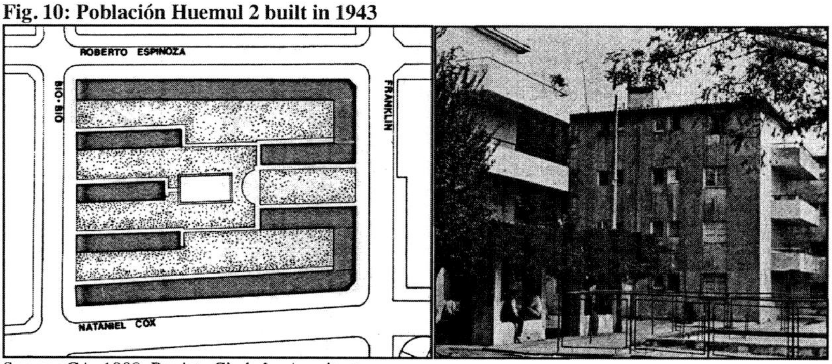

Source: CA, 1988. Revista Ciudad y Arquitectura

Frontyards were included, one and more storeys were mixed and the first estate of social housing was built in the *población* Huemul 2 which reached a density of 826 inhabitants per hectare (Fig. 10). According to Hidalgo (1999), the original idea of the Caja de la habitación was to continue building estates, though most of the new *poblaciones* were eventually built in extension. While the city was experiencing many independent interventions and the overall growth rate was still high, it lacked an urban plan that embraced the whole city as one cohesive unit.

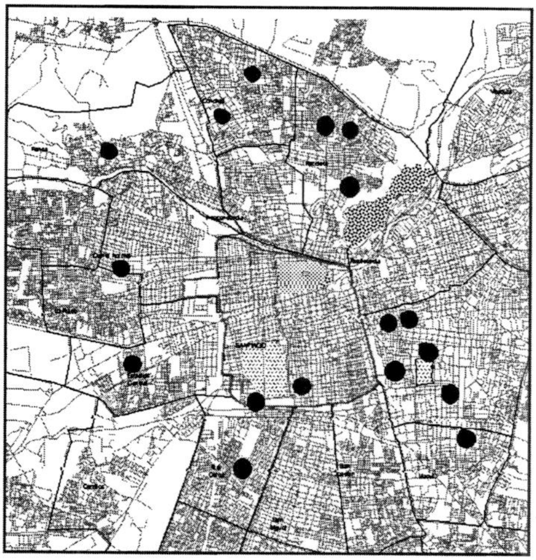

Map 02: Social housing between 1925-1953

Source: Data location from Hidalgo, 2002

A first attempt at developing such a plan was made by Austrian planner Karl Brunner who finished a Master Plan of Santiago at the beginning of the 1930s. This plan included a new ring road and defined the location of services, housing and industry (de Ramón, 2000:221) [(17)].

However, this plan was not fully implemented, and its results were constrained to some interventions in the core of the city. Nevertheless, every district or "*comuna*" was working on its own "*plan regulador*" or regulatory plan. The improvement of public transportation, and private automobiles encouraged the suburbanisation of middle and high-income families, who continued migrating preferably to the eastern "*comunas*" of Providencia, Las Condes and Ñuñoa. The first multi-storey office buildings appeared downtown, and some apartments for middle and high-income families were built in the *comuna* of Providencia and Santiago (de Ramón, 2000).

[(17)] *Camino de cintura*: The first ring road that was created by the intendant Vicuña Mackennain 1875, currently makes up the borders of the district of Santiago.

Fig. 11: "Chalets" built through Pereira´s Law

Source: CA, 1988.
Revista Ciudad y Arquitectura

However, the Chilean "ideal" of the single-family house was still dominant in private and public housing alike. After 1948, the so-called *"Law of Pereira"* incited private involvement in social housing destined to middle-income families by a drastic reduction of taxes. This legislation fixed the maximal price per square meter that could be taken for social housing to no more than 60% of "basic" wages. As a result, within a period of two years, more than 16.000 single-family dwellings were built (Silva, 1997:269).

4.4 The Dreams of "Welfare Times" 1953-1973

After the Second World War, the Chilean economy was relatively stable, and the state was slowly becoming more involved in many areas of social policies such as health, education, social security and housing. The country was also already highly urbanised, compared with other Latin American countries at the time, with more than 60% of the country's population inhabiting urban areas and close to 20% concentrated in Santiago (Gilbert, 1998:26; de Mattos, 1999:41). In addition, the pace of urban growth decreased between 1940 and 1960, but the overall population still increased by over 3% (Fig. 7).

Consequently, urban problems were on the rise, especially because there was no plan to direct urban growth. As a result, squatters continued emerging in the periphery of the cities. As a matter of fact, the first "*toma*", or big land invasion, took place in the late 1950s in the southern periphery of the city (Richards, 1995:522).

The need for planning the growth of the city was evident, and in 1953m the former general ordinance for urbanisation and construction, OGUC, was reformed and transformed into a law. This measure gave the government more instruments to plan future developments. An important result was the first metropolitan inter-borough plan for the city, PRIS, which was conceived in the 1950s and finally enacted in 1960. Two main contributions of this plan were the creation of a new institutional framework for planning, and the basic coordination of different public ministries and agencies for its implementation (Silva, 1997:271-272).

Housing policies were also providing more integral solutions for the habitations of the poor. The government launched new programmes that included beneficiary participation (Haramoto, 1988:58) such as the "*Programa de autoconstrucción y ayuda mutua*" (self-construction and mutual help). Moreover, separate housing institutions were merged into the "*Corporación de Reconstrucción y de la Vivienda*" (CORVI or Corporation for Reconstruction and Housing), which took over responsibility for projecting, financing and building social housing. The CORVI also assumed the tasks of promoting housing research and technological innovation, which included the development of new materials for construction, the elaboration of master plans for every city and the expropriation of land considered as of public interest. It was further in charge of building schools and responsible for the coordination with other agencies to implement other social facilities.

Complementary to these efforts, all public financial institutions were fused in the relatively "young" *Banco del Estado* (State's Bank), which held the responsibility of receiving people's savings, giving preferential credits for social housing and managing mortgage portfolios (Silva, 1997:271). For social housing, two strategies were followed by the government: the design and construction of new *poblaciones* as well as the provision of sites and services accompanied by technical assistance for their construction (Fig. 12). The latter was done in cooperation with the United States government in the frame of a financial and technical agreement between CORVI and the Institute for Inter-American affairs (Haramoto, 1988:58).

Fig. 12: Población Riesco, 1953-55. Built by self-construction and mutual help.

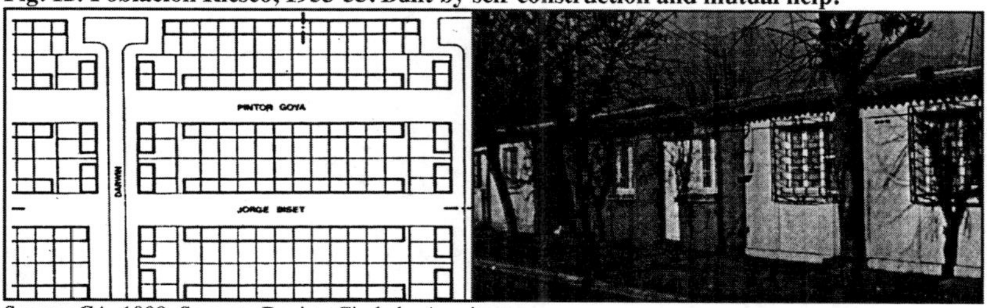

Source: CA, 1988. Separata Revista Ciudad y Arquitectura

As can be seen in the Figures 12-13, the main pattern of design followed the orthogonal lines of the streets, with straight façades, attached housing in one to three storeys, and densities between 170 and 350 inhabitants per hectare. However, in 1959 a new pattern was introduced that resembled German "*Siedlungen*", and showed the increasing influence of the modern movement in Chile.

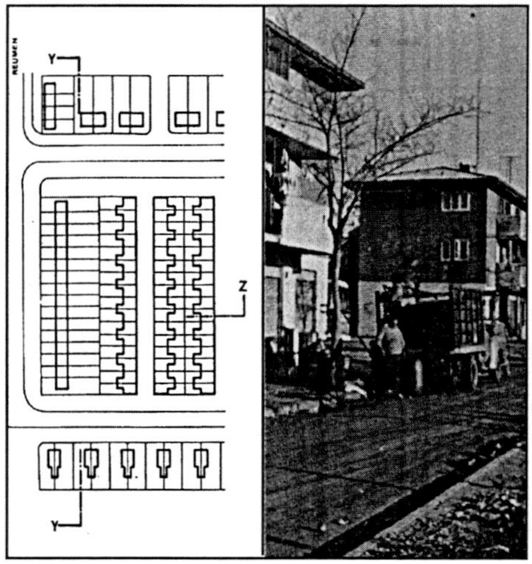

Fig. 13: Población Davila, 1956, built and designed by CORVI

Source: CA, 1988.
Separata Revista Ciudad y Arquitectura

Various large housing compounds were built in the periphery of the city, mainly in former agricultural areas , where land was cheap and close to industrial areas (Gurovich, 1988:65). The *población* J.A. Rios, for example, was one of the first housing developments with "super-*blocks*" that became more popular in the 1960's and 1970's and which broke with the former squares of the classical gridiron. Built in the northwest of the Mapocho River and outside of the formal city, the compound included a mixture of one and two storey single houses as well as isolated estates, reaching a total density of 520 inhabitants per

Fig. 14: Plan Juan A. Rios, 1959

Fig. 15: Attached housing and blocks

Source: CA, 1988. Revista Ciudad y Arquitectura

hectare (CA, 1988:45-48) (Fig. 14-15).

In spite of the outward growth of the city, Santiago was still preserving its unity and compactness. Every neighbourhood was developing its own character, and through public transportation, they had more or less equal access to the focal centre where the main commercial and service facilities were located. In addition, public services and infrastructure were being introduced into every sector. Distances were still not too long, and social "mobility" was a normal feature in a society where public education and health were affordable.

Social housing programmes were not able to reach the poorest segments of the population, and shantytowns or *"callampas"* (literally, mushrooms) were spreading even into affluent districts or *"comunas"*. Indeed, the 1960s and early 1970s were marked by an increase of shantytown movements demanding housing solutions in consonance with an increasing political "polarisation" which divided the nation into three clear forces: left, centre and right wing parties that were almost in a balance.

According to Kusnetzoff (1990), there was an undeclared acceptance of land invasions which led to their escalation over time; while in 1968 only 13 *"tomas"* were made, by 1970 more than 100 were accounted for. As a result, the city expanded at higher rates than population growth (Kusnetzoff, 1990:53). Moreover, housing began to be used as a political instrument, and every government started to promise a solution through detailed

Fig. 16: Población Lo Valledor, 1965

Source: CA, 1988. Revista Ciudad y Arquitectura

plans and programmes. However, no policy was able to control the augmenting quantity of land invasions or "*tomas*", and they continued to form part of some radical political movements (Kusnetzoff, 1990).

In this context, a series of programmes to provide land and basic infrastructure through upgrading actions was created. The government combined private and public initiatives by encouraging the saving of money through savings and loans associations for moderate-income families and governmentally supported savings institutions for low-income families (Rojas, 1997).

In the early 1960s, during the government of the right-wing president Alessandri (1958-1964), massive evictions were undertaken, and sites and services were the main response to those displaced families. But, land invasions did not cease in spite of the fact that police repression caused dozens of victims.

On the positive side, Alessandri held national sponsored contests to design and build huge compounds of social housing. However, they were mainly oriented to moderate lower and middle-income households. Most of these developments were favoured by the decree DFL No. 2 of 1959 which offered huge tax exemptions of up to twenty years, for houses that were less than 140 square meters in size (Kusnetzoff, 1990: 49). Because the savings and loans associations related to worker's activity (private or public) financed the construction of most of these compounds, they usally concentrated people with the same background and origin (Richards, 1995).

Fig. 17: Operación Sitio, 1970

Source: CA, 1988. Revista Ciudad y Arquitectura

The social democratic government of Frei (1964-1970) considered housing as "a right" and as "a basic need" and promoted its affordability for every type of family regardless of their income level (Haramoto, 1988:58). In his governmental plan, he offered to solve the invasions problem by developing subsidies and by promoting assisted self-construction. In 1965, the Ministry of Housing and Urbanism was created, in order to supervise both housing provision and urban development.

After 1966, CORVI began to act as an autonomous public enterprise in charge of designing, planning and executing urbanisation and housing plans and projects. Its tasks included the designing of prototypes for minimal housing with possibilities for future expansion and the implementation of basic social infrastructure. In addition, many other public enterprises

Fig. 18: Población Santa Anita, built in 1972

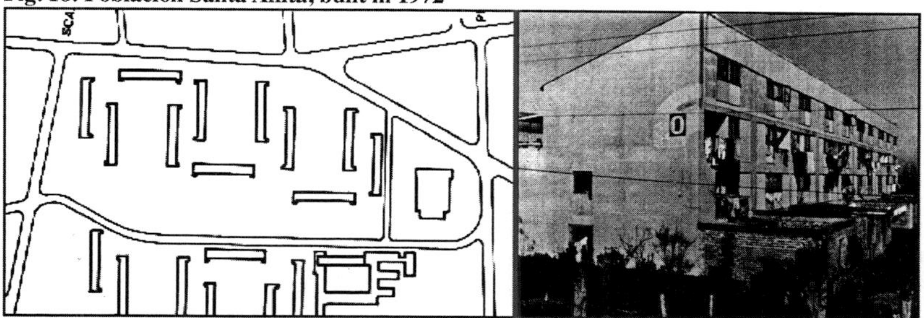

Source: CA, 1988. Revista Ciudad y Arquitectura

were created in the period such as CORHABIT and CORMU which were in charge of housing services and urban development respectively .

Moreover, the Ministry of Housing (MINVU) also controlled other public enterprises such as the water supply, sewage, and urban roads. These tremendously institutionalised enterprises demonstrate how consolidated the public apparatus was by that time (Silva 1997).

While the objective of Frei's government was to build complete dwellings with an average of 50 square meters, in the course of his presidency, these expectations were reduced to an "extensible" unit of 27 sqm.

Nonetheless, other programmes to cope with invasions were initiated such as *"Operación Sitio"* (Operation Site), and when the resources started lacking *"Operación Tiza"* (Operation Chalk) (Kusnetzoff, 1990:51).

"Operación Sitio" consisted of the delivery of totally urbanised plots of land on which the beneficiaries could build their own housing later, *"Operacion Tiza"* only assigned demarcated lots.

The socialist government under Allende (1970-1973) not only understood housing as a right, but believed that the state should be responsible for its provision in case people could not afford it. Housing was considered a means to develop human and social values, and *"it cannot be the object of lucre, it cannot be governed by economic rules, but must be based on social conditions and needs"* (Haramoto, 1988:58 - author translation).

Anti-segregationist policies were passed, and the government used the existing public enterprises to build houses not only where land was cheap, but also in well-off districts such as Las Condes and Ñuñoa. Initially, self-construction was not promoted out of respect for working class free time and leisure. This attitude also pursued the creation of employment by modernising the construction industry as a means to reactivate the economy (Haramoto, 1988:59).

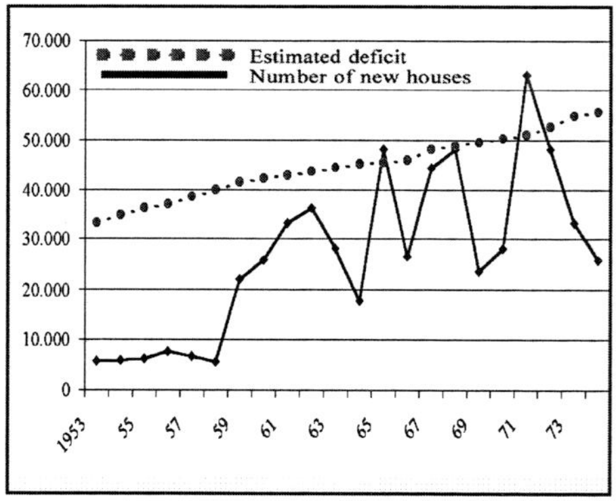

Fig. 19: Dwellings needed and built, 1953-1973

Source: Adapted from Rojas, 1999:10

However, popular expectations increased and invasions not only continued but were also encouraged by more radical groups. As a result, a programme was created through which the beneficiaries could participate in the design of their environments which included voluntary work in the construction. Other participative initiatives involving beneficiaries, ministerial officials and architects were also attempted (Haramoto, 1988; Kusnetzoff, 1990).

In spite of economic difficulties and socio-political distress, during Allende's rule a historical record of housing construction was reached: more than 60,000 dwellings by 1972 (Fig. 19).

4.5 The Neo-Liberal Agenda (1973-1989)

In September of 1973, a military coup d'etat headed by the General Pinochet overthrew Allende's democratic government and directed what some authors called a "neo-liberal revolution" (Richards, 1995; Moullian, 1997). Indeed, Chile was one of the first countries in the world to implement structural adjustment long before the International Monetary Fund (IMF) or the World Bank (WB) began widely to promote similar policies in the "developing world". "It was a revolution which saw full-scale privatisation, deregulation of capital markets, a shift to export-led growth" (Richards, 1995:515), as well as a complete restructuring of the role and structure of the government.

Within the frame of the neo-liberal agenda led by the "Chicago Boys"[(18)], the government assumed a subsidiary role as "facilitator", and promoted the expansion of the private sector into different social areas such as education, health, the retirement pension system and social housing. These changes resulted in a two-tier system -one public and one private-, which established a drastic difference in terms of affordability and accessibility of social services. However, such drastic shifts not only faced two severe economical crises (1975-76 and 1982-84), but also led to an increase in poverty, unemployment, and social protest [(19)] (Richards, 1995; de Ramón, 2000).

In addition, the government took other measures that strongly affected the urban and housing arenas. First, in 1979 the land markets were deregulated under the premise that scarcity of land was artificially produced by excessive state control. All the land restrictions existing in the still prevailing metropolitan regulatory plan of 1960 were eliminated, and the potentially urbanisable area was increased from 36,000 hectares to 64,000 (Harberger 1979; Kusnetzoff, 1990; de Mattos, 1999; Smolka and Sabatini 2000). But the explosion of urban sprawl, speculation and increase in land values finally made the regime "reduce those excessively free-market oriented principles in 1985" (de Mattos, 1999:44).

---

(18) Many of the ministers under Pinochet that took key positions in this period were postgraduated students of the Chicago School where one of the most influential professors was the Nobel Prize Laureate economist Milton Friedmann, widely known as a fierce promoter of a neo-liberal free-market economy.

(19) In 1982, overall unemployment reached 20%. In the construction industry -which usually serves as a mirror of economic trends-, it reached over 40%. While people living in poverty reached 39% in 1979, they were close to 50% in 1984-86 (Kusnetzoff, 1990; Richards, 1995; Ferraz, 1998). Successive and sustained demonstrations against the regime began from 1983 and continued until the plebiscite of 1988.

Second, between 1979 and 1985 a process of radication and eradication started, and new districts were created by the partition of the 17 former districts into 34. The eradication process resulted in the eviction of more than 28,000 families that were transferred, mainly from areas of higher land value, to districts located in the southern, northern and western periphery (Rodriguez and Icaza,1989; CED, 1990). On the other hand, the partition of districts facilitated the homogenisation of areas according to social classes. While some better-off districts such Las Condes and Ñuñoa lost most of their poorest inhabitants, rural and already poor areas received most of the evicted ones. The most dramatic case occured in La Pintana which was then still a rural area yet increased its population by 90% in two years (1982-4) (Kusnetzoff, 1990:61)

Third, land invasions were strictly repressed and a new phenomenon was created: *"los allegados"* ('drop-ins'), people who have to share a home, usually with their relatives, under overcrowded conditions. Actually, in the 1980s, it was common to find many houses in *poblaciones* with one to three shacks in the backyard; between three to six households were living in the same typical plot of 100 m2. According to Kusnetzoff (1990:60-62), by the late 1970s more than 142.500 households or 600.000 people were living as *allegados*. Nevertheless, impoverishment and political discontent led to two important land invasions or "*tomas*" in 1983 which received support from the Catholic Church, a fact that prevented major repression and assured that the occupants, close to 8,000 families, could remain in the place.

Fourth, after some trials and errors the subsidiary system for housing production was enhanced both through improvements in the application system and by the creation of new programmes targeted at low-income families [(20)]. As early governmental interventions on housing were very limited and could not cover the increasing demand, the MINVU developed a subsidiary system for housing in 1978 (Silva, 1997). This system was based on a combination of three main elements: beneficiary savings, public subsidy and private loans

According to Gilbert (2001:8) the influence of the neo-liberal perspective was clearly visible in the fact that *"the subsidiary system pursued to stimulate housing demand rather than housing supply"* and *"introduced the idea that housing was a good that could only be obtained through one's own efforts"*. The system was delineated demand-driven with the

[(20)] Between 1973 and 1979, the military regime carried out direct interventions such as buying and commercialising housing, giving credits to cooperatives and directly assigning subsidies to poor households (Silva, 1997:275-276).

expectation that housing production and finance would be performed by the private sector, and families could use their subsidies to buy the house that they wanted. However, housing remained unaffordable for many families.

They were "excluded" not only because the system had high savings requirements and indebtedness, but also because the market did not give them loans (Richards 1995; Silva, 1997).

4.5.1 The Birth of the Current Housing System

Various scholars agree that despite of all the *"free market rhetoric"*, the government was not completely insensitive to the social effects of its policies, and through a *"pragmatic decision"* persisted along with the long tradition of intervening in social policies (Richards, 1995; Rojas, 1999; Gilbert 2001).

In 1984, the leader of the Chilean Chamber of Construction (CChC) became Minister of Housing. His main aims were, without affecting public expenses, to increase the amount of available subsidies to the lowest income families and to reactivate construction activities. Accordingly, most of the existing programmes were reformulated, housing standards were reduced and the ministerial budget was reorganised (Richards, 1995; Silva, 1997)[(21)].

As private banks were not providing loans for low-income families, and therefore, no offer of affordable housing existed for them, the MINVU filled the gap both calling for bids for tenders and bringing directly long-term credits to the poorest families. The government continued assisting moderate and middle-income families with subsidies, but the amount of these subsidies was reduced, and they continued relying on market offer and loans.

In addition, MINVU had already been restructured and many of its functions deconcentrated by the creation of the *Secretarias Regionales Ministeriales* (SEREMIs) and the *Servicios Regionales de Urbanización* (SERVIUs). While MINVU kept its role in the formulation and supervision of plans and programmes, SEREMIs assumed the role of representing the ministry at the regional level and the task of preparing regional plans and programmes, while SERVIUs took over executive tasks (Silva, 1997)[(22)].

[(21)]The Chilean Chamber of Construction continues to be an influential actor to this day. It is important to take into account that the construction industry was one of the sectors most affected by the two economical crises, and therefore, it was very interested in revitalising construction activities (Richards, 1995:522).

[(22)] Most of the remaining departments of the former CORVI, CORHABIT, and CORMU, etc. were merged into the SERVIUs and SEREMIs.

In this context, the most important shift was a new emphasis on making subsidies effectively reach the poor through a means-tested system. Accordingly, in 1984 the questionnaire *ficha* CAS [(23)] (register of socio-economic stratification) became a requirement for the application procedure, in order to measure the socio-economic situation of potential beneficiaries (Richards, 1995; Ferraz, 1998; Rojas, 1999). Some authors point out that the idea was not only to continue helping people living in shantytowns, but also to address the needs of the allegados (Richards, 1995; Ferraz, 1998).

Consequently, in 1984 the *Programa de Vivienda Básica* was consolidated through the decree D.S. 62/84 [(24)]. The programme was conceived to solve the problems of "marginal" families by providing a minimal solution, consisting of a flat or an "attached" house (terraced in Britain) of 30 to 35 m2 with at least two bedrooms, a living-room, kitchen and bathroom (Minvu, 1984). For the financing of the solution, the government provided a subsidy of up to 75% of the cost of the dwelling, and a long-term credit for up to 20 years with minimal mortgages.

The *Programa de Vivienda Básica* was and remains as one of the most important housing programmes in Chile. In order to be elegible for this programme, applicants had to score within the lowest ranges of the *ficha* CAS and prove that they hold the minimal savings required by the system. In addition, the applicants needed to be registered at the regional SERVIU until they fulfilled their obligations and had accumulated enough time in waiting, which also passed to be part of the scoring requirements of the system.

According to Gilbert (2001:10), this kind of system not only pursued to encourage savings [(25)], but also to reinforce the idea that housing is a good that requires *"sacrifice and time"*. The registration in a waiting list performed the function of controlling demand, making planning easier to the government.

---

(23) The *ficha* CAS is administered by the municipalities and consists of a concise questionnaire that provides detailed information on the socio-economic situation of the household and living conditions (type of dwelling, number of people in the house, assets held by the family, etc.). Based on this information, the *ficha* CAS assigns a range of points between 380 and 770 points. People with less than 500 are considered extremely poor, and those between 500 and 540 as poor. In order to attenuate the impact of the withdrawal of the government from social policies, the military regime used the *ficha* CAS to allocate a wide range of subsidies such as access to free health, family allowances, nutritional programmes and free kindergartens (Richards, 1995:520-524)

(24) The Supreme decree number 62 of 1984 is the legal instrument that regulates the *Programa de Vivienda Básica* or "Basic housing programme".

(25) Figures from 1997 indicate that -in this year- there were more than 1.38 million savings accounts for housing with a total amount of around US$ 686 million (Pardo, 2000:5).

In Chile, two modalities are differentiated: a) the assistance of social housing production through subsidising the demand and b) the direct production of housing through bids for tender. They are known as "*Programas Privados*" and "*Programas SERVIU*" respectively. Even today, these two modalities represent the backbone of Chilean housing policy (see Boxes 1-2).

As a matter of fact, the democratic government that was installed in 1990 neither changed the basis of the economical system (Neo-liberalism) nor the type of subsidiary system for housing. Nevertheless, a renewed emphasis on social aspects was made. Many social indicators improved such as poverty which was reduced from 44% in 1987 to 28,5% by 1995 (Mideplan, 1999).

In order to cover the expected housing demand and to prevent massive "pent-up" land invasions, after 1990 many modifications of the social housing policy were passed and new subsidy lines and programmes were created especially targeted at the poorest segments of Chilean society.

Among the changes made to improve the affordability of housing, the MINVU again reduced the amount of subsidies aimed at assisting middle-income families and introduced the idea of "progressive" housing -a remake of sites and services-, which included the participation of the people and the support of NGOs.

The scheme of *Programas Privados* and *Programas SERVIU* remained but with a clear effort of reducing the importance of the latter and reinforcing the "private" alternative. The *Programas* SERVIU relied on three main actors: the applicants -later beneficiaries-, the Ministry of housing through its regional SERVIU's and the Construction companies. The types of actions that they must perform are presented in Box 1.

Within this system, other actors such as the municipalities play a secondary role. The municipality has to complete the *ficha* CAS and send it to SERVIU, and it also has to deliver construction permits and the acceptance of the final works. However, even the task of safeguarding the type of construction to be done in its territory is undermined by the central authorities: if a municipality does not want to accept a new development, the respective regional SEREMI has the right to decide for them.

The second scheme of housing provision, the *Programas Privados*, relies mainly on private offers and the involvement of beneficiaries. It also aims at involving other agencies such as NGOs, local governments and charity institutions. In this case the participation of the three main actors is presented in box 2.

Box 1: Programas SERVIU - Actors and actions

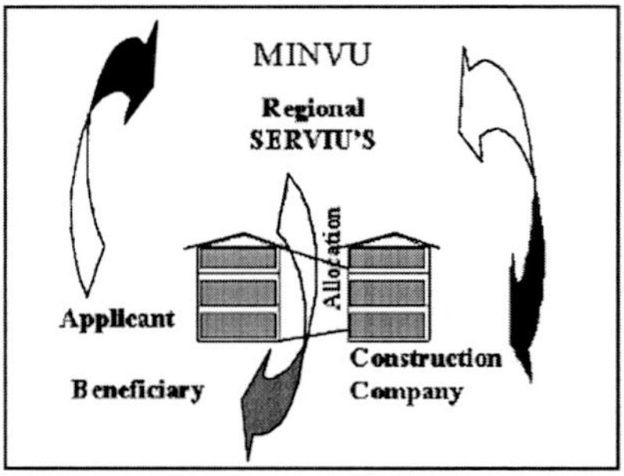

The Applicants

· Request the ficha CAS (a) in their local municipality
· Fill-out the registration form in their respective regional SERVIU.
· They can apply individually or in groups.(b)
· Complete the requirement of savings (c)
· Receive or refuse the assigned dwelling and sign a mortgage contract.

(a) The ficha CAS must be updated every six months. The municipalities send it directly to SERVIU.
(b)Encouragement is given to people who apply collectivelly (Score)
(c) A registered interested person does not become a proper applicant until he/she has completed the savings requirement and other personal data such as the ficha CAS are updated.

SERVIU

· Maintains a list of applicants and -usually- goes through three processes of selection of beneficiaries per year.
· Prepares and calls bids for tenders for a determined number of houses to be financed in every period.
· Determines the minimal standards, the higher price of the solutions and the schedule.
· Supervises, receives and accepts the work done by the construction company and pays the complete amount of the contract.
· Allocates the applicants located at the top of the scoring system in the received dwellings
· Brings loans to the beneficiaries and maintains the mortgage portfolio.

The Construction Company

· Participates in the bid for tender by offering the requested number of units at the best price.
· Can apply for cash advances under the respective bank guarantees.
· Designs and builds the requested dwellings - Usually located on their own plot of land-- and delivers them to SERVIU.
· Receives the complete back payment from SERVIU.

Box 2: *Programas Privados* - Actors and actions

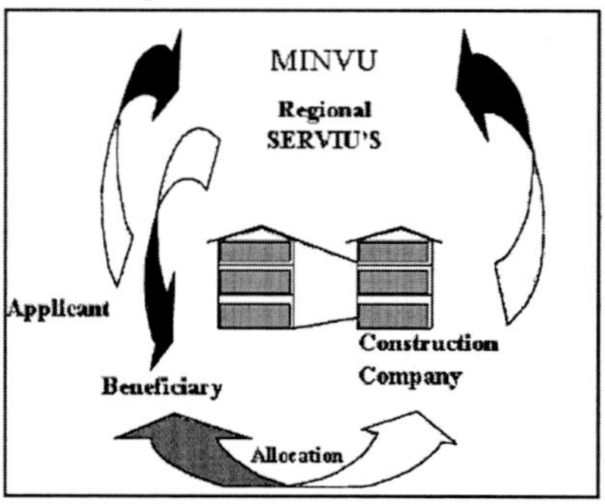

The Applicants

· Applicants undergo the same procedure of application as in the Programas SERVIU. However, they can include their own plot of land instead of the requested savings
· Once applicants have been selected and have received their "voucher", they can either contract a construction company that is interested in building the dwelling/s or buy an existing new or used dwelling on the market.
· As of 1997, Applicants can apply for an extra subsidy in order to obtain technical assistance from NGOs or other private institutions (only within programmes for the lowest-income sector).
· Receive a loan from a private bank or from the government.

SERVIU

· Maintains a list of applicants and, after the process of selection, hands out "vouchers" (a) or *"certificados de subsidio habitacional"* to the favoured beneficiaries.
· It approves -or not- the solution proposed by the beneficiaries · It exchanges the vouchers for cash when the beneficiaries have actually received a dwelling
· Also brings loans to those families that could not receive private loans (and manages the respective mortgage portfolio).

The Construction Company

· Enters a contract with the applicants in exchange for subsidy "vouchers" *(a)*.
· It can apply for advances in cash from SERVIU by showing a signed contract with the beneficiaries and their respective "vouchers".
· Designs and builds the dwellings on its own land or on a plot provided by the beneficiaries.
· After the municipality approves the works, they exchange "vouchers" for cash in the SERVIU.

(a) Most of the authors (Richards, 1995; Ferraz, 1998) that have written about the Chilean housing system have used the translation "vouchers" for this type of subsidy in order to differentiate it from other types of subsidies .

The operation of the Chilean housing system cannot be explained without a brief reference to the financial instruments created to support it. First, the savings system for housing that accumulates a considerable amount of resources and commits the applicants to a determined amount of disciplined and constant savings. And second, a complex system of mortgage-backed bonds that provides an important source of financing because bonds can be easily commercialised in the exchange market -under determined rules of securitization [26]. These financial aspects of Chilean housing policies have already been the main subject of manifold studies for example by Ferraz (1998), Pardo (2000) and Rojas (1999), among others.

4.6 Main Current Housing Programmes

Among the programmes designed for low-income households, the most important one in quantitative terms has been the *Programa de Vivienda Básica* (PVB). It provides a small complete dwelling, usually in estates or attached housing in one- to two-storey buildings. The PVB functioned in an experimental form from 1978 until its formalisation in 1984. It has also been successively improved in order to target lower-income families. While in the early years it existed only as part of the *Programa*s *SERVIU*, in recent years a private modality has been incorporated which is now favoured by the authorities.

The programme also includes the possibility of reserving dwellings to be rented by senior citizen households (*Programa del Adulto Mayor*). Another important programme that attends to families with the lowest-income is the *Programa* de *Vivienda* Progresiva (PVP) which provides land and basic infrastructure and has also been used to complete interventions built through former sites and services operations. This Programme began in 1990 and has since operated according to private as well as the SERVIU modality.

Last but not least, the *Programa de Subsidio Rural* (PSR) supports infrastructure provision and basic shelter in non-urban areas, including mining and fishing settlements.
Because its potential beneficiaries usually live in isolated settlements without very many construction companies that could participate in bids for tenders, this programme has been mainly carried out as a *Programa Privado*.

---

[26] According to Pardo (1995:12-13), the current housing finance system dates from 1976, a time when banks were authorised to offer mortgage-backed bonds using an inflation-protected bond called *Unidad de Fomento* (U.F) The system is based on long-term loans, with a twelve- to twenty-year term, that are funded through letters of mortgage credit issued to the payee. They are for the same amount, term, and interest rate as the underlying mortgage contract.

Fig. 20: Main Current Programmes and their characteristics (Values in U.F[27] and US$)

HOUSING PROGRAMMES	Targeted Population	Main Features	Maximum Price UF and US$	Finance System in UF		
Programas SERVIU First two Quintiles				Subsidy	Minimum Saving	Maximum credit
Programa de Vivienda Progresiva **PVP**	Those families with monthly income below 7 UF or US$ 170	It consists in a site-and services + complete urbanisation. The solutions vary from 6 to 20 m2 in a plot of minimum 60 m2	140 UF US$3.400	132	8	0
Programa de Vivienda Básica **PVB**	Households with an income not below 5 UF (US$ 120) and able to assume a monthly mortgage of 0,6 UF (US$15)	Typologies A, B & C It considers a new dwelling with at least two dormitories, living-room, bathroom and kitchen + complete urbanisation. It area varies between 35 and 45 m2	250 UF US$6.070	140	10	100
Programa de Subsidio Rural **PSR**	Rural Inhabitants, fishermen, mining workers or other people who live in non-urban areas	Typologies A & B It permits to build both in villages and in isolated settlements. Its area varies between 35 and 45 m2	267 UF US$6.480	150 to 200	10	Variable
Programas Privados First three Quintiles						
Programa de Vivienda Progresiva, First Stage **PVPP-1**	Those families with monthly income below 7 UF or US$ 170 which have their own plot of land or the commitment to buy it.	It consist in a site-and services + complete urbanisation. Solutions vary from 6 to 20 m2 in a plot of minimum 60 m2	140 UF US$3.400	132	0 to 8	0
Programa de Vivienda Progresiva, Second Stage **PVPP-2**	Those families with monthly income below 7 UF or US$ 170 which have already received a PVP first stage or a site-and services	Typologies A & B At least one additional room to be added to a site-and services	70 UF US$ 1.700	18 to 35	0 to 8	35 to 47
HOUSING PROGRAMMES	**Targeted Population**	**Main Features**	**Maximum Price UF and US$**	**Finance System in UF**		
Programas SERVIU First two Quintiles				Subsidy	Minimum Saving	Maximum credit
Programa de Vivienda Básica Libre Elección **PVBP**	To families with an income not below 6 UF (US$146) and able to assume a monthly mortgage. Owners of a plot of land or with the commitment to buy it.	Typologies A, B & C Open the access to build or to buy a new or used dwelling - not bigger than 140 m2- in both rural and urban areas	260 UF US$ 6.320 400 UF US$ 9.700 600 UF US$ 14.570	140	20	100
Programa Especial para Trabajadores **PET**	To workers groups organised through unions or other associations and with a monthly household income not below 11 UF or US$ 250	Typologies A, B & C It considers the access to a new minimal dwelling with at least two dormitories, living-room, bathroom and kitchen + complete urbanisation. Its area varies from 40 to 60 m2	400 UF US$ 9.700 600 UF US$ 14.570	90	40	Variable
Programas Privados 3rd to 5th Quintiles						
Subsidio General Unificado **SGU**	For middle income households that are able to take a loan from a private institution. It considers three different alternatives of financement according to families income	Typologies A, B & C Open the access to build or to buy a new or used dwelling - not bigger than 140 m2- in both rural and urban areas	500 UF US$ 12.140 1.000 UF US$ 24.280 1.500 UF US$ 36.420	70 to 90 110 to 130 110 to 130	50 100 150	Variable
Subsidio de Renovación Urbana **SRU**	For middle income families willing to live in areas subject of urban renewal and able to take a loan from a private institution	Diverse Typologies Permits to build or to buy a new or used dwelling - not bigger than 140 m2- in those areas subject of urban renewal programmes	1.500 UF US$ 36.420			
Leasing Habitacional	To middle and higher income households without savings	Diverse Typologies with the chance of buying it in stages	Variable and Fragmented subsidy + Saving + monthly rent			

Source: Information recollected from MINVU
** Unidad de Fomento

(27) The U.F. or Unidad de Fometo is the Chilean inflation-protected bond, and its exchange rate is calculated on a daily basis relative to Chilean currency. This exchange rate is based on inflation in the last two months, so that the real purchasing power of one UF remains the same, but its value fluctuates in relation to the Chilean (C$) peso. The exchange rate used in table 3 relates to the Value of the UF and the Dollar in May 2003: 1UF = C$ 17.024,34; 1US$= C$ 699,98 UF to Dollar: 1 UF =US$ 24,321.

Fig. 21: MINVU's housing typologies

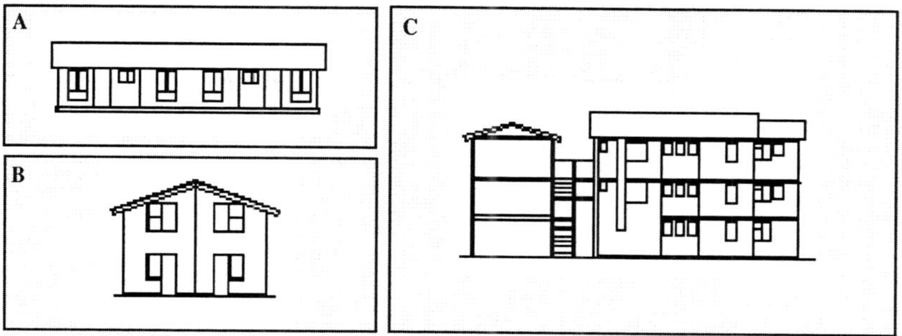

Source: División Técnica de Fomento Habitacional, MINVU

In spite of the fact that design typologies slightly differ among constructions firms, they are mostly based on three types already defined by MINVU. These typologies are known as types A, B and C. The type A corresponds to one-storey dwellings usually attached to one or more units. The type B defines single-family housing of two to three storeys and could be attached as well. Finally, type C corresponds to collective low-rise estates of three to four floors.

Besides programmes focused on low-income recipients, a series of other programmes also attends to middle-income families such as the *Subsidio General Unificado* (General Unified Subsidy), and the *Programa de Renovación Urbana* (Urban Renewal Subsidy). All these programmes operate under the system of *Programas Privados* (Fig. 20).

As can be seen in figure 20, the Programmes designed for the two poorest quintiles of the population include higher subsidies, while upper-middle and higher income segments are meant to deal directly with developers and private banks. However, the *Programas Privados* cater both to low and middle-low income groups that are eligible for private or governmental mortgages and are able either to buy a house in the market or to contract a private developer for its construction.

4.6.1 Additional Programmes and Measures

In addition to housing programmes, MINVU has been taking steps to improve other urban deficits related to housing developments such as basic and social infrastructure. Indeed, most of the housing programmes carried out in the 1980s lacked basic infrastructure such as community centres, schools, playgrounds, as well as road paving and green areas. The programmes MINVU offers are the "*Programa de equipamiento comunitario*", the "*Programa de Parques Urbanos*" and the "*Programa de Pavimentación participativa*".

The *"Programa de equipamiento comunitario"* aims at reducing the large shortage of social infrastructure in most of the housing compounds built before 1993. This instrument finances projects to build multipurpose fields, community centres and playgrounds, etc., in *comunas* that require central resources because they cannot finance improvements by themselves. Municipalities apply with a project idea which, after a ministerial evaluation, can be approved and financed by MINVU.

The *"Programa de Parques Urbanos"* tackles the imbalance in the stock of green areas in the city of Santiago through the construction of parks and afforestation, particularly in low-income neighbourhoods. As a result, at least four new inter-borough parks have been built in the last decade in areas with high deficits of green areas such in southern and western districts. Since Santiago suffers from air pollution, the implementation of greenery plays not only an aesthetic and social role, but also reduces the impacts of smog.

Finally, the *"Programa de Pavimentación Participativa"* provides a legal framework for the pooling of resources for the pavement of streets and passageway pavement. It is called "participatory" because its financial resources come from the municipality, the central government and beneficiaries. The main objectives of the programme are to improve the accessibility of neighbourhoods that lack paved roads and to reduce sickness related to muddy and flooded roads. The paving of roads also reduces air pollution because one of the main sources of pollution in Santiago is particles of dust.

4.6.2 Upgrading Policies and Estates Problems

Besides sectoral programmes, the MINVU also cooperates with other ministries in the *"Programa Chile Barrio"* which is an integral programme focused on slum-upgrading. This holistic programme aims at improving the living conditions of families in shantytowns through the provision of shelter and basic infrastructure as well as capacity-building programmes. The programme involves eight governmental agencies including the *Ministerio de Educación*, the *Ministerio del Trabajo* and the *Servicio Nacional de la Mujer.* Besides on-site measures, many slum settlements in Chile have been eradicated and their inhabitants relocated in new *poblaciones* of *Vivienda Básica* and *Vivienda Progresiva.*

In addition, MINVU has implemented some measures designed to improve the existing housing stock in recent years. The social housing stock in general, and collective housing areas in particular, not only lacks social infrastructure and services, but also has evidenced construction and maintenance problems. Moreover, current difficulties in finding available -and cheap- land for social housing projects within the urban area has given these measures further importance.

Since 2001, the *"Fondo Concursable Para Proyectos Habitacionales Solidarios"* is the legal instrument for providing people with governmental subsidies to acquire or improve existing housing. This subsidy requires collective applications and the backstopping of a public or private agency (Municipality, NGO, etc.) which takes charge of organising the applicants and developing the project that will later be evaluated by the MINVU. However, this fund is restricted to families that have not received any housing subsidy before and, therefore, cannot be used by former beneficiaries that aspire to upgrade their social dwellings.

Yet, problems that have been appearing in estates of social housing have triggered some additional measures in recent years. Problems include issues related to low building standards such as construction pathologies, lack of maintenance and early decay.

As there is no tradition of living in collective housing in Chile, especially for low-income families, social relations have also proven to be difficult (Ducci, 1997). As a result, in 1998 a reform of the *"ley de copropiedad horizontal"* (law 19.537) -which regulates cohabitation in every block of flats- was implemented in order to include estates of social housing into the same ruled system.

In order to introduce this legislation to the beneficiaries of estates and to prepare them for living collectively, a capacity-building programme in cooperation with the Ministry of Planning has been implemented in some compounds within the last two years. This process is supposed to encourage people who live in estates to organise themselves and to apply for support to improve their dwellings. However, the law restricts this aid to the following interventions:

a) to actually obtain the legal right to manage the condominium
b) to improve common spaces such as stairs and roofs through painting or replacing obsolete structures;
c) to cover fire and other insurance expenses and,
d) to repair basic sanitary and electric installations.

4.7 General Achievements of Current Housing Policy

Undoubtedly, exclusion from housing has been increasingly tackled by current Chilean housing policy. Indeed, the operation of its programmes has increased affordability through its subsidiary approach. While former systems were unable to reach the poorest segments of society, which forced many poor to "conquest" the city through land invasions, the current system has proven to be efficient in providing the necessary flow of funds towards housing in order to assure enough production. As a matter of fact, for the first time in history housing production has been sustained at levels above the yearly increase of households and the needs for replenishment of the stock. Moreover, according to Rojas (1999:9), by 1997, almost 30% percent of the dwellings built in the country corresponded to the *Programas Privados* and 28% of them were *Programas SERVIU*, resulting in a total of more than 50% of housing developments with governmental support. In 1990, this figure was close to 80%.

The efforts made by the current system to reach the poorest segments of the society are particularly impressive. Housing programmes are progressively increasing the proportion of beneficiaries in the first two income-quintiles while reducing the amount of those situated in upper quintiles. According to Nieto (2000:37), while between 1974 and 1989 not more than 18% of the beneficiaries belonged to the first income-quintile, within the period 1990-96 this figure had increased to more than 25%. In spite of the fact that not all the poor applicants are reached by the system, the Programmes *Vivienda Progresiva* and *Vivienda Básica* show a high percentage of beneficiaries in the lowest income levels, as can be seen in figure 22.

Fig. 22: Targeting of the Programmes Vivienda Progresiva (PVP) and Vivienda Básica (PVB) in percentage

Criteria	Factor	*PVP*		*PVB*	
		Applicants	Beneficiaries	Applicants	Beneficiaries
Income	(a) Indigent	55,8	47,5	56,1	52,8
	(b) Poor	31,0	35,0	28,3	26,2
	Low-income (a+b)	86,8	82,5	84,4	79,0
	No Low-income	13,2	17,6	15,6	21,0
Housing Situation	Without potable water	55,9	66,7	44,3	60,1
	Without sewerage	57,6	72,7	44,8	62,8
	Without electricity	18,1	15,0	9,5	13,4
	Poor roofing	59,5	54,2	43,8	54,2
	Poor flooring	54,7	39,1	38,7	39,5
	Poor walls	71,0	65,5	58,9	69,1

Source: MINVU, 1995 quoted from Rojas and Greene 1995 (Rojas, 1999:13)

Apart from the importance of these achievements, the Chilean housing system still lacks more integral approaches to urban problems. There is still very little relation between urban planning and housing policies, for example. This shows in the way social and basic infrastructure has been provided only after social compounds were already built. The current social housing stock also shows signals of inadequacy and early decay. There is an apparent need to upgrade existing dwellings, especially the huge amount of estates built in the last decades, which are also becoming the source of social conflicts. Indeed, the predominantly quantitative approach has disregarded other problems such as social disintegration and urban fragmentation. Some of these impacts, in particular those concerning exclusion through housing, will be further discussed in the following chapter through the analysis of the city of Santiago and three case studies.

4.7.1 Residential Satisfaction and Construction Pathologies

Some of the problems related to dwelling quality and residential satisfaction have already been studied by the Ministry of Housing (MINVU). An increasing amount of criticism of Chilean current programmes, has led the MINVU to elaborate a series of studies concerning residential satisfaction and the presence of construction pathologies in dwellings erected through the *Programa de Vivienda Básica*. The studies seem quite "benevolent" and do not coincide with all the matters observed in this research.

In spite of the fact that the study about residential satisfaction is quite critical of housing design, standards and construction quality, its main conclusion is that most residents are actually satisfied due the following reasons:

1) people think they can live a satisfactory life in their dwellings.
2) the relation between the number of rooms and beds and number of inhabitants is adequate.
3) most family activities can be done at home.
4) dwelling gives couples room for privacy.
5) family activities are carried out in the corresponding area.
6) many people have reformed their dwellings (extensions).

Between 1995 and 1998, another study evaluated construction pathologies existing in *Vivienda*s *Básica*s built since 1990 (MINVU, 2001). The study does not make a differentiation between single-family housing and estates, but presents some of the classic problems to be found in social housing in general.

Box 3 : Study about Residential Satisfaction, Programa de Vivienda Básica - MINVU, 2002: some selected results.

- **Residential Satisfaction:** Dissatisfaction with dwellings is three times higher among estate residents than among families living in single-family housing.
- **Displacement from comunas of origin:** In the metropolitan region more than 50% of the beneficiaries were displaced from their former residential areas to another *comuna*. They left stable social networks.
- **Previous dwelling situation:** most families (56,8%) came from houses where they lived in conditions of overcrowding with relatives or in a rented shack (30,2%) in the backyard of a house. Only 2,2% of them came from slums
- **Contradictory satisfaction:** most of the people were satisfied because they had reached their dream of owning, yet the new dwelling did not necessarily fulfill their expectations
- People in houses were prouder than those in estates: 77% of the people living in single housing and 51,1% of those living in estates declared to be proud of their neighbourhoods
- **Collective applications improved residential satisfaction**. Among the beneficiaries of estates, 67,3% of those that applied collectivelly and 58,2% of those that applied individually were satisfied.
- **People made extensions**: most people had already made or at least had the desire to make transformations, especially through extensions. However, **the study does not mention extensions in estates.**
- **Promiscuity and overcrowding were acute problems.** Newer estates presented lower levels of overcrowding.
- **Desire to stay or to move:** 33,5% of the people living in estates and 52,2% of those living in houses expressed the desire to stay in the same dwelling. Yet, the longer they lived there, the greater their desire to move.
- **Delinquent youth, bad reputation and stigma**. Focal groups showed that the main problems with youth were related to drugs and alcoholism. People living in estates felt more insecure than those living in houses and believed they were stigmatised because of being poor.
- **Disintegrated spatial configuration:** Urban tissue was usually ignored because estates are usually built in huge plots or "super-blocks". Estates showed a low hierarchy of organisational spaces, and usually included left-over areas that lacked social control and showed strong symptoms of decay.
- **Lack of infrastructure and low maintenance:** Social infrastructure was usually scarce or presented problems such as lack of maintenance or low standards.
- **Social networks and participation.** People living in single housing were more predisposed to do community work and participate actively in their environment.
- **Uncontrolled areas:** The backyards of estates were usually appropriated by the people in order to secure them.
- **Construction defects and design.** People were more aware of construction defects than of design failures. The main complains were are about isolation, rainwater infiltration through walls, roofs or windows and sanitary installations.

Source: División Técnica de Fomento Habitacional, (MINVU, 2002)

According to this study about construction pathologies, at the national level more than 30% of the housing analysed within the periods from 1990-1994 and from 1996-1997 presented pathologies. In the metropolitan region, problems were found in 20,8% of the dwellings. Typical problems were:

- cracks in doors and window structures and in their fixations
- erosion and cracks in concrete floors
- problems with general finishing
- cracks and deviations in inner thin walls and ceilings
- damage in window and door locks
- water filtration through walls, roofs and guardrails
- problems with electric and sanitary installations.

Fig. 23: Examples of construction pathologies

Structural cracks
Broken front door
Water filtration in bathroom
Floor erosion

Source: División Técnica de Fomento Habitacional, (MINVU, 2001)

Chapter 5: Housing Policy in Santiago

5.1 Introduction

The following section briefly analyses and categorises the main possible relations between the implementation of the current housing policy and social disintegration in the city of Santiago. It aims to recognise the main socio-spatial features of the city of Santiago in relation to social housing developments. The analysis leads to a classification of different districts with the same type of housing, yet apparently different performance and impacts.

The abovementioned classification results in the selection of particular areas - case studies- where a field exploratory approach could explain what makes the difference. In other words, why do some areas present "better" performance in terms of maintenance of the dwellings and their environment? And which factors have influenced these results?

Box 4: The specific objectives of the city level study

- To give a general overview of the spatial and social characteristics of the city of Santiago,
- To identify how has been the urban growth tendency of Santiago in the last decades and its relation with social housing developments,
- To distinguish the main characteristics of every districts, both in social terms (type of population, educational level, etc.) and in terms of its access to the main urban facilities (transport, work, health, etc.).
- To find out which districts are more representative -in terms of different shares of social housing types, diverse periods of construction, and their relation with divergent social indicators - in order to make a further comparative analysis.

Box 5: Type of indicators

- To give a general overview of the spatial and social characteristics of the city of Santiago,
- To identify how has been the urban growth tendency of Santiago in the last decades and its relation with social housing developments,
- To distinguish the main characteristics of every districts, both in social terms (type of population, educational level, etc.) and in terms of its access to the main urban facilities (transport, work, health, etc.).
- To find out which districts are more representative -in terms of different shares of social housing types, diverse periods of construction, and their relation with divergent social indicators - in order to make a further comparative analysis.

Map 03: Santiago´s Urban Districts

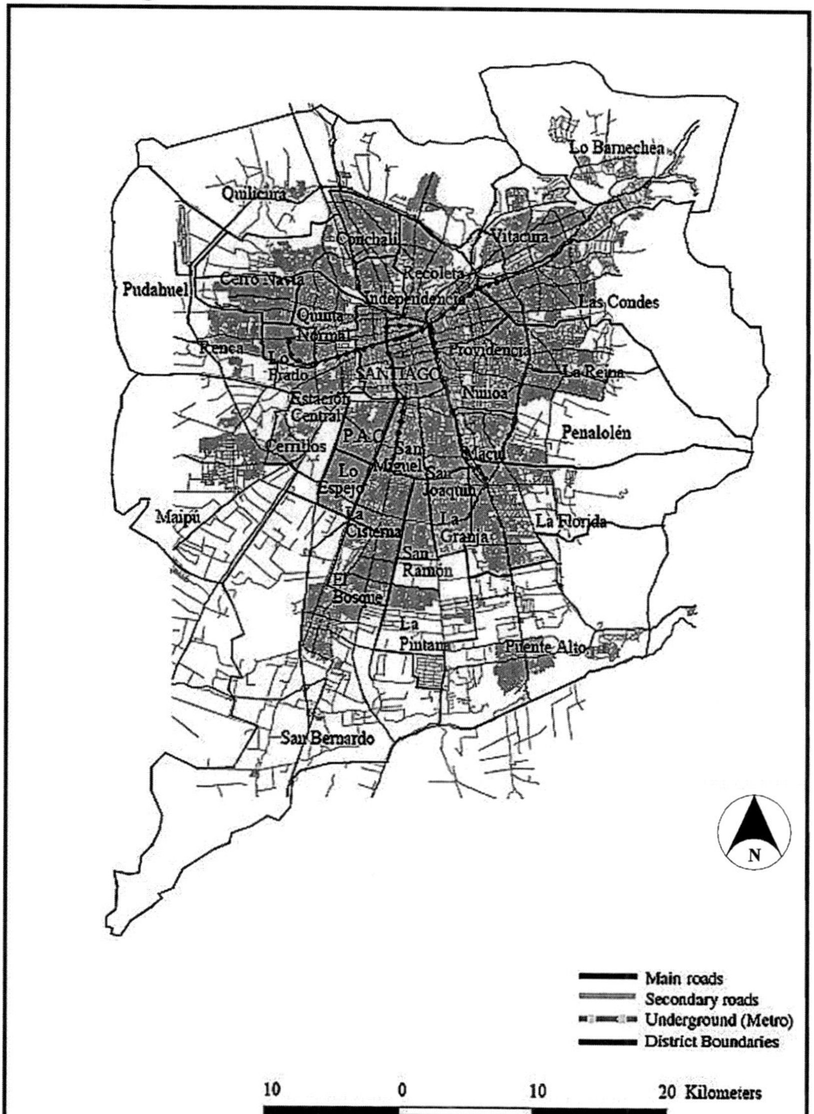

5.2 Impacts of Housing Policy on the City

Two decades of application of the same housing policy have had noticeable impacts on the city. In spite of impressive achievements -represented by the massive quantity of social housing built and a more or less balanced serving of the poorest families-, Chilean housing policy has also played an important role in sharpening historical residential segregation and social exclusion.

Current housing policies have certainly continued with the long tradition of central governmental intervention in social affairs. However, two main shifts can be made out in relation to former paradigms. First, as land markets were deregulated, housing location began to be defined exclusively by land prices and did not follow any other social concerns[(28)]. Second, standards for social housing oriented towards the lowest-income families were drastically reduced, not only in terms of the dwellings' area and the type of construction materials, but also in relation to infrastructure and social facilities.
In addition, the massive programme of radications and evictions carried out between 1979 and 1985 not only permitted the clearance of 246 slums and their removal from many better-off sectors, but also marked the starting point of the "consolidation" of *comunas* according to social classes. According to Paquette-Vassalli (1998:231), 77% out of the 142,500 displaced families were resettled in just five *comunas*: La Pintana, La Granja, San Bernardo, Puente Alto and Peñalolén, all located in the south and southeast of the city. The tendency to locate social housing has been subsequently applied all throughout the last decades, as will be later analysed.

In addition, areas that used to concentrate most of the low-income families in the southern, southeastern and western parts of the city also experienced population increase. While in 1970 they represented 59% of the total population and occupied an area of 10.559 hectares, by 2002 their population share had reached 71% involving an area of 34.333 hectares. The most representative cases of this tendency are the former villages of Maipú and Puente Alto which were not only added to the city, but that also explosively increased their densities and shares in population. Yet, until the 1970s, Santiago was still quite a compact city. Most of its districts had more or less good accessibility to the focal centre, or CBD, where most of the working places and main services were and are still located. Unfortunately, the last decades have given way to thriving sprawl which had included the urbanisation of former agricultural areas at the periphery and the annexation of adjacent

[(28)] According to Rojas, (1999:15):*"The cost of land is a large component of affordable housing, often representing up to 40% of total cost. Seeking to reduce costs, developers offer houses in peripheral locations where undeveloped land is less expensive, greenfield projects allow greater control of costs and make possible the short delivery schedules required to reduce financial costs"*.

Fig. 24: Eastern Comuna

Fig. 25: Pericentral Comuna

Fig. 26: EasternPe-ripheral

villages. Today, the urban landscape is characterised by a strong differentiation between "modern" districts, the "decadent" ones and districts of social housing. While the Eastern parts of the city with high-standard infrastructure, skyscrapers and high quality of life represent the economic success of the country, central *comunas* are being abandoned, and the periphery is increasingly concentrating low-standard housing even lacking many basic services.

5.2.1 The Distribution of Social Housing in the City

The amount of public intervention in the country's housing market is made clear by comparing the proportion of houses that were acquired through subsidies and those acquired directly through private transactions without governmental aid. Figures from the Chilean Chamber of Construction (CCC) and the National Institute of Statistics (INE) indicates that 62,91% of all housing built in Chile between 1981 and 1998 received public support (Nieto, 2000)[(29)]. In the city of Santiago, the figures show that at least one-third of the total housing built between 1984 and the year 2000 was destined to the low-income population [(30)].

However, within the frame of a market-driven economy, this high level of intervention is not reflected in the decisions about housing location. As a matter of fact, since location depends on private offer and land markets are deregulated, low-income housing has been mostly developed in unattractive poor areas where slums or other social housing already

[(29)] This percentage includes all the programmes destined both to middle and low-income families through the diverse programmes existing in the current policy. Between 1992 and 1998, 81,6% of the housing built in Santiago correspond to subsidised units (Nieto, 2000:35).

[(30)] This figure represents those developments made by the Ministry of Housing (MINVU) through the *Programa de Vivienda Básica* (PVB), the *Programa de Vivienda Progresiva* (PVP), and the *Programa Especial para Trabajadores* (PET). It does not takes into consideration the large programme of sites and services directed by the Ministry of Internal affairs through which many slums were upgraded or evicted between 1981 and 1995.

Fig. 27: Comunas with the highest proportion of social housing (1978-2000)

Comuna	LOC (1)	Number of dwellings	Percentage of total	Cumulative %
Puente Alto	SE	31489	14,08%	14,08%
La Pintana	S	21563	9,64%	23,73%
San Bernardo	S	20297	9,08%	32,80%
La Florida	SE	19868	8,89%	41,69%
Maipú	W	15458	6,91%	48,60%
Peñalolén	SE	14217	6,36%	54,96%
Renca	W	13615	6,09%	61,05%

Source: MINVU's yearly reports and self-processed.

(1) LOC: Location.
S: South,
SE: Southeast, W: West
N: North
E: East
CBD: Central Business District

Map 04: Districts concentrating 90% of Social housing built between 1982-2000

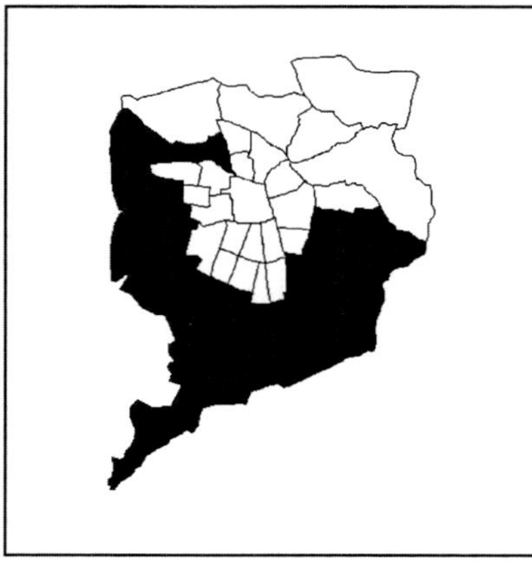

existed because land was cheaper. Analysis of the distribution of social housing within Santiago shows that almost 90% of the dwellings built between 1978 and the year 2000 were located in no more than 15 out of 34 urban *comunas*. Of these dwellings, 65,7% were built in the south and southeastern *comunas*. In contrast, the *comuna* of Santiago (traditional CBD) and the *comunas* located in the eastern part of the city together received less than 3% in the same period.

Even the western *comunas* received an important share -that reaches 25,45% of the total. Thus, some scholars refer to these new *poblaciones* as "our Soweto" (Collados, 1996)[31].

Map 05: Social housing built 1982-1991

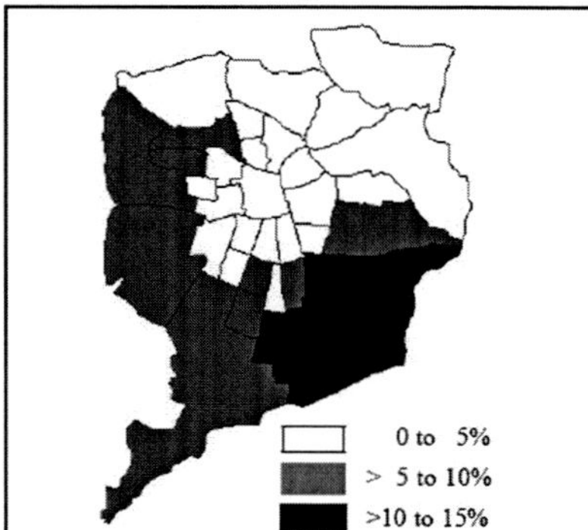

Data from MINVU and self-elaboration

Map 06: Social housing built 1992-2000

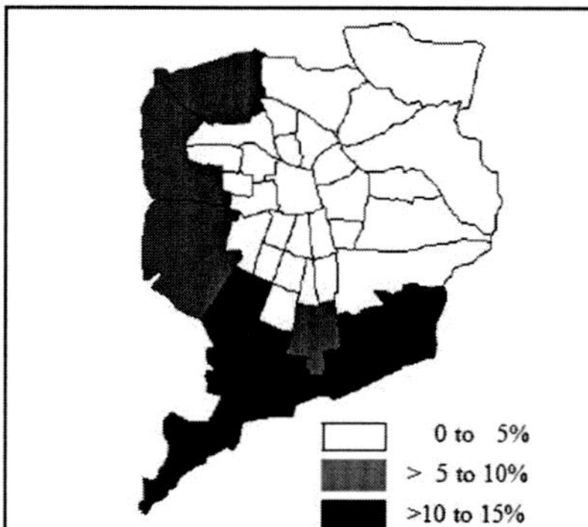

Data from MINVU and self-elaboration

[31] Referring to the southwestern territories in former South African Apartheid

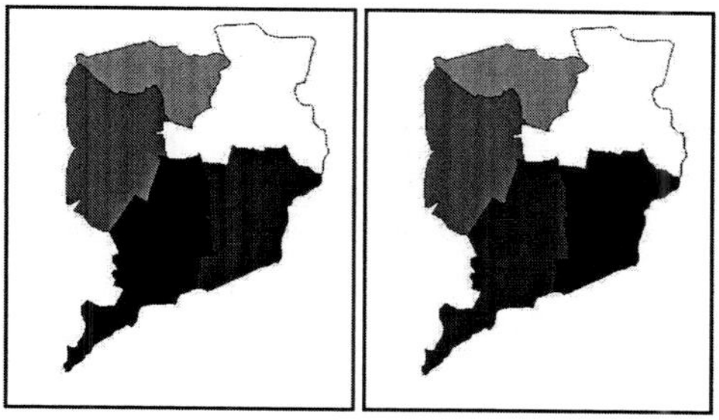

Map 07: 1982-1991

Map 08: 1992-2000

Zone	1982-1991	Zone	1992-2000
South	41,47 %	South	29,64 %
South-east	23,35 %	South-east	34,02 %
West	24,84 %	West	22,08 %
North	3,07 %	North	11,69 %
CBD & East	2,28 %	CBD & East	2,57 %

Fig. 28: Housing by zones 1982-2000

A breakdown of these figures -housing distribution data- into two periods[32] brings to light that over time, less and less *comunas* have concentrated the majority of social housing built in the city.

From 1982 to 1991, the *comunas* congregating close to 90% of the total housing amounted to fourteen, while from 1992 to 2000 they were reduced to twelve.

In spite of the continuing tendency to locate the highest proportions of social housing in the southern and southeastern districts, some slight but relevant differences can be distinguished such as the increasing preference for peripheral *comunas*. While the *comunas* of La Pintana, La Florida and Puente Alto were preferred in the earlier period[33], the second period shows a strong concentration of social housing in Puente Alto and in the peripheral *comunas* of San Bernardo and Quilicura in the extreme south and north respectively.

Some scholars such as Nieto (Sugranyes, 2000:41) explain this displacement from La Pintana to Puente Alto as the result of the lack of available land. However, an explanation might also be that at the beginning of the 1990s, La Pintana was one of poorest *comunas*

(32) This breakdown responds to the need of comparing this information with other social indicators coming from the three last censuses (1982-1992 and 2000).

(33) Between 1979 and 1985, most of the efforts of the housing policy were concentrating on upgrading programmes related to the evictions done within this period. Accordingly, most of the 46.230 new social housing units built within the period -both sites and services and small dwellings of *Vivienda Básica*- were located in the southern *comunas* (50,14%), and in the southeastern ones (27,09%).

in Santiago, and the democratic government received the district's permanent refusal to receive more social housing. Many other local authorities disliked the arrival of social housing because that it could affect "attractiveness"[(34)].

Unlike the first period, after 1992, some attempts were made to build in pericentral *comunas* such as Pedro Aguirre Cerda and Cerrillos. However, these interventions were limited by the lack of available cheap land, and thus, their replicability was denied by public officials, disregarding the social benefits higher levels of infrastructure could achieve for the people[(35)] .

5.2.2 The Growth of the City and Social Housing

One of the clearest features of Santiago's urban development is its continuous growth in extension. Although the average yearly rate of growth is lower than the high percentages reached in the periods between 1940-50 and between 1960-70 (see figure 7 and 30), absolute figures show an increase. While between 1940 and 1970 the city added 25.341 hectares -or an average of 845 hectares per year-, between 1970 and the year 2002 this amount reached 30.095 hectares. In other words, in the last 32 years, 940 hectares per year have been urbanised.

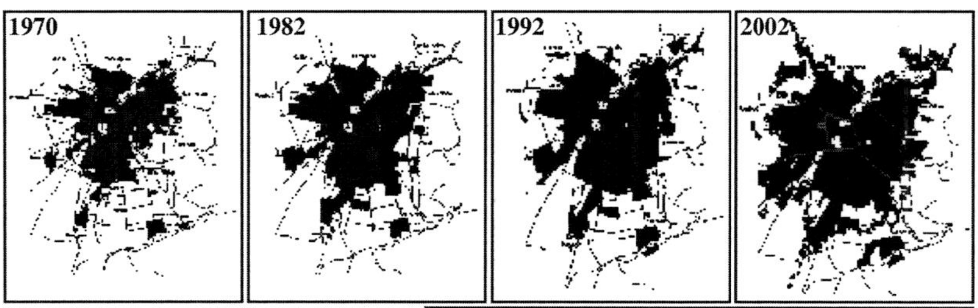

Fig. 29: Urban Growth between 1970-2002
Sources: Minvu and de Mattos 1999

Fig. 30: Population & urban growth between 1970-2002
Sources: Source: INE, Censuses 1970, 1982, 1992 and 2002

Year	Hectares (a)	Variation Period in %	Average Increase %	Density Inh./Ha
1970	31.841	50,44	4,03	89
1982	42.080	32,16	2,31	92
1992	49.270	17,09	1,57	96
2002	61.936	25,71	2,28	87
Year	**Population (b)**	**Variation Period in %**	**Average Increase %**	**Ratio a / b**
1970	2.821.000	40,63	3,38	1,19
1982	3.877.000	37,43	3,63	0,88
1992	4.750.000	22.52	2.02	0.78
2002	5.392.840	13,53	1,27	1,80

(34) These kinds of comments were frequently heard by the author at the time of working at MINVU, and by bringing technical assistance to groups of applicants that were looking for available land and found out the disfavour from local governments.

(35) Cummings and DiPasquale (1997) and Olivares (2002) have studied the long-term advantages of building social housing in more central comunas.

Urban sprawl is not only expressed in terms of area, but also in the fact that in spite of one hundred years of continuous and intensive urbanisation, population density has remained unchanged since 1895, (figures 1 and 30).

As has the ratio between urban growth and population increase: the city has grown almost at the same rate as its population. Between 1992 and 2002, urban expansion has even outpaced population growth (figure 30).

Fig. 31: Population and land increases

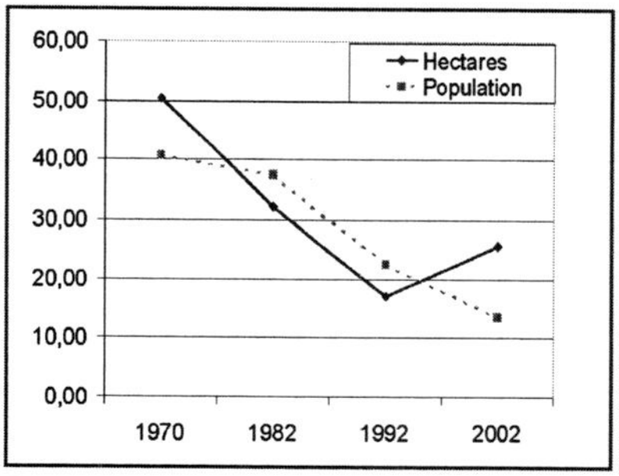

Fig. 32: Social Housing & Growth (1982-2000)

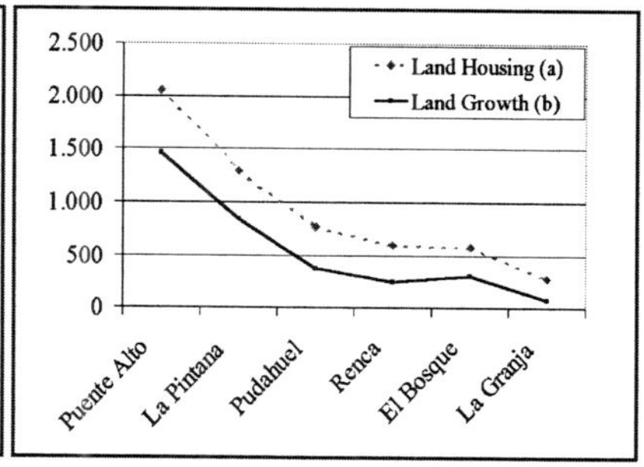

Sources: Source: INE, Censuses 1970, 1982, 1992 and 2002 and self-processed

Nowadays, migration has slowed down, land invasions are almost non-existent and the city counts with a new metropolitan master plan [36]. It, therefore, seems evident that the main sources of Santiago's extensive growth are unstopped middle and high-income suburbanisation on one hand, and social housing policies on the other (Ducci, 1998).

According to Zegras and Gakenheimer (2000:124), though increased motorization and consumer desires have change the patterns of settlement leading to further migration of well-to-do families, urban expansion cannot only be linked to these phenomena. Especially so, if we take into consideration that better-off *comunas* have undergone a process of densification through the replacement of former mansions with apartment buildings. Therefore, one of the questions that arises is how much of this urban growth is related to housing policies? If the city has grown by 14.635 hectares between 1982 and 2000 and social housing accounts for an estimated 6.248 hectares, it follows that at least 40 % of this growth could be imputed to the production of social housing.

(36) The *Plan Regulador Metropolitano de Santiago* (PRMS) enacted in 1994 explicitly pursued to increase the density of the city and to limit its growth. Nevertheless, once more, planning has been surpassed (MINVU, 1994).

Map 09, 10 and 11:Social housing, area and population growth 1982-1991

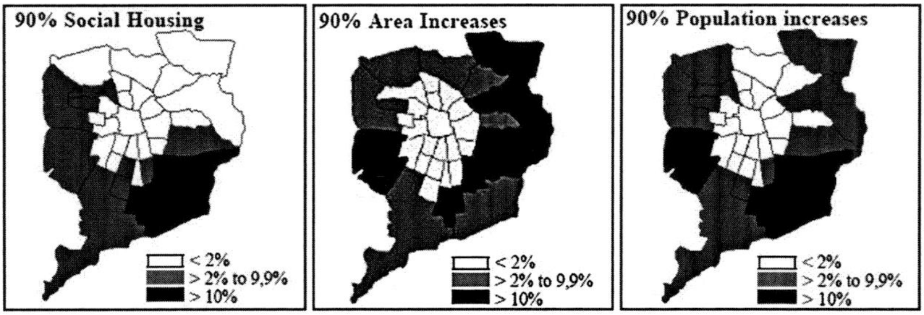

Map 12, 13 and 14: Social housing, area and population growth 1992-2002

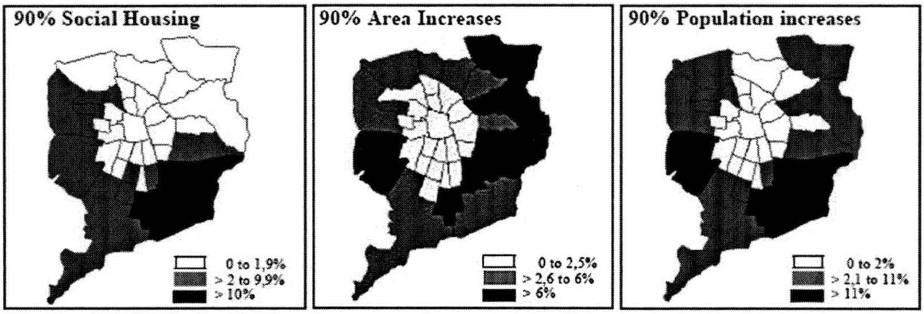

Data from MINVU and self-elaboration

These relations are quite unclear, due to the fact that no exact information exists about how much of the land used by social housing was actually added to the *comuna* and how much of this increase corresponds to processes of densification. However, the relationship between the city's growth and the production of social housing seems to be evident, in some cases, especially when analysing those *comunas* with the highest proportion of social housing. In these *comunas* the quantity of hectares added by social housing developments is much bigger than the growth of the district's area, a fact that brings an idea of the possible correlation between urban growth and housing production.

This correlation is verified through the analysis of the growth during the two periods under examination. As a matter of fact, *comunas* such as La Pintana, La Florida and Puente Alto that received the largest amount of social housing between 1982 and 1991
also rank among the first five districts with higher increases in area. In addition, the same correlation applies to demographic growth: these three *comunas* rank among the first four districts with the highest population increase in the period .

Within the second period the pattern is almost the same, but the tendency towards peripheral growth is sharpened and shows a stronger correlation with housing policies. As a matter of fact, in this last period, the *comunas* with highest area, housing and population increases are those of Puente Alto, Quilicura and San Bernardo.

Conversely to this peripheral pattern of growth, central and pericentral *comunas* show a progressive reduction of the share of population. Moreover, a second CBD has been developed in the eastern districts of Las Condes, reducing the traditional importance of the district of Santiago. While by 1970 close to 50% of the population lived in central districts and just 25% in peripheral ones, nowadays 56% of the population lived in the periphery and just 20% in the central districts (INE, 1970;2003) (37). The most representative cases of this tendency are visible in the former villages of Maipú, Quilicura and Puente Alto, which were not only added to the city, but that also explosively increased their shares in population. In addition, the *comunas* located in the south, southeast and west have also experienced a dramatic change in terms of population densities (Maps 15, 16 and 17), while those ones in the east has been decreasing.

Map 15, 16 and 17: Population densities 1982 - 2002

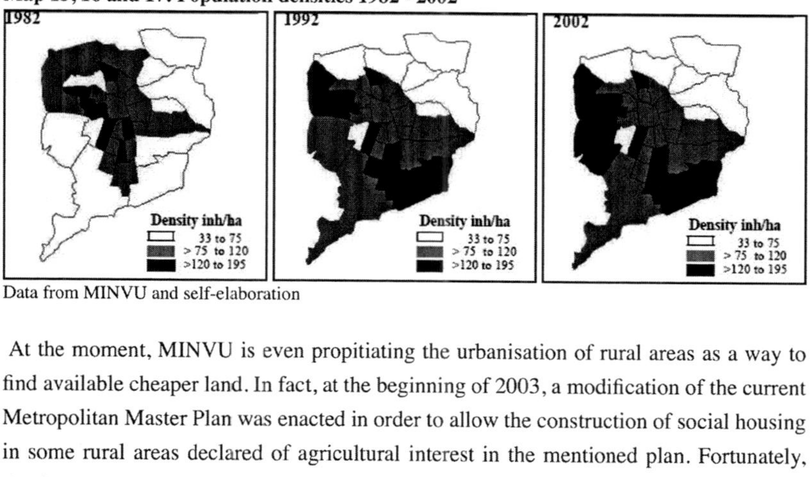

Data from MINVU and self-elaboration

At the moment, MINVU is even propitiating the urbanisation of rural areas as a way to find available cheaper land. In fact, at the beginning of 2003, a modification of the current Metropolitan Master Plan was enacted in order to allow the construction of social housing in some rural areas declared of agricultural interest in the mentioned plan. Fortunately, the Supreme Court rejected this modification after an appeal presented by the Chilean Association of Architects (Colegio de Arquitectos, 2003)(38) .

(37) According to the figures from the 2002 census (INE,2003).

(38) This information appeared in the Internet web page of the Colegio de Arquitectos de Chile in May 2003.

In spite of this novel decision, the metropolitan SERVIU has been buying large tracts of land in the neighbouring rural *comunas* of Buin, Colina, Melipilla and Paine in an attempt to recover the former tradition of counting on public land for housing developments. In fact, according to Roman (2000:42), 54% of the land bought between 1990 and 1998 is located in rural areas. In addition, the same author affirms that in the same period, close to 15% of the total social housing built in the region was done in rural *comunas* such as Colina, Melipilla, Peñaflor and Talagante. Another factor that contributes to this process of "rural-urbanisation" is the fact that many groups that are pursuing to buy a tract of land cannot afford the increasingly high prices within the urban areas. Therefore, in many cases they are also buying land in rural areas, and thereafter, pressuring the government to modify planning regulations [(39)].

According to Moffat (2000:190), the lack of affordable land for social housing contributed to the intensification of socio-spatial segregation because it concentrated low-income families only in areas were land was cheap and usually adjacent to slums or risky areas at the periphery. Moreover, most of these areas lacked basic amenities, social infrastructure or, in other words, were simply not "prepared" to receive a massive increase of newcomers [(40)].

Nevertheless, the process of "rural urbanisation" responds not only to low-income housing developments, but also has been a solution for better-off families. Indeed, well-to-do families have been building their "enclaves" in rural areas such as Chicureo, Chacabuco and Colina where gated communities are increasingly being built through "mega-projects" by private developers (Zegras and Gakenheimer, 2000:87-105). However, their migration is not only outward, and new gated communities have also been built in the low-income *comunas* of Huechuraba and Peñalolén which gives some scholars reason to claim that segregation is being reduced in scale (Sabatini, 1999).

However, a recent comparative study of segregation in Mexico and Chile (Fischer, 2003) asserts that in spite of the fact that in the case of Santiago de Chile residential segregation has historical roots, several indicators show a sharpening in the small scale of

[(39)] The Metropolitan Master Plan, as well as local planning instruments defines which areas can be urbanised and which ones are protected as an agricultural resource. Nevertheless, the ministry of Agriculture can authorise land use changes. In recent years, many groups of applicants received subsidies by certifying that they have a tract of land (owners of land do not need savings to apply for a subsidy). Yet, they had to follow a long process to obtain a concrete solution... some of them never obtained it.

[(40)] For example, the *comuna* La Pintana was a former low-income agricultural settlement surrounded by slums and received most of the social housing built in the 1980's. This *comuna* did not count, either with enough infrastructure and services for its population share or the resources to implemented them. As most of its population are low-income families, the municipal budget counts with minimal revenues, and "market" oriented services are not interested in serving this type of *comunas*.

this partition. According to the same authors, Santiago shows a higher segregation at the level of *comunas* than other Latin American cities. Besides the fact that social housing is increasingly concentrated in merely some *comunas*, many indicators show that the city is also partitioned according to social status. Today, Goethe's sentence -paraphrased- *"tell me where you live and I will tell you who you are"*, has become a normal question for the inhabitants of the city, which leads to other urban and social problems such as stigmatisation and disintegration.

5.2.3 A Socially Partitioned City

Analysing the distribution of poverty according to zones, it become clear that the highest percentage of poor families lives in the southern periphery. Indeed, the south and southeastern *comunas* concentrate more than 65% of the total poor of the city, while the western *comunas* have 22,5% of them, those in the north concentrate 8,49% and those in the east have just 3,09% of them (Mideplan, 1998)[41].

However, the percentage of low-income families per district is not the single instrument to measure segregation in a given city. Massey and Denton (1988), for example, developed five indices to measure different aspects of the segregation phenomenon. The main objective of these indices is to look at the classification and distribution of certain groups -low-income families, ethnic minorities, foreign people, etc.- over predefined discrete spatial units such a "census tracts" in the United States and districts or boroughs in Britain. A brief description of these indices is as follows:

- *Evenness*: also known as the dissimilarity index, is used to measure the general distribution of certain groups over the spatial units.
- *Exposure:* measures the probability of contact among different groups located in different spatial units
- *Concentration:* is developed to measure the extent to which one group inhabits only some restricted area in the city
- *Clustering:* is used to measure the concentration of areas with the same type of groups
- *Centralisation:* measures the tendency of some groups to locate themselves close to the central business district.

[41] Includes the *comuna* of Santiago (CBD). This data was extracted from the survey of socio-economic characterisation CASEN (1998).

Map 18, 19 and 20: Poverty in % and segregation Indicators

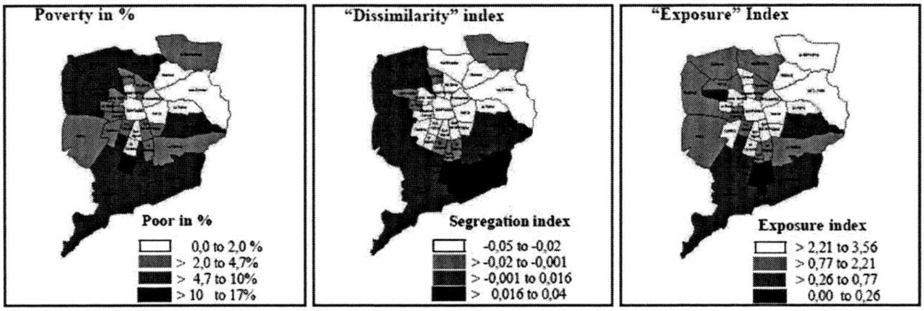

Data from MIDEPLAN (CASEN Survey 1998) and self-elaboration

Using the exposure [42] and dissimilarity[43] indices, important distinctions can be made. The districts with the highest dissimilarity index value are again mainly in the southern *comunas* La Pintana, Puente Alto and El Bosque as well as in the western *comuna* Cerro Navia. The southern district La Pintana is the *comuna* with the highest index of exposure, followed by Puente Alto, San Bernardo, Peñalolén and Cerro Navia.

In addition to these indicators, a market study conducted by the private firm Novomerc (1999) [44] provides useful information to identify the socio-economic categories of every *comuna*[45]. According to their data, in some *comunas* in the south, such as La Pintana, more than 80% of the population is considered low-income. At the other extreme, *comunas* in the east have up to 79% of all high income families (Vitacura). Evidently, most middle-income families are to be found in pericentral areas. However, this data does not reveal whether poor families live in social housing or whether social housing is merely built in *comunas* with higher percentages of low-income families. Indeed, a test of the level of correlation between the existence of social housing and the concentration of low-income families using, for example, the Parson's[46] Coefficient (Castañeda, 1996:140)[47] resulted in a very low value of 0,21.

Restricting the analysis to the 15 districts with the highest share of social housing, this coefficient reaches a value of 0,67 which at least indicates that most of the social housing is located in low-income neighbourhoods. This correlation is even stronger when comparing

---

[42] The exposure index is equal to: (Poor/total poor)*(Poor/total population)*100

[43] The segregation index is equal to: Number of not poor in the district/Total not poor - Number of poor in the district / Total poor

[44] Data gathered in the web page: www.novomerc.cl

[45] The categories are ABC1: Managerial level, C1 and C2 professional and small entrepreneurs, D: low-income employees and E: low-income informal workers. In order to make these categories operative, they were aggregated as follow: ABC1: High-income, C1+C2: Middle-income and D+E: Low-income.

[46] The Parson's coefficient (r) serves to make a correlation with a pair of data (x and y), where the value 1 means a clear strong correlation and 0 no correlation.

[47] Values close to 1 are just to be found in eastern comunas such as Providencia, Las Condes and Vitacura.

Map 21: Income per household **Map 22: Human development**

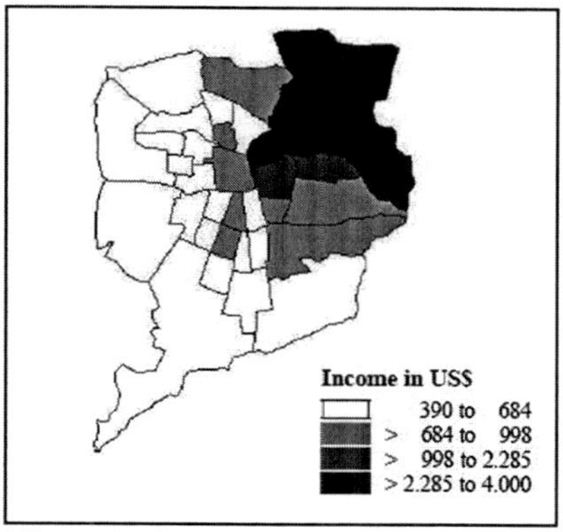

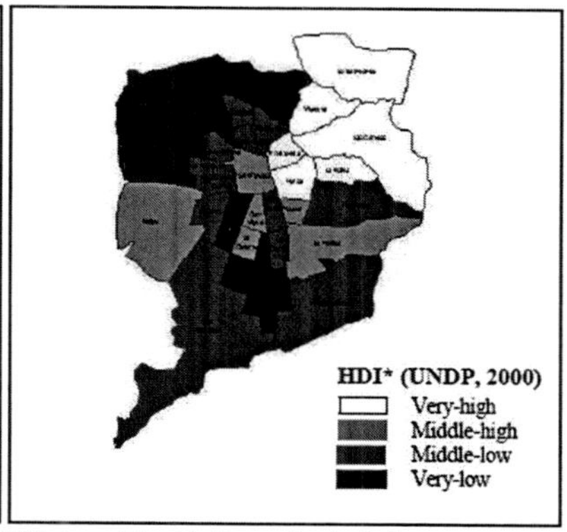

* Human development index elaborated by UNDP (2000). A combined indicator that includes access to education, health and poverty. Source: UNDP 2000 and self-elaboration

social housing and incomes per household, reaching a value of 0,77. On the other hand, there is a moderate negative correlation of -0,43 when comparing the index of dissimilarity with the share of social housing and a positive stronger coefficient of 0,68 by relating housing to the exposure index.

There are at least four reasons that could explain why it was not possible, at the city level, to verify a more direct correlation between social housing policy and poverty. Firstly, as there is not enough quantifiable data about former social housing developments, the analysis was restricted to the current policy. Secondly, there is no information about poverty at the *comuna* level in former periods. Thirdly, data at the *comuna* level does not provide detailed information about people living in specific types of housing. Fourthly, the current indicators used by the government to measure poverty bring an important weight to aspects such as access to basic services (water, electricity, and sewerage) and housing conditions. Therefore, most of the people who have received a dwelling, especially within the frame of the *Programa de Vivienda Básica*, are not necessarily considered poor. In addition, looking at the distribution of families according to other social indicators such as unemployment, dependence on food subsidies, average years of education and health standards also presents some difficulties. Some of the poorest districts correspond to those districts that contain high proportions of social housing, while others do not. However, all of these districts include a certain amount of social housing.

This brief analysis confirms the requirement of complementing this examination with other indicators, such as possible differences in access to infrastructure and the quality of the living environment as well as the need to concentrate the study on some selected cases.

Fig. 33: Selected Social Indicators and Performed average

Unemployment			Years of Education			Health Quality		
Comuna	LOC (1)	Indicator	Comuna	LOC (1)	%	Comuna	LOC (1)	%
Renca*	W	0.00	Cerro Navia	W	0.34	La Granja*	S	0.00
La Granja*	S	0.08	La Pintana*	S	0.53	San Ramón*	S	0.02
Cerro Navia	W	0.22	Cerrillos	W	0.45	La Pintana*	S	0.03
Lo Espejo	S	0,29	Renca*	W	0,33	Recoleta	N	0,05
La Pintana*	S	0.32	San Ramón*	S	0.34	Huechuraba	N	0.07
El Bosque*	S	0.36	Huechuraba	N	0.18	San Joaquín	S	0.11
Lo Prado*	W	0.45	Lo Espejo	S	0.00	Lo Espejo	S	0.15
Overcrowding			**Food/subsidies**			**Performed HDI** [20]		
Comuna	LOC (1)	%	Comuna	LOC (1)	%	Comuna	LOC (1)	%
La Pintana*	S	0.00	Cerro Navia	W	0.44	La Pintana*	S	0.00
Recoleta	N	0.02	La Pintana*	S	0.00	Cerro Navia	W	0.04
P. A.Cerda	S	0,07	San Ramón*	S	0,18	Lo Espejo	S	0,08
Conchalí	N	0,14	Lo Espejo	S	0,45	Renca*	W	0,09
Lo Espejo	S	0,14	Renca*	W	0,40	Quilicura*	N	0,11
Cerro Navia	W	0.27	Peñalolén*	SE	0.30	San Ramón*	S	0.11
San Ramón*	S	0,27	Conchalí	N	0,59	Huechuraba	N	0,12

*Districts with a high proportion of social housing. Author's self-elaboration
Sources: Data from Casen 1998 and Zegras and Gakenheimer, 2000. Author's self-elaboration

5.2.4 Social Housing and Infrastructure

Segregation it is not only expressed by income or socio-economical factors. The city also presents different levels of infrastructure and accessibility to urban opportunities such as employment and services. For example, in spite of the fact that the *comunas* of Santiago, Las Condes and Providencia represent just 10,5% of the total population of the city; they concentrate most of the working places. As a matter of fact, more than 50% of the total land uses devoted to commerce, 15,4% of the industry and 70,6% of the offices are located in these three districts. Other public services such as education and health facilities reach percentages of 43,1% and 21,4% respectively (Zegras and Gakenheimer, 2000: 23-24).

Fig. 34: Percent Share of Metropolitan Area's Land Uses (1997)

Commercial			Education			Residential		
Comuna	LOC	%	Comuna	LOC	%	Comuna	LOC	%
Santiago	CBD	36,9%	Santiago	CBD	29,9%	Las Condes	E	9,3%
Las Condes	E	7,4%	Providencia	E	9,0%	Santiago	CBD	6,4%
Providencia	E	6,3%	Ñuñoa	E	6,9%	Maipú	W	6,3%
Recoleta	N	4,8%	San Miguel	S	4,9%	La Florida	SE	5,9%
Ñuñoa	E	4,3%	Las Condes	E	4,2%	Providencia	E	5,7%
La Florida	SE	3,3%	Recoleta	N	4,2%	Ñuñoa	E	5,7%
						Puente Alto	SE	5,6%

Industrial			Offices			Health		
Comuna	LOC	%	Comuna	LOC	%	Comuna	LOC	%
Santiago	CBD	15,4%	Santiago	CBD	43,3%	Santiago	CBD	21,0%
Quilicura	N	8,4%	Providencia	E	17,6%	Providencia	E	20,5%
San Joaquín	S	7,1%	Las Condes	E	9,7%	Independencia	N	12,9%
Macul	SE	6,5%	Quilicura	N	2,5%	Ñuñoa	E	6,7%
Maipú	W	6,1%	Ñuñoa	E	2,5%	Vitacura	E	6,6%
Quinta Normal	W	6,0%	Vitacura	E	1,9%	Puente Alto	SE	6,6%
Cerrillos	W	5,6%						

Source: Mideplan, 1998a; quoted from Zegras and Gakenheimer, (2000:24)

The concentration of working places in the central areas and in some peripheral industrial *comunas* results in various degrees of their accesibility. Indeed, travel times to work are considerably unbalanced between *comunas*. While most of the people living in the eastern areas need an average of twenty minutes to reach their working places, those in the south need at least forty.

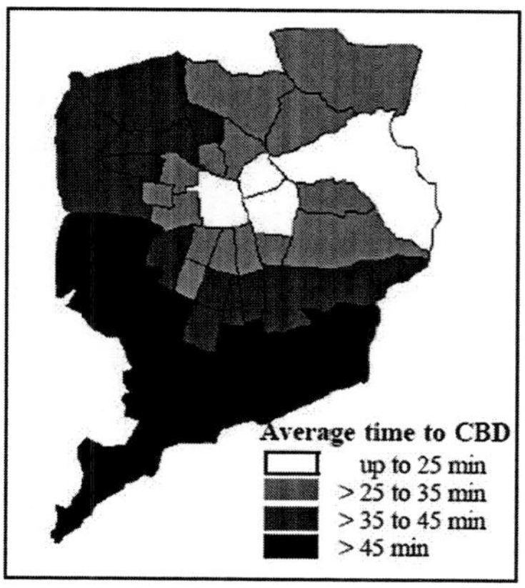

Map 23: Travel time/work
Source: Jiménez, 1999. See Table 36

As most of the social housing completed between 1978 and 1989 lacked basic amenities, a programme to supply social infrastructure was performed in the early 1990's. This programme aims at the implementation of communitary centres, kindergartens and playgrounds through the municiplaities. In addition, since 1993 the regulation requiring the provision of this sort of social infrastructure has been tightened, avoiding previous "misinterpretations"[(48)].

The chronic lack of these basic services is usually exacerbated by the fact that social houses -as real estate- do not need to pay taxes and, therefore, municipalities do not receive enough revenues to implement such services. In addition, some authors such as Rodriguez (2000:128) claim that even though most of the districts do include basic infrastructure, the quality of the services diverges, especially in terms of access to good education: *"poor districts have not only bad schools but also bad results"* [(49)].

In a seminal study by the Centro de Estudios para el Desarrollo (CED, 1990), it was found that most of the poorest neighbourhoods in Santiago included basic services such as water, but that their inhabitants consume much less than better-off people and commonly owe their bills. Though this is not current information, it is possible to assume that no substantial changes have occurred.

Map 24, 25 and 26: Selected Infrastructure Indicators

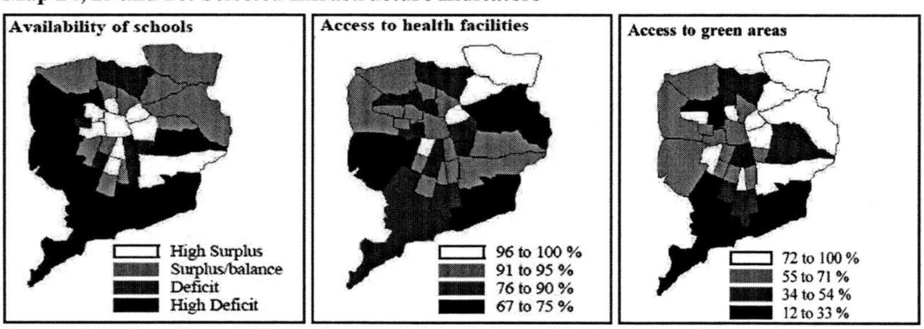

Sources: Data from Casen 1998 and Zegras and Gakenheimer, 2000. Author's self-elaboration

---

(48) It is important to notice that this requirement was not completely absent in the previous legislation, but the problem was that the construction firms used to avoid it. In fact, the legislation did require that every new development of more than 100 social dwellings should consider some basic social infrastructure. Nevertheless, construction firms used to divide their offers up to a maximum of 99 dwellings, despite the fact that they could be in adjacent plots.

(49) The authors make a reference to the results obtained in the governmental test -to measure educational attainment- *Prueba SIMCE* of 1997 which showed a clear difference between *comunas*; in particular those in the eastern districts present the best performance in this test (Rodriguez and Winchester, 2000:129).

5.2.5 The Architectural and Physical Differences

Besides social factors and spatial location, the partition of the city is also expressed in its morphology. This difference used to be expressed through typical qualitative aspects of buildings such as height, materials used, size, appearance, monetary value as well as through the symbolical significance that they had for their dwellers.

These attributes of the housing stock also contribute to exclusion and disintegration[(50)] and, therefore, deserve some attention, particularly in the case of Santiago where the consolidation of such physical divergences becomes apparent. In spite of the fact that this study cannot embrace all aspects for the whole city, the most relevant aspects linked to social housing will be highlighted.

First, average housing areas sharply contrast among districts. Once more, *comunas* in the eastern part of the city that coincide with well-to-do settlements have the highest average of square meters per housing, reaching up to more than 200 sqm per dwelling (Rodriguez, 2000:133). *Comuna*s that concentrate most of the low-income families and huge proportions of social housing average no more than 50 sqm per dwelling. Second, one of the features of the city is its low-height construction. In fact, the relation between the amount of single-family houses and the amount of apartment buildings is almost 5:1 (77% are houses and 21% apartment buildings).

Map 27: Average sqm Dwellings

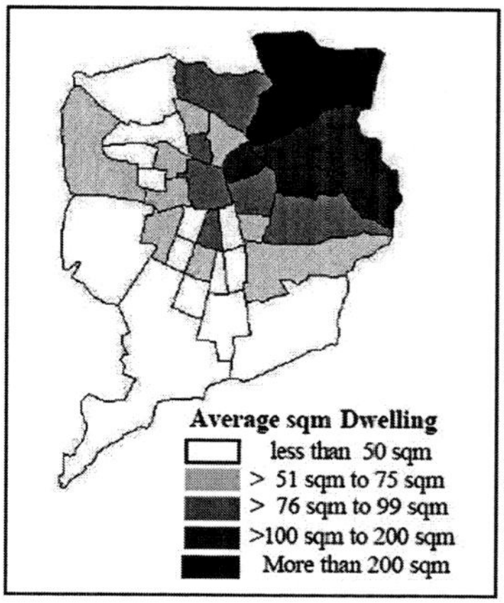

Fig. 35: Average sqm in some districts

Comuna	LOC (1)	Average m2	*Comuna*	LOC (1)	Average m2
Barnechea	E	209	Cerro Navia	W	41
Vitacura	E	209	San Ramón	S	41
Las Condes	E	159	La Pintana	S	42
La Reina	E	121	Lo Espejo	S	42
Providencia	E	105	La Granja	S	43
Ñuñoa	E	90	El Bosque	S	44
Huechuraba	N	87	Lo Prado	W	45
Peñalolén	SE	87	San Bernardo	S	48
Independencia	N	81	San Joaquin	S	48
San Miguel	S	81	Puente Alto	SE	49
La Florida	SE	79	Maipú	W	50
Santiago	CBD	77	Quilicura	N	50
Est. Central	W	75	Renca	W	50
LaCisterna	S	67	Cerrillos	W	56
Conchali	N	66	Recoleta	N	58
Macul	SE	66	Qta. Normal	W	59

Source: Rodriguez and Winchester, 2001

(50) Assuming that a place and its attributes such as the disparities in access to urban opportunities or environmental quality directly affects attractivity or stigma.

However, almost half of the apartment buildings existing in the city are built in only four districts out of 34 (see figure 36). In three of them, this ratio is inverse: more than 50% of the construction are middle to high-rise buildings. This is the case of Providencia (80,5%), Ñuñoa (56,77%) and Las Condes (56,22). Even in the central district of Santiago -where the main CBD is located- the proportion of high-rise buildings is quite low. In spite of the efforts to renew and repopulate the *comuna* of Santiago with the construction of residential estates[51], just 36,17% of its dwellings are middle- or high-rise buildings (INE, 2003).

Map 28: Social estates

Fig. 36: Flats in the City

Comuna	LOC (1)	% of Total
Santiago	CBD	14,40%
Las Condes	E	13,03%
Providencia	E	11,30%
Ñuñoa	E	9,23%
Puente Alto	SE	4,83%
La Florida	SE	4,21%
Maipú	W	4,01%
San Bernardo	S	3,49%
Vitacura	E	2,85%
Macul	SE	2,52%
Lo Prado	W	2,41%
Quilicura	N	2,28%
Est. Central	W	2,03%
La Pintana	S	1,74%
San Miguel	S	1,73%
Pudahuel	W	1,61%

Third, significant differences can also be perceived in population densities. These are much higher in *comunas* with great shares of social housing rather than in the eastern *comunas* withthe greater amount of high-rise buildings. For example, Puente Alto has 165 inhabitants per hectare, Lo Prado 156 and La Pintana 123. On the other hand, Providencia has 85 inhabitants per hectare, Las Condes 64 and Vitacura just 28. Visually, this is expressed by the fact that most of the eastern *comunas* have much higher proportions of green areas, wider streets and larger plots of land. Fourth, the garden-city building typology or single-family house with front and/or backyard that use to be the most common througout the social classes is being displaced by collective housing in middle- and high-income neighbourhoods either in the form of gated communities or apartment buildings surrounded by green areas and surveillance. While the garden city paradigm included a kind of integration between different neighbourhoods -because the main difference rested in the size and not in the type of buildings [52]-, gated communities and high-rise residential

[51] A new renewal programme, highly subsidised by the government, has resulted in the construction of many middle and high-rise buildings destined to middle-income families and employees that work in downtown areas. This process is certainly changing the morphological structure of the pericentral *barrios*. It is also, however, causing gentrification.

Fig. 37: Hige-rise buildings in Vitacura

buildings stand for an increasing distancing of status classes. Nevertheless, this process it is not exclusive to high-income *comunas*; middle-income ones are following the same pattern.

Fifth, the preferred typology for social housing used in the last decades has consisted of low-rise buildings or estates of three to four storeys, which are also known in Chile by the English word "*blocks*". While until 1989 *blocks* or estates represented a minimal

Fig. 38: Social housing at the southern periphery

Fig. 39: Estates in La Pintana, late 1980s

Fig. 40: Estates in Puente Alto, early 1900s

Source: Author's photo

(52) Both in middle and low-income neighbourhoods it was common to find houses that resemble, on a small scale, the façades of mansions and architecture to be found in well-to-do areas.

proportion of the total social housing built in the city, they make up 86% of social housing built between 1990 and the year 2000. Nowadays, the estates built between 1982 and 2000 make up 45,8% of the total social housing built in the same period.

While the traditional pattern of building one- to two-storey social housing on a single plot had the advantage of facilitating further individual improvements -as is the case in many old *poblaciones*-, estates are much harder to be transformed, because of the fact that they are collective units. In addition, this type of construction usually requires much more maintenance and community organisation to solve conflicts. As a result of all these aspects, some *comunas* of the city have a clear chance to continue evolving through market actions and to continue attracting investments and people, whereas others are born with the handicap of being unattractive, isolated and stigmatised places.

5.2.6 Summary of Findings

Indicators at the city level tend to confirm the role played by the government in reinforcing socio-spatial segregation and fragmentation according social classes through social housing policies. In the main categories, the findings are presented according to the following categories: Location, Social indicators, Physical attributes, Infrastructure and Demographic indicators.

Location

- Social housing has been progressively located in more and more peripheral areas of the city,
- Almost 90% of the dwellings built in the last decades have been located only in 15 out of 34 urban *comunas*,
- South and southeastern districts concentrated 65% of the social housing built between 1978 and the year 2000.
- Land values and market interest have become the most important factors that have guided housing location.

Social indicators

-Low-income families are mainly located in the southern periphery

- Many social indicators such as unemployment, school abandonment and overcrowding coincide with patterns of housing location
- There is almost no social housing in those areas categorised as high-income and middle- to high-income districts.
- Segregation is taking another shape (gated - communities versus social housing)

Physical and architectural attributes

- Unbalanced average of square meters devoted to housing. Poor districts have much fewer sqm per inhabitant than the richest areas.

- High standard apartments are concentrated in three districts.

- Central and eastern areas have lower densities

- Land prices and property taxes reflect socio-economic segregation.

- 3-4 storey social housing dominates some sectors in poor districts

Infrastructure and opportunities

- Working opportunities, main health facilities and a big amount of green areas are located in central and high-income districts.

- A deficit of schools, green areas and educational facilities affects districts in the southern periphery.

- Travel times are not necessarily related to distance. Districts in the south do not possess enough transportation means; the road system is not as developed as the one existing in central and eastern areas.

Demographic and urban growth

- Housing policies have played an important role in urban growth, especially in some peripheral districts. However, real estate developments for middle and high-income families seem to be more relevant.

- Central and pericentral areas are becoming depopulated while both the periphery and some nearby rural areas are becoming urbanised (rural-urbanisation process)

- Urban growth has taken a higher pace than population increase. Densities remain as low as one hundred years ago.

5.3 Clustering and Selection of Case Studies

In order to select three *comunas* for a field study that includes direct observation and exploratory interviews, a cluster analysis and indicator performance was done. This process consisted of a normalisation of indicators combined or added according to the following categories: a) Social Aspects, b) Infrastructural aspects, c) Demographic aspects and d) Physical aspects.

In the end, these four aspects were treated as one set of general indicators that facilitated a tentative cluster. This experimental clustering assisted the selection of three case studies that fulfilled the following criteria: first, all three districts include a proportion of social

Map 29, 30, 31 and 32: Comparative Clustering according to four categories

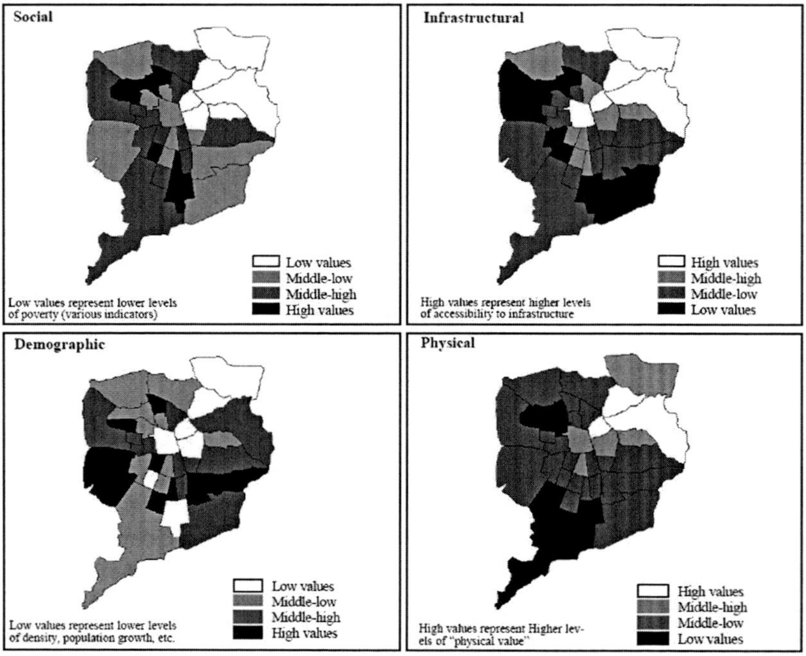

estates completed through the *Programa* de *Vivienda Básica*; second, they have divergent socio-economic characteristics and different levels of access to urban opportunities and third, each district has a distinctive symbolic significance.

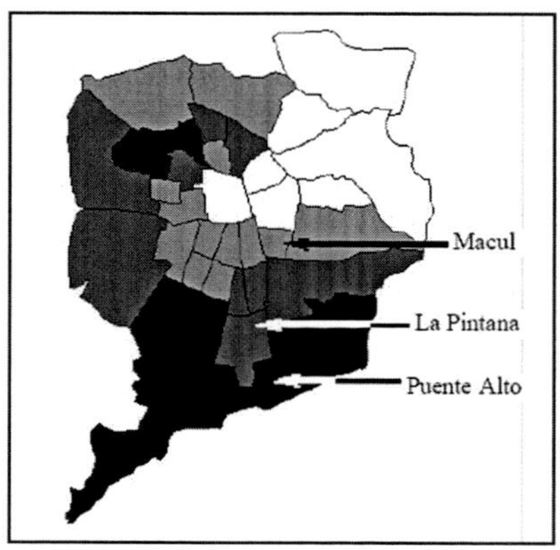

Map 33: Cluster and selected districts

In finding a combination of characteristics and taking into account that the eastern and central areas of the city almost do not contain social housing, three districts that fall under those abovementioned categories were selected to further analysis about the needs for upgrading and reintegration. The other final criteria for the selection of the three districts and the *poblaciones* was the result of the direct observation of some pre-selected *comunas*, looking for the following aspects:

a) districts that contain blocks of apartments that were built in different periods;
b) apartments with diverse typology in terms of architecture and distribution of the blocks, and
c) developments that present different standards of maintenance both of the buildings and their immediate environment.

A city partitioned according to access to opportunities and other social classes:	**A city partitioned in terms of general image:**
- ***Central and pericentral districts,*** predominately middle class that still contain quite a mixture of social classes and have more or less good connections and access to opportunities such as Macul, Peñalolén, Estación Central.	- ***"Postmodern" districts*** that concentrate most of the highest advances in terms of "modernity" (parks, health and educational facilities, architecture, etc.) and that show the success of the Chilean economy.
- ***Former Villages*** that have been incorporated into the city due to urban sprawl which are mainly inhabited by middle- and low-income families and have their own centres (in spite of the fact that population growth has rendered them insufficient) such as Puente Alto, Quilicura and Maipú.	- ***Old central districts*** with a mixture of decadent turn-of-the-century housing and neighbourhoods where new programmes of renewal are "gentrifying" former middle- and low-income areas
- ***Traditionally poor districts*** or semi-rural areas that have been transformed into social housing districts and have little access to main urban opportunities such as Cerro Navia, La Pintana, and El Bosque.	- ***Peripheral districts*** that are "warehousing" the poor with a clear character of "dormitory" zones for those that have no other option in the market.

The above summarised analysis also allowed the making of a kind of classification of districts that represent the current "partitioning" in relation to social housing policies. This classification is shown in the following boxes:

Chapter 6: Case Studies

6.1 Villa San Ricardo, La Pintana

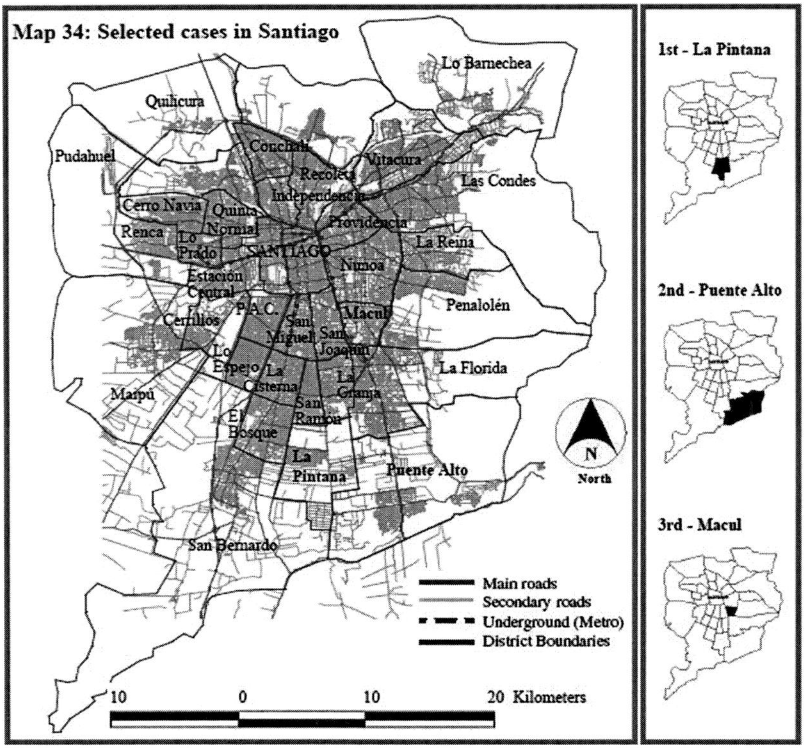

First case: Villa San Ricardo	Second case: Villa Horizonte	Third case: Villa Las Cumbres
The first compound selected is located in the most stigmatised *comuna* of Santiago. A former rural area, La Pintana was the district that received most of the evicted families during the military regime (1973-1989). Villa San Ricardo was built in 1980 and is one of the early developments of social housing completed in the block or estates form under the current housing policy.	Villa Horizonte was built in 1994 and is located in the former village of Puente Alto -on the southeast side of Santiago-but quite far from the historical centre of the village. Puente Alto is the district that contains the highest proportion of social housing completed in the last decade. Villa Horizonte is located on the southwestern border of the district near rural areas.	Villa Las Cumbres is located in Macul, an old relatively central district, predominately middle class, with "spots" of diverse types of housing. Macul is one of the districts with the lowest quantity of social housing completed in the last twenty years. Villa las Cumbres is located at the southeastern edge of the districts and was built in 1989 at the end of the military regime.

6.1.1 The District in the City

La Pintana is located at the southern periphery of the Santiago about 18 km from midtown. It is one of the poorest districts in Santiago and is known as a distressed district that concentrates poverty, drugs and crime. Its bad reputation emerged after the district received a very high proportion of low-income people evicted from high-income *comunas* during the military regime[53].

Fig. 41: Aerial Photo of Comuna La Pintana

Sources: Municipality of La Pintana, Casen 1998 and Census 2002.

General Data		Social Data	
Population (Inh.)	190.085	Unemployment (%)	15.20
Area (Hectares:Ha)	3.060	Poor (percent)	30.91
Density (Inh./Ha)	63	No Poor (percent)	69.09
Total Dwellings	41.398	Illiteracy rate (%)	3.9
Permanent Dwellings	41.152	Average studies (years)	8.7
Households	45.301	Child mortality (1:1000)	12.6
Owners (percent)	74,26	Early pregnancy (%)	20,6
Tenants (percent)			

Indeed, La Pintana holds the biggest proportion of social housing completed under the military government during the early stages of the current housing policy. It is also representative of the changes that have occurred in former rural areas located at the outskirts of the city which have been dramatically transformed through the implementation of such policies[54]. Moreover, the massive implementation of programmes of sites and services and new social housing resulted in an explosive increase in population and the

---

(53) According to information gathered in the municipality of Puente Alto, the three *Comunas* of San Bernardo, La Granja and Puente Alto received more than 75% of the evicted families coming from Las Condes, La Reina, Providencia and Ñuñoa. In addition, La Pintana continued receiving further housing programmes carried out over the period from 1984 -1989.

(54) In spite of the fact that between the late 1960s and early 1970s La Pintana experienced some land seizures (*"tomas de terreno"*), its rural character was still present until the early 1980s; the landscape was predominately conformed by both big plots of agrarian land and rural social housing known as *"Huertos Obreros"* (workers orchards), which was an experimental cooperative development of single family housing in a plot of half an hectare.

Fig. 42: Housing growth in La Pintana

Census	Number of dwellings (a)	Average Growth (a')	Number of inhabitants (b)	Average growth (b')	(b) / (a)	Cumulative social Housing Nº	Cumulative social Housing %
1982	15.060		73.932	(*) 5,35%	4,91	2.149	14,26
1992	38.942	8,84%	169.640	7,86%	4,36	17.113	43,94
2002	41.398	0,61%	190.085	1,14%	4,59	28.094	67,86

(*) Calculated according to the 1970 Census, which accounted 37.994 inhabitants that year.
(**) Data year 2000)

Fig. 43: Social housing in La Pintana

Range of unites by *Poblacion*	Number of *Poblaciones*	Estates *Poblaciones*	Type of Unites	Number of unites
Between 70 and 200	6	2	Total Social Housing	21.563
Between 201 and 500	22	11	Social single unites	16.581
Between 501 and 1.000	9	1	Social Estates	4.982
more than 1.000	2			

spatial concentration of homogeneous low-standard social housing. In addition, the spatial location of the new *poblaciones* did not follow any urban plan of development; they were simply spread where land was available, as places of repetitive, plain-looking housing typologies.

This growth was not followed by the implementation of social facilities such as schools, green areas, sport or community centres, and, in many cases, even basic infrastructure such as paved roads was not provided. During this period, the relatively new(55) district was not prepared to receive such a forced growth in population. In addition to this, most of the displaced people also lost their former social networks, and their access to workplaces and services became much more difficult to access (CED, 1990).

Nowadays, La Pintana's urban tissue is characterised by a combination of fragments, the most relevant being big empty areas(56) and dense residential compounds consisting of some 39 *poblaciones* built between 1980 and 1999. While the population density reaches close to 130 inhabitants per hectare, most of these compounds have net densities between 300 and 800 inhabitants per hectare. Since the return to democracy in 1990, various democratic local governments have attempted to reduce infrastructure and service defects

(55) La Pintana was instituted as a *comuna* in 1981. Previously, it was administratively the rural area of the *Comuna* of La Granja, which was partitioned that year in the framework of an administrative and spatial reorganisation done by the military regime.

(56) These non-urbanised or vacant areas include an experimental university Campus for Agrarian and Veterinary Sciences, as well as former agricultural land which is destined to receive the new city zoo.

as well as to stop the construction of more social housing in the *comuna*. Indeed, the new Plan Regulador *Comunal* of 1996 has fixed the quantity of residential areas of 60% of the *comuna*'s territory. One of the results of this municipal intervention is that[57] the average rates of dwelling and population increases have shown a dramatic reduction in the last decade (see figure 35). However, La Pintana is still a stigmatised residential *comuna*[58] that lacks industry or enough employment sources and where commercial, educational and health facilities are scarce. In addition, former middle-income residents in small agricultural areas have been leaving in search of better environmental conditions.

6.1.2 The Selected Case: Villa San Ricardo

The main reasons behind the selection of Villa San Ricardo for a case study out of a total of 14 *poblaciones* that include estates or *blocks*, are manifold. One of the reasons is that Villa San Ricardo was built in 1980, and therefore, it represents one of the early developments of social housing estates completed during the experimental phase of the *Programa* de *Vivienda Básica* (1978-1984). Also, its architectural typology and dwelling sizes are exceptional compared to the type of construction implemented in following years.

San Ricardo	Data
Population	4.290
Households	895
Single family housing	337
Multifamily unites (Blocks)	384
Total Social Housing	661
Households in Estates	330
Flats dwellers	2.030
Density (Inh/Hectare) Estates	390
Construction Index (*) Estates	0,20
Year of construction	1.980

(*) Built area in first floor divided total area

Fig. 44: San Ricardo's surroundings

Fig. 45: San Ricardo compound

Fig. 46: General data San Ricardo

Source: Photo Minvu and self-digitalised location

[57] The Municipality of La Pintana has been investing in several programmes to alleviate poverty and to improve urban and social conditions. Nowadays, most of the *comuna* possess basic infrastructure such as paved roads and the implementation of a civic centre -close to the municipality- as well as the development of squares and new green areas.

[58] In spite of the fact that many social indicators have improved, the district -and some specific poblaciones- usually occupies the front pages of newspaper and TV news as the place of drugs and high criminality.

A third reason for selecting Villa San Ricardo is that it shows evidence of resident interventions, both in public and private spaces, which seem to be relatively well maintained. In the end, most of its inhabitants are the original beneficiaries of the social housing programme or their relatives which means that many have been living there for more than 20 years.

6.1.3 Spatial Configuration and Architecture

Fig. 47: Typical "Block" San Ricardo

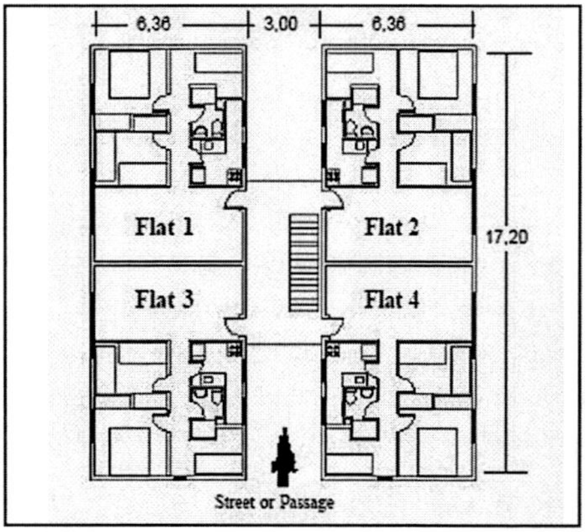

Fig. 48: "Blocks" Assembling

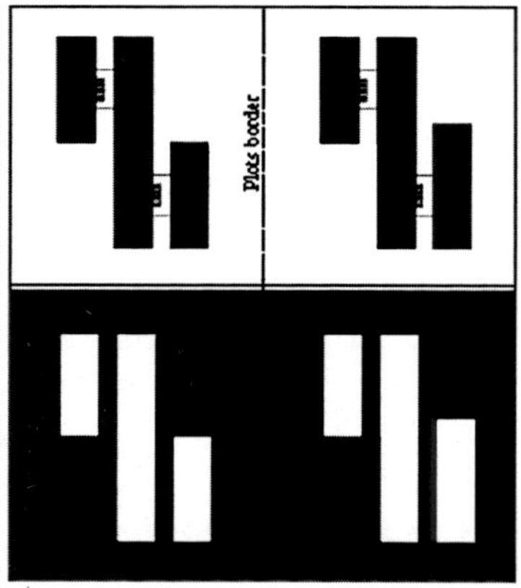

Source: Author's drawings

Villa San Ricardo is located around 2 km from the geographical and services centre of the *comuna* and only 700 meters from the main avenue Santa Rosa which facilitates the accessibility to both transportation means and community services.

Built in an area of eight hectares, it is compoused of a combination of single-family units -built in attached two-storey houses- and 48 multi-family units or estates of 4 storeys built up in an area of five hectares that includes free areas to be used by the whole *población*.

Fig. 49: Staircases in San Ricardo

Source: Author's Photos

Fig. 50: Façades San Ricardo

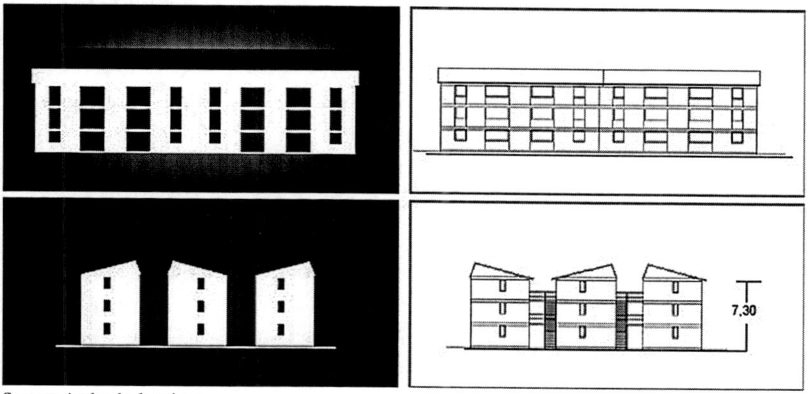

Source: Author's drawings

As many others compounds of social housing estates, San Ricardo ignores the urban tissue by breaking the continuity of the gridiron street pattern and appears as a "spot" of middle-rise buildings without relation to the surrounding single-storey *poblaciones*. This fragmented image is reinforced by the presence of some abandoned empty land which used to be the place for illegal deposition of rubbish (wastelands).

Every estate is made out of two *"blocks"* of three storeys and 4 flats per floor, joined by a stair system that serves the 8 upper flats. The distance between *blocks* is three meters and functions as a sort of hall that is used for drying clothes and storing bikes and plants.

This configuration permits each estate composed of two *blocks* to form a more or less independent community of 12 flats always enclosed by a main fence door. Some of these *blocks* or estates are isolated although most of them are assembled into a greater estate that composed a joint pair and aids in determining a clear concept of space where the *blocks* generate interstitial areas in a graduation from public to private domain.

Fig. 51: Extension in San Ricardo

Fig. 52: Typical extension types

Source: Author's drawings and Photos

Composed and isolated units of estates alike are placed in independent plots that are legally defined as common land. The predominant structural materials used in the buildings are reinforced[(59)] red brick walls and concrete-poured beams and flagstones. Asbestos planks cover the roof. All façades have windows facing the street and pedestrian ways, and the relation between void and solid surfaces softens the monotony of the massive brick constructions. In addition, this proportionality also creates a direct relation with the surrounding areas and the chance to have a social control -through the windows- over them.

Every flat has an area of 53,86 sqm and includes one living room, three bedrooms, a bathroom and a kitchen with a small loggia. The internal distribution of space clearly separates the living room from bedrooms through a corridor, which facilitates the detachment of uses and privacy. All inner division materials are flexible walls that can be easily modified.

Fig. 53: Flat in San Ricardo

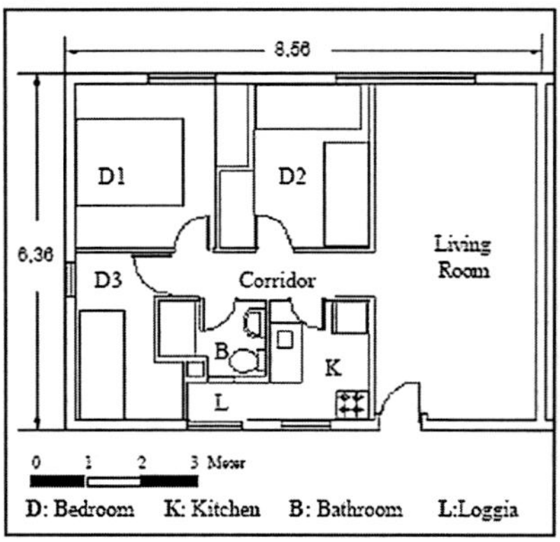

Fig. 54: Extension in San Ricardo

Fig. 55: Extensions in San Ricardo

[(59)] This type of construction does not considered concrete- poured pillars due to the fact that the bricks are vertically reinforced with metal structures.

6.1.4 Resident Interventions

The estates show many interventions done by the beneficiaries. Indeed, most of the people living in the first floor have made illegal extensions(60) or at least occupied the immediate surrounding area with gardens and/or parking lots.

Besides these extensions and "privatised" public spaces, the surrounding areas of the estates have been developed with open public greenery and playgrounds in cooperation with the municipality.

Nevertheless, not all the estates or *blocks* and their surroundings have the same condition of maintenance: some of them are perfectly painted and cared for, while others are neglected and show a decadent upkeep. Extensions of first floor flats are also irregular, some of them occupying just the immediate surroundings and others having expanded their area taking up a big part of the public space.

Order	Interviewee	Sex	Age	Floor	PP (*)	HH (**)
1	Petronila Aguayo	F	48	1	8	2
2	Claudio Carmona	M	42	1	8	2
3	Adrián González	M	48	1	8	2
4	Isidora Riquelme	F	45	1	6	1
5	Esteban Mora	M	37	1	8	2
6	Juanita Avalos	F	42	2	3	1
7	Jorge Ramirez	M	42	1	7	2
8	Isabel Montecinos	F	32	1	4	1

(*) PP : Number of people per dwelling
(**) HH: Number of households per dwelling

Fig. 56: Interviewees from San Ricardo

In comparison with other compounds, San Ricardo is relatively well designed. Dwellings are larger than the average of social housing built under the current policy, their configuration facilitates the formation of small communities, and -besides the irregularities- their state of maintenance seems quite appropriate.

(60) Although the main function of these extensions are bedrooms, some of them allocate workshops or commercial shops.

6.1.5 Resident Perceptions

The simple fact of living in La Pintana, along with its practical and symbolic burden, became the most important aspect at the moment of exploring resident perceptions. Indeed, most of the answers expressed their dissatisfaction with the flats, but in particular, with their environment. In addition, feelings of stigmatisation and weak community bonds are held responsible for neighbourhood decay, according to the interviewees.

6.1.5.1 Sense of Belonging and Community Bonds

In spite of the fact that the majority of families have been living in Villa San Ricardo for more than two decades, their feelings of belonging appear to be weak. Less than a third of the interviewees said to have friends there and expressed confidence in their neighbours. Moreover, some of them expressed that disturbing neighbours and delinquent youth were among the main problems of living in these estates. The main reasons people continue living in the compound were because they have relatives, because they are owners of their flats and because they feel that they have no other alternative.

Fig. 57: Belonging and bonds

Order	Owners	Relative	From a far away district	More than 5 years here	Family here
1	X		X	X	
2	X		X	X	
3	X		X	X	X
4	X		X	X	X
5	X			X	X
6	X		X	X	
7		X			X
8	X			X	

Fig. 58: Dwelling adequacy

Original m2	M2 Extension	Current Area	M2 p/p Original	M2 p/p Current
54	3	57	6,75	7,13
54	9	63	6,75	7,88
54	6	60	6,75	7,50
54	6	60	9.00	10.00
54	9	63	6.75	7.88
54		54	18.00	18.00
54	3	57	7.71	8.14
54		54	13.50	13.50

6.1.5.2 Dwelling Adequacy and Image

Overcrowding seems to be an intense problem in San Ricardo. Because, in many cases, up to eight persons and two households share one flat, most of the interviewees expressed a desire either to move or to increase the inner area. All of them expressed that a main problem of living in Villa San Ricardo is the bad material quality of the flats. Lack of privacy[(61)] was also mentioned in many cases, but usually in relation to conflicts with neighbours rather

(61) However, a successful movie based on truth facts called *"El Chacotero Sentimental"*, and television special reports Programmes (*El Mirador and Contacto*) have shown the difficulties that many couples faced to have a "healthy" sexual life in these conditions of overcrowding.

than to the unsuitability of the flats. Desired changes also include structural improvements, improvement of common spaces, and in particular, modification of the appearance of the estates by painting or building fences.

6.1.5.3 Living Environment and Stigma

Apparently, dwellers in San Ricardo distrust their environment. Indeed, most interviewees avoid passing through nearby vacant lots or wastelands, and half of them neither feel secure in the streets nor when traveling in buses. Although communal statistics about drugs abuse, alcoholism and delinquency are below regional averages and even unemployment is not the most acute problem in the eyes of the interviewees, still, these are the main conflictive issues related with their neighbourhood.

Fig. 59: Environment and stigma: most mentioned problems

Order	Insecurity	Youth behaviour	Alcohol/ drugs	Bad infra	Bad services	Unemployment	Delinquency	Vandalism
1	X	X	X	X	X	X	X	X
2	X	X	X	X	X	X	X	X
3			X	X	X		X	
4	X	X	X	X		X	X	X
5			X		X	X		
6	X		X	X			X	X
7						X	X	
8		X	X	X		X	X	X

These opinions demonstrate the residents' low self-esteem which tends to be reinforced by the fact that many of them not only think badly of their neighbourhood, but have also experienced prejudices from outsiders[(62)].

Fig. 60: Green areas in San Ricardo

[(62)] Some of them avoid giving their address when asking for a job while others have already received questions such as *How can you live there? Are there not too many robbers there?*

Fig. 61: Aerial Photo Comuna Puente Alto **Fig. 62: General Data Puente Alto**

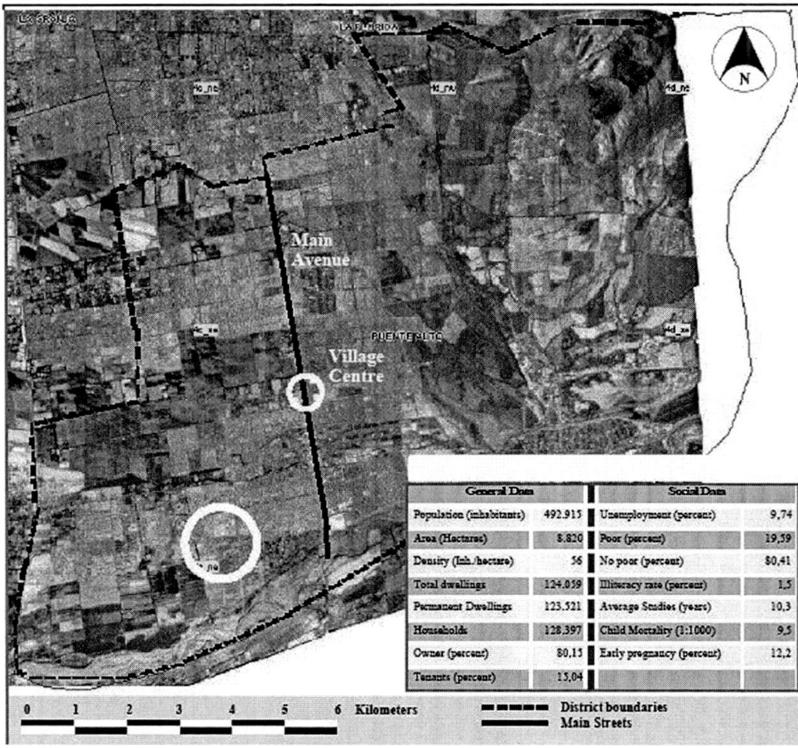

General Data		Social Data	
Population (inhabitants)	492.915	Unemployment (percent)	9,74
Area (Hectares)	8.820	Poor (percent)	19,59
Density (Inh./hectare)	56	No poor (percent)	80,41
Total dwellings	124.059	Illiteracy rate (percent)	1,5
Permanent Dwellings	123.521	Average Studies (years)	10,3
Households	128.397	Child Mortality (1:1000)	9,5
Owner (percent)	80,15	Early pregnancy (percent)	12,2
Tenants (percent)	15,04		

6.2 Villa Horizonte, Puente Alto

6.2.1 The District in the City

The *comuna* of Puente Alto represents a case similar to that of many other formerly "independent"(63) villages around the city of Santiago such as Maipu, Quilicura and Lo Barnechea which have merged, over time, with the rest of the metropolitan area. Puente Alto is located at the southeastern foothills of Santiago and is near to one of the richest

(63) Puente Alto was created in1898 and declared the head district of the Cordillera province in 1958, It was slowly growing encompassed with the establishment of industry and agricultural activities. The biggest Chilean paper factory and the principal water treatment plant for Santiago are located since decades in the comuna.

Fig. 63: Housing growth in Puente Alto

Census	Number of dwellings (a)	Average Growth (a')	Number of inhabitants (b)	Average growth (b')	(b) / (a)	Cumulative social Housing N°	Cumulative social Housing %
1982	25.034		113.211	(*) 3,20%	4,52	1.472	5,88
1992	64.331	8,79%	254.673	7,69%	3,96	12.433	19,32
2002	124.059	6,34%	492.915	6,37%	3,97	(**) 31.489	25,38

(*) Calculated according to the 1970 Census, which accounted 76.694 inhabitants that year (**) Data year 2000). Source: Data from Minvu.

Fig. 64: Social housing in Puente Alto

Range of unites by *Población*	Number of *Poblaciones*	Estates Poblaciones	Type of Unites	Number of unites
Between 70 and 200	14	14	Total Social Housing	31.489
Between 201 and 500	17	10	Social single unites	16.356
Between 501 and 1.000	12		Social Estates	15.133
more than 1.000	10			

agricultural areas of Santiago. It is among the *comunas* with high rates of population growth during the last decade, and indeed, the most populated one in the country. Puente Alto also holds the highest absolute number of social housing in the whole country.

The case of Puente Alto shows how current Chilean housing policy has supported a tendency of city growth towards peripherialsation and "rural-urbanisation". The reasons why Puente Alto's urban area has grown as much as it has are, at least, threefold. First, the evictions carried out in the 1980s [64] resulted in a massive relocation of people in new settlements, second, the fact that the largest amount of social dwellings built in the 1990s -estates in particular- was located is this *comuna*[65] and third, that some areas of Puente Alto are still interesting locations for middle-high income families.

As a matter of fact, the *comuna* contains numerous country houses (*parcelas de agrado*) and other real estate developments for middle- and high-income families due to its environmental attractiveness. It lies close to rural and mountainous areas. Nevertheless, the existence of different types of families does not result in social integration because different social classes are spatially segregated in the *comuna*. While most of the 53 different

[64] According to the 1992 Census, almost 15% of Puente Alto's inhabitants corresponded to those evicted. Information collected at the Municipality of Puente Alto.

[65] Figures from MINVU indicate that between 1992-2002, almost 30% of the housing build in the district was destined to the lowest-incomes (PVB and PVP). Likewise, many other developments also received subsidies oriented to middle-income segments of the population; however, there is no exact data about the quantity of units subsidised by the Programa de subsidio unificado (SGU).

"Poblaciones" or *"Villas"* are located in the southwestern periphery of the district and far from the centre of the village, middle- and high-income areas are mostly in the eastern parts.

Unlike other districts that are trying to reduce their growth, Puente Alto is a dynamic and swelling district. It has already urbanised 36,18% of its 88,2 km2, and according to its new *Plan Regulador Comunal* approved in 2003, another 14,9 km2 are still left to be urbanised in the future[66]. Moreover, its centre is quite well-serviced with banks, commerce, health services and transportation facilities, including a future extension to the metropolitan underground. Nevertheless, the relation between population and availability of working places is still negative, and educational facilities do not cover the augmenting demand.

6.2.2 The Selected Case: Villa Horizonte

Puente Alto includes many examples of *poblaciones* [67]; however, Villa Horizonte appeared as one of the most interesting ones for many reasons. First, it presents a high level of interventions done by the beneficiaries which include not only extensions in first and second floors such as those visible in other estates, but also self-made constructions on the third floor. Second, the buildings correspond to a classic typology known as "scissors" which had been widely spread since the late 1980s and abandoned just a few years ago following a lot of criticism. Third, it is located close to geologically precarious areas and

Fig. 65: General Data Horizonte
Fig. 66: San Ricardo´s surroundings
Source: Photo Minvu and data from Municipality of Puente Alto & Census 2002

Villa Horizonte	Data
Population	2.113
Households	500
Single family housing	296
Multifamily unites (Blocks)	78
Total Social Housing	374
Households in Estates	84
Flats dwellers	428
Density (Inh/Hectare) Estates	1.296
Construction Index (*) Estates	0,35
Year of construction	1.993

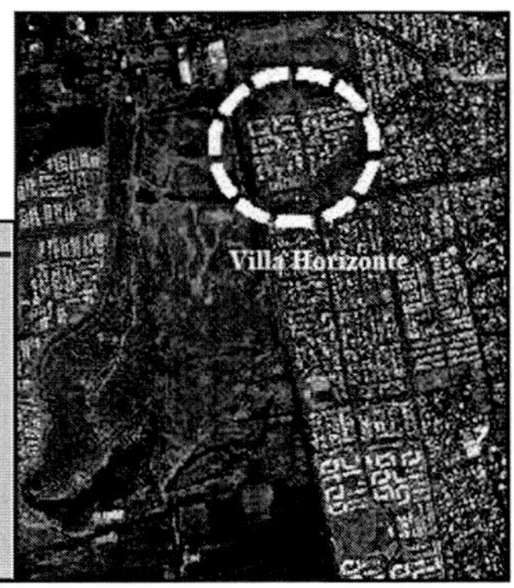

[66] The *Plan Regulador* determined that 12,2 km2 are urbanisable with restrictions, and 5,7 km2 are deemed industrials areas. On the other hand, 25% of the district˝s territory -22,4 km2 are defined as not urbanisable because they correspond to hills, mountain cords and ells for grave extraction.

[67] One of the most notorious is Villa El Volcán which was an initial option for the study due to the fact that it characterises the massive low-quality and construction pathologies existing in current social housing developments. El Volcán was on the front pages of the news and public debate after strong rainstorms in the winter of 1997 evidencing the poor quality of construction -walls absorbing rain water-. This Villa was called "the polythene's población" due to the fact that after those storms, the people covered them with huge pieces of plastic.

surrounded by nothing but low-income, sinlge-floor housing and is far from schools and other social facilities. Fourth, most of its residents are young families that have applied for housing in a collective manner, so they have strong familiar ties in the neighbourhood.

6.2.3 Spatial Configuration and Architecture

Villa Horizonte is located in the southwest of the district, around 3,5 km from the civic and commercial centre of Puente Alto where most of the communal services are located. The compound includes 296 *viviendas progresivas* (sites-and services) built on independent plots of 100 sqm each with 84 flats distributed in three estates of 3 storeys completed through the

Fig. 67: Hozonte Compound

Programa de *Vivienda Básica* and built on a single plot of 3,300 sqm. Unlike *poblaciones* built before 1993, the compound also includes some basic social infrastructure[68].

Fig. 68: Typical "Block" Horizonte

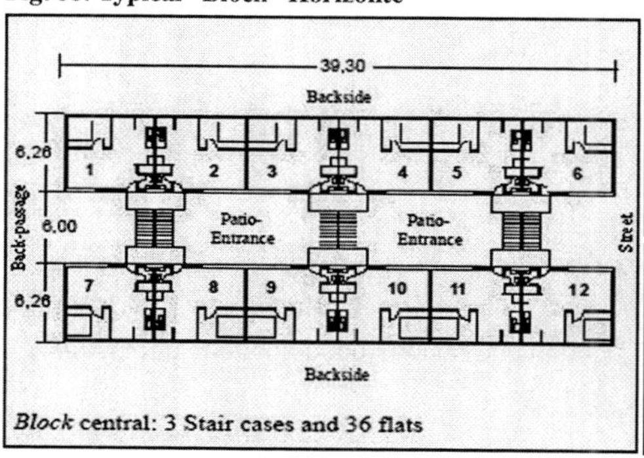

Fig. 69: Blocks Assembling

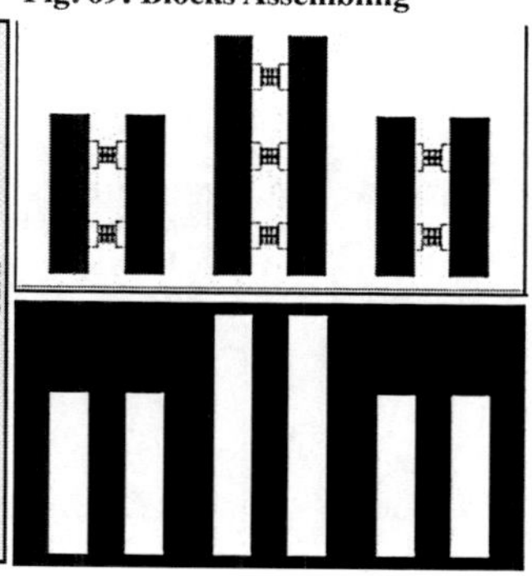

[68] The compound includes some social infrastructure such as two multiple-use playgrounds of 910 sqm. each located at the extremes of the compound (Capture 49) and free area of 1000 sqm. reserved for a future green area. There is also a reserved area for a community centre.

The compound is surrounded not only by more *poblaciones*, but also by rural and large vacant areas that include a huge pit for the extraction of gravel which is considered a source of dust and even danger due to the geological risks of erosion. Moreover, this type of surrounding gives the impression of both decadence and dereliction. The estates are

Fig. 70: Staircase and extensions in Villa Horizonte

located at the southernmost extreme of the compound and are assembled into three groups of *blocks*, two of them with 24 flats each and the central one with 36 flats. These *blocks* share a 6-meter wide patio entrance with a system of stairs commonly known as "scissors" -because of their crossing form- which is used as a playground for small children and for socialising within the estate. The buildings are arranged in a linear shape, perpendicular to the access street. They do not include more open spaces than the patio entrances and the backsides which are commonly used by the expansions of first floor residents. In

Fig. 71: Façades Villa Horizonte

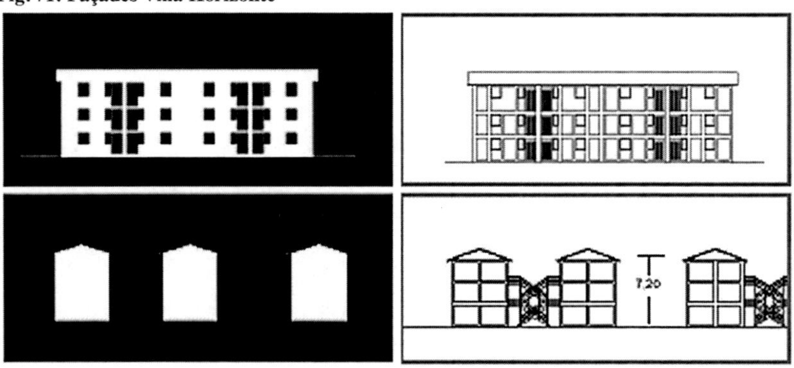

Fig. 72: Typical falt Horizonte

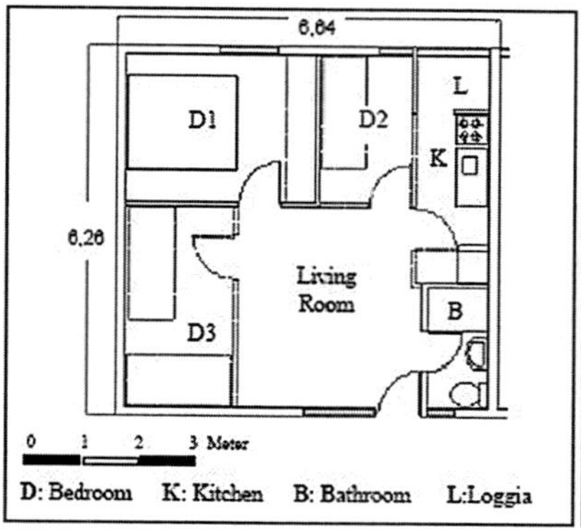

Fig. 73: Extensions in Horizonte

addition, these "barrack"-like estates[69] are isolated in a single shared plot and have neither a morphological, nor a spatial relation to the rest of the Villa. This appearance is confirmed by the massive type of construction made up of red brick walls and concrete-poured braces, with a minimal quantity of voids in the façade surfaces. Neither the façade facing the access street, nor the one facing the back passage has windows.

All flats have the same shape with a small difference in area: those at the extremes of each block have an area of 41,18 sqm, the rest only have 40,78 sqm. They include three bedrooms, a living room, a bathroom and a kitchen with a loggia. The living room is the core of the internal distribution, and all other rooms converge to it. Therefore there is no transitional space that could facilitate a graduation between private and collective spaces. In spite of the fact that Villa Horizonte was built in 1993, it already shows signs of decay, which are visible both in the dereliction of common spaces and occurance of vandalism[70].

6.2.4 Resident Interventions

Interventions by the residents are especially visible at the backside of each block -opposite to the patio entrance. Interventions have been made in order to extend the flats on the first floor, either with a finished construction -usually a bedroom- or a private yard.

[69] Besides aesthetic concerns, other important criticisms have been originated due to the fact that in spite of been economically suitable, this configuration does not clearly define a sense of community. On one hand, they do not configure community spaces and, on the other hand, the patios are too small to promote common uses and too big to produce an appropriation.

[70] Broken stairs and fences, graffiti and destruction of public lights and telephones cabs.

Fig. 74: Extensions in Horizonte

Fig. 75: Extensions in Horizonte

Fig. 76: Extensions in Horizonte

Fig. 77: Interviewees Villa Horizonte

Order	Interviewee	Sex	Age	Floor	PP (*)	HH (**)
1	Luis Inostroza	M	52	1	4	1
2	Cecilia Calfante	F	31	1	8	1
3	Patricia Mansilla	F	34	2	5	1
4	Mónica Hermosilla	F	32	1	4	1
5	Gloria Ruíz	F	28	3	7	2
6	Mirta Baez	F	41	2	10	3
7	Manuel Perez	M	70	3	2	1
8	Rosa Alvarado	F	38	3	6	1

(*) PP : Number of people per dwelling
(**) HH: Number of households per dwelling

In addition, this compound includes extensions on second and third floors and even in the shared patio entrance. It is important to highlight that these kinds of extensions are not only illegal, but also quite dangerous in a seismically-active country as Chile.

6.2.5 Resident Perceptions

The sample interviews aid the assumption that the levels of confidence and socialisation in Villa Horizonte are intensive features: most people have familiar ties. Yet, most of the concerns of the interviewees are related to the type of dwelling and their environment rather than to community problems. However, problems of appearance, insecurity and dereliction of common spaces are also relevant.

6.2.5.1 Belonging and Community Bonds

As most of the beneficiaries of social housing, the families living in Villa Horizonte originally came from a different district (other than Puente Alto) and are the original owners since they were allocated here in 1993. Because most of them applied as a group, there are many parental relationships between neighbours, and therefore, many of the interviewees expressed that one of the reasons to continue living here was the existence of familiar ties. According to some of the interviewees, neighbourly ties keep them informed about practical matters such as social services and job opportunities and are also a base for mutual help. On the other hand, this closeness was also said to have some negative effects such as noise and lack of privacy.

Fig. 78: Belonging and Bonds

Order	Owners	Relative	From a far away district	More than 5 years here	Family here
1	X		X	X	X
2	X		X	X	X
3	X		X	X	X
4	X		X	X	X
5	X		X		X
6	X		X	X	
7		X		X	
8	X		X	X	X

Fig. 79: Dwelling adequacy

Order	Original m2	M2 Extension	Current Area	M2 p/p Original	M2 p/p current
1	41	9	50	10.25	12.50
2	41	9	50	5.12	6.25
3	41	13	54	8.20	10.80
4	41		41	10.25	10.25
5	41	3	44	5.85	6.29
6	41	7	48	4,10	4,80
7	41		41	20,50	20,50
8	41	6	47	6,83	7,83

6.2.5.2 Dwelling Adequacy and Image

Although most of the interviewees have already made extensions to their flats -mainly to be used as bedrooms-, a further increase of flat space remains the top priority on the list of desired changes. However, overcrowding is not seen as an apparent problem. Only two of the interviewed families share a flat with another household which might be explained by the fact that most of the households are young families. Other changes desired by the majority of the interviewees are related to the appearance of the buildings. Painting and changing windows appear as the most desired interventions. The improvement of the structure and the quality of common spaces also form part of the changes agreed among most of the interviewees.

Fig. 80: Environment and stigma: most mentioned problems

Order	Insecurity	Youth behaviour	Alcohol/ drugs	Bad infra	Bad services	Unemployment	Delinquency	Vandalism
1		X	X			X		X
2	X		X	X	X	X	X	X
3	X		X			X	X	X
4	X		X			X	X	X
5	X	X	X			X		
6			X			X	X	
7	X		X				X	X
8	X	X		X	X			X

Fig. 81: Playground in Villa Horizonte

6.2.5.3 Living Environment and Stigma

One of the main reasons for moving (as a desire) to another *barrio*, stated by the majority of the interviewees, was their feeling of insecurity due to high levels of delinquency, vandalism and troublesome youth. Alcoholism and unemployment were also mentioned as being major problems of living in Villa Horizonte. In addition, almost half of the interviewees feel stigmatised by the mere fact of living in such a minimal type of housing, and the majority think that they are disciminated from outsiders because of this [(71)].

6.3. Villa Las Cumbres, Macul

6.3.1 The District in the City

Macul is one of two districts created in 1981 after the *comuna* of Ñuñoa was split into three *comunas* - Ñuñoa, Peñalolén and Macul. It is located in the southeast of midtown Santiago within the first metropolitan ring road and is a middle- and middle-low-income pericentral district close to some of the richer districts such as Providencia, Las Condes and Ñuñoa. Macul is an old consolidated district that has already used most of its urbanisable area and has, in addition, experienced a reduced population growth over the past decade.

In addition, it is a district that includes a variety of land uses, for example, an important share of industry, commerce and diverse typologies of housing. In spite of the fact that Macul is a predominantely middle class district, it still preserves mansions from the early 1900s, *poblaciones* from different periods that targeted low-income families and middle-income employees, as well as some already upgraded slums from the 1960s and 1970s.

[(71)] That is expressed in comments such as *"people believe I live in a slum"*, *"everybody thinks we are the worst"* or *"people ask me why am I living here?"*

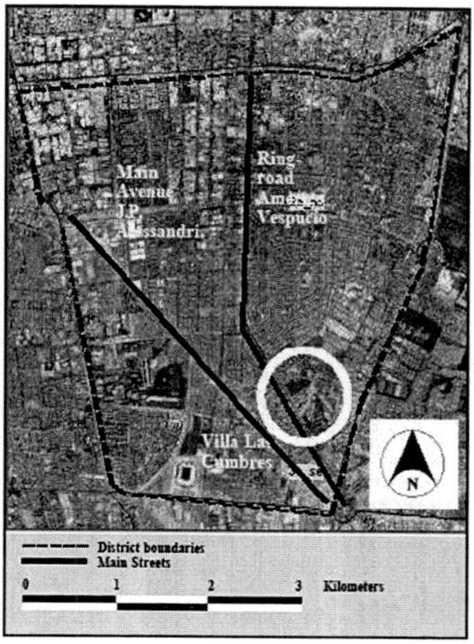

Fig. 82: Aerial Photo of Comuna Macul

Fig. 83: Macul, General Data

General Data		Social Data	
Population (inhabitants)	11253	Unemployment (percent)	9,80
Area (hectares)	1.23	Poor (percent)	13,21
Density (Inh./hectare)	9	No Poor (percent)	86,79
Total Dwelings	28.00	Iliteracy (percent)	2,3
Permanent Dwelings	27.73	Average studies (years)	11
Households	31.20	Child mortality (1:1000)	9,6
Owners (percent)	66,27	Early pregnancy (percent)	10,4
Tenants (percent)	18,2		

Apart from programmes to upgrade former slums, the district has not received massive developments of social housing under the current housing policy. As a matter of fact, only five *poblaciones* -all of them in three-storey *blocks*- were built between 1986 and 1990. Most of these *poblaciones* are concentrated at the eastern and at the southeastern boundaries of the *comuna*, adjacent to the metropolitan ring road Americo Vespucio.

Fig. 84: Housing growth in Puente Alto

Census	Number of Dwellings (a)	Average growth (a')	Number of inhabitants (b)	Average growth (b')	(b)/(a)	Cumulative social housing	Cumulative social housing %
1982	23.762		123.100	(*) 4.25%	5.18	2.778	11.69
1992	28460	1.80%	120.708	-0.20%	4.24	4.553	15.99
2002	29870	9,48%	112.535	-0,70%	3,77	4.553	15,24

(*) Calculated according to the 1970 Census, which accounted 76.694 inhabitants that year
(**) Data year 2000)

Fig. 85: Social housing in Puente Alto

Range of unites by *Población*	Number of *Poblaciones*	Estates Poblaciones	Type of Unites	
Between 70 and 200	2	2	Total Social Housing	4.553
Between 201 and 500	2	2	Social Single unites	0
Between 501 and 1.000	1	1	Social Estates	4.553
more than 1.000				

Most of the existing *poblaciones* in Macul and its industrial areas form a dense urban fabric built up mainly in one- to two-storey housing that includes frontyards and trees along the streets. Although Macul does not have a clear civic or commercial centre, it does include many important axes where commerce and services are located such as the ring road and the J. P. Alessandri Avenue. Thus, most of the *poblaciones* located in this *comuna* have quite good access to transportation means, commerce and services.

6.3.2 The Selected Case: Villa Las Cumbres

Villa Las Cumbres was built in 1989 and represents one of the latest developments completed during the military regime. Even though Macul does not include many examples to choose from, Villa Las Cumbres was selected for the following reasons: first, its typology is the predecessor of the "scissors" type, largely developed in following years. Second, the general composition of *blocks* aims to create communitary spaces between them. Third, it is close to other compounds of estates completed at different periods in time -one from the 1970s and another from the 1990s. Fourth, it has an important share of tenants and fifth, its state of maintenance is irregular.

Fig. 86: Las Cumbres' surroundings

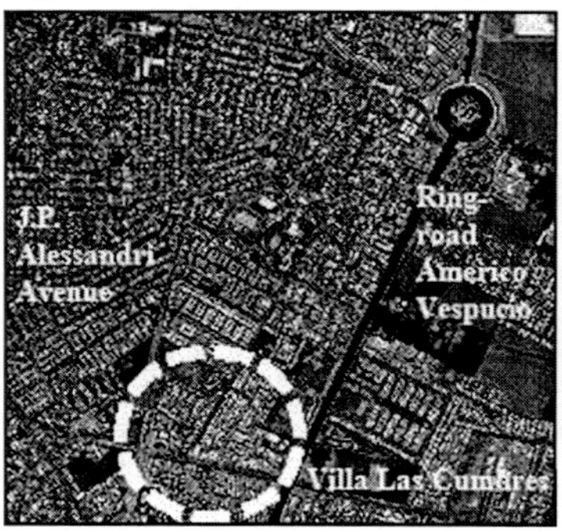

Fig. 87: General data Las Cumbres

Villa Las Cumbres	Data
Population	2.300
Households	492
Single family housing	0
Multifamily units (*Blocks*)	492
Total Social Housing	492
Households in Estates	520
Flats dwellers	3.450
Density (Inh/Hectare) Estates	740
Construction Index (*) Estates	0,12
Year of Construction	1.989

(*) Built area in first floor divided total area

6.3.3 Spatial Configuration and Architecture

Villa Las Cumbres is located at the southeastern corner of the *comuna* of Macul adjacent to the main metropolitan ring road, about 400 meters from the border to the *comunas* of Peñalolén and La Florida, where several commercial and transportation facilities are available. It is a compound of 37 three-storey estates built in an area of three hectares, which includes internal pedestrian walkways and open spaces destined for communal

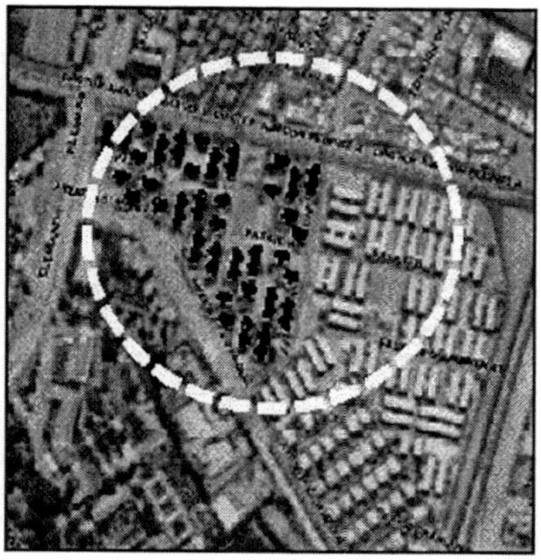

Fig. 88: Las Cumbres Compound

uses. The compound of estates does not strongly contrast with surrounding constructions because it is located next to other estates, and a wide avenue with trees disconnects Villa Las Cumbres from the one- to two-storey houses located on its northern side.

Fig. 89: Typical "Block" Las Cumbres

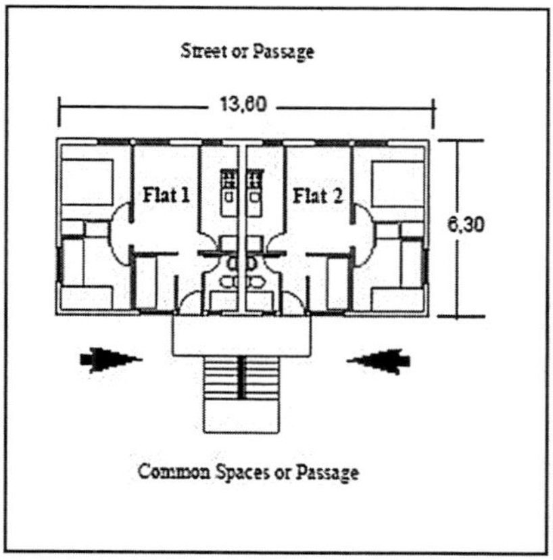

Fig. 90: Blocks Assembling

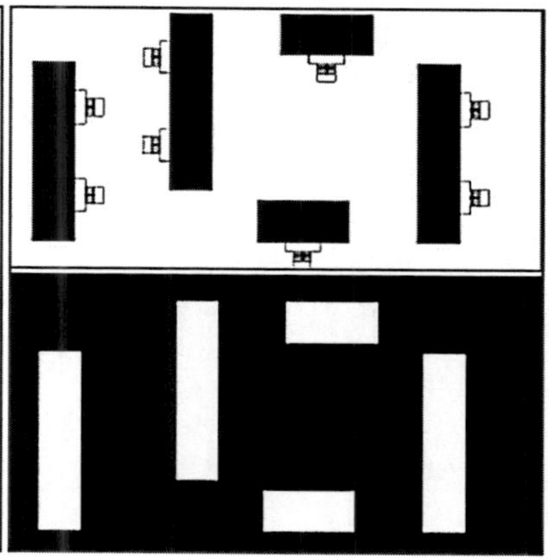

Fig. 91: Block & Staircase

Fig. 92: Façadess, Las Cumbres

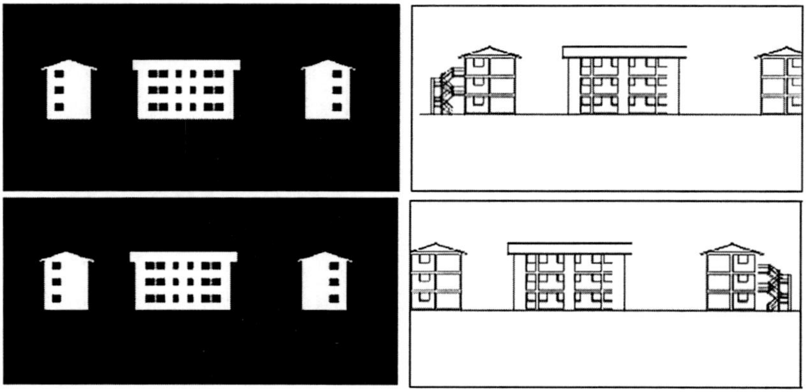

The 37 estates are composed of 55 modular units of three storeys with one external staircase, which provides access to the flats. In 20 of the cases, the estates are assembled so as to form two attached modules. In all of the *blocks* the entrance way is located on the inner side of the compound with an orientation toward the pedestrian passageways or open spaces. This typology does not provide transitional spaces between the public and the private realm, considering that the stairs are completely public and do not facilitate the "enclosement" of every block.

On the other hand, the distribution of the estates results in communal open spaces that have been mainly filled with playgrounds, green areas and sport fields. Unlike most of the compounds of estates, Villa Las Cumbres is not enclosed by fences, and all the pedestrian

Fig. 93: Typical flat Las Cumbres

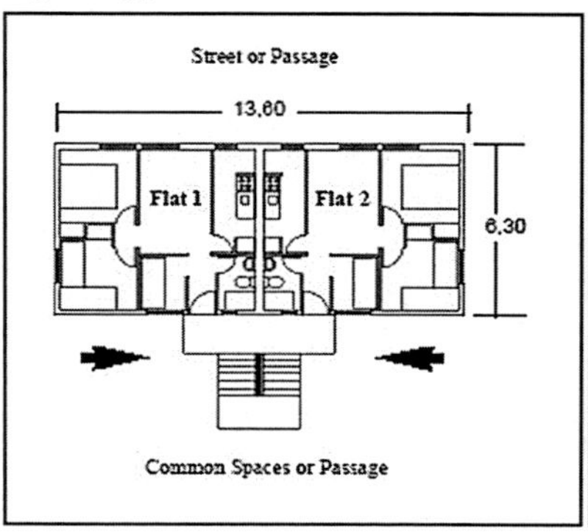

Fig. 94: Las Cumbres Surroundings

passageways and squares are open to the public. However, some greenery and low, wooden fences tend to insinuate a differentiation between public and private spheres surrounding some of the *blocks*.

Like in other compounds, the dominance of materials such as red brick walls with concrete braces and the imbalance between solid and void surfaces give the estates a "cumbersome" appearance. However, this appearance is slightly lessened through the existence of windows on all of the fronts, and in particular, because a considerable amount of façades face the main streets.

There are basically two flat sizes: type A with 45,54 sqm and type B with 44,88 sqm. Their internal distribution is the same, the only differences are related to their position in the general assemblage. The flats include a central living room, a bathroom and a kitchen on one side, two bedrooms on the opposite side and a third bedroom can be installed onto the living area. As in the case of Villa Horizonte, this internal distribution does not allow the separation between private and common uses.

6.3.4 Resident Interventions

Villa Las Cumbres does not exhibit as many extensions as other compounds. Nevertheless, resident interventions are visible on first floors where the immediate surroundings of every flat have been occupied, mainly by private yards and/or semi-public gardens and even some rooms used as bedrooms, workshops or small grocery stores.

Fig. 95: Typical extensions

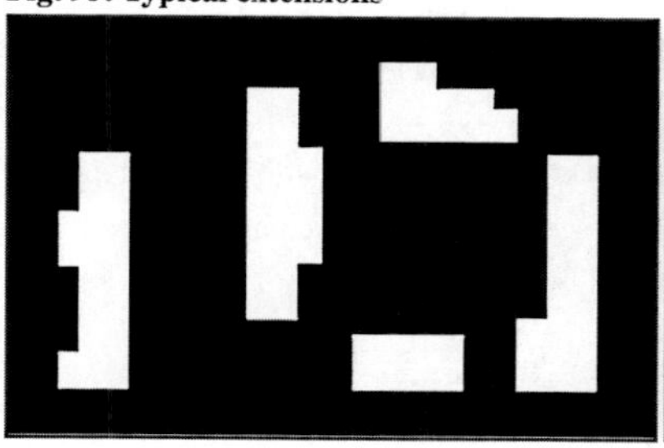

Fig. 96: Extension in Las Cumbres

The buildings are not all completely surrounded by barriers, whereas windows and entrance stairs are almost always fenced in. Other interventions include a sports field built by the municipality and small green areas with benches built by individual initiatives. As every estate is practically a single house with a common staircase, their maintenance varies not only among estates, but also among floors. Some dwellings are plastered, painted, or even include enlarged windows and fences, but some others do not.

Fig. 97: Interviewees Villa Horizonte

Order	Interviewee	Sex	Age	Floor	PP (*)	HH (**)
1	Gerohina Poblete	F	27	2	6	1
2	Jorge Rodriguez	M	38	1	10	2
3	Patricia Rios	F	32	1	8	1
4	Esteban Soto	M	34	3	8	2
5	Margarita Sepulveda	F	45	1	6	1
6	Roberto Alvarado	M	54	1	4	1
7	Clementina Caceres	F	36	3	8	2
8	Cipriano Alegria	M	38	2	8	2

(*) PP : Number of people per dwelling
(**) HH: Number of households per dwelling

Fig. 98: Extension in Las Cumbres

6.3.5 Residents' Perceptions

The interviewees in Las Cumbres felt no conflict with their *comuna* of residence -which provides them with access to many opportunities- but rather with the type of dwellings they live in and their immediate stigmatised environment. Moreover, communitary bonds seem to be weak, and people also believe to be sourrounded by delinquents. However, most of them are willing to introduce changes not only into their private dwellings, but also into communal spaces.

6.3.5.1 Belonging and Communitary Bonds

In comparison to other districts located at the periphery where most of the residents are owners, Macul has a larger proportion of tenants. This is underlined by the fact that, of the eight randomly chosen interviewees, two were tenants and another two were relatives of the original owner who no longer lived in the compound. In addition, almost half of the interviewees relayed that they had been living in Villa Las Cumbres for one to five years, yet confessed to have neither very many friends nor relatives within the compound. These facts may explain the lack of neighbours' commitment to community activities

Fig. 99: Belonging and bonds

Order	Owners	Relative	From a far away district	More than 5 years here	Family here
1	X		X	X	X
2	X		X	X	X
3	X		X	X	X
4	X		X	X	X
5	X		X		X
6	X		X	X	
7		X		X	
8	X		X	X	X

Fig. 100: Dwelling adequacy

Order	Original m2	M2 Extension	Current Area	M2 p/p Original	M2 p/p current
1	41	9	50	10,25	12,50
2	41	9	50	5,12	6,25
3	41	13	54	8,20	10,80
4	41		41	10,25	10,25
5	41	3	44	5,85	6,29
6	41	7	48	4,10	4,80
7	41		41	20,50	20,50
8	41	6	47	6,83	7,83

which are clearly inferior to those observed in the other two cases. This could also explain why many people feel that they belong to the *comuna* but would like to move to another neighbourhood.

6.3.5.2 Dwellings Adequacy and Image

The inadequacy of the dwellings becomes apparent in the levels of overcrowding: in five cases, eigth to ten people were sharing a flat. Moreover, half of the interviewees share a dwelling with more than one household. Therefore, most of the interviewees would like to increase the area of their flats, and complain about lack of privacy.

The improvement of common spaces, solving structural problems and the desire to change the buildings appearance were also aspects mentioned by the majority of the interviewees. This shows a high concern about the image of the whole compound. The most typical changes already introduced are fences and paint, as well as the replacement of sanitary devices and windows.

6.3.5.3 Living Environment and Stigma

The feelings of stigmatisation in Villa Las Cumbres do not differ substantially from those encountered in peripheral districts. Stigmatisation is mostly felt in the discrimination through outsiders. Yet, people usually hide or modify their address when applying for a job [72].

With the exception of one of the interviewees [73], none of them feel protected by the police, and the majority believe that Villa Las Cumbres is an insecure neighbourhood. Yet, most of the interviewees expressed that school abandonment, delinquency, vandalism, alcoholism and drugs are the main problems of these estates.

---

(72) Typical comments were like: *"my family think that this is my grave"*, *"I hide where I live...people think we are robbers"* or *"That is the worst... Police never protect"*.

(73) According to some of interviewees, one of the neighbours that participate in this exploratory study was a well-know dealer, fact which could explain some of his answers.

Fig. 101: Environment and stigma: most mentioned problems

Order	Insecurity	Youth behaviour	Alcohol/ drugs	Bad infra	Bad services	Unemployment	Delinquency	Vandalism
1	X	X	X			X	X	X
2	X		X	X			X	
3	X	X	X				X	X
4		X					X	
5	X	X	X			X	X	X
6	X	X	X	X		X	X	X
7		X	X	X	X	X	X	X
8		X		X				

Fig. 102: Playground in Villa Macul

6.4 Comparative Summary of the Three Cases

	Villa San Ricardo	Villa Horizonte	Villa Las Cumbres
Location	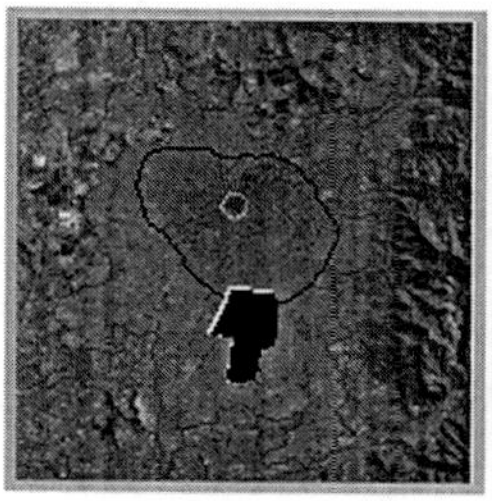	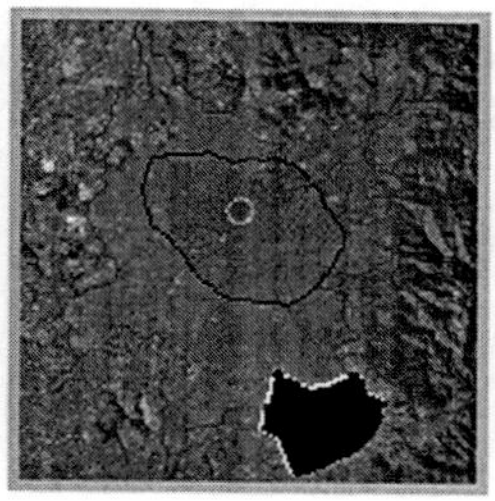	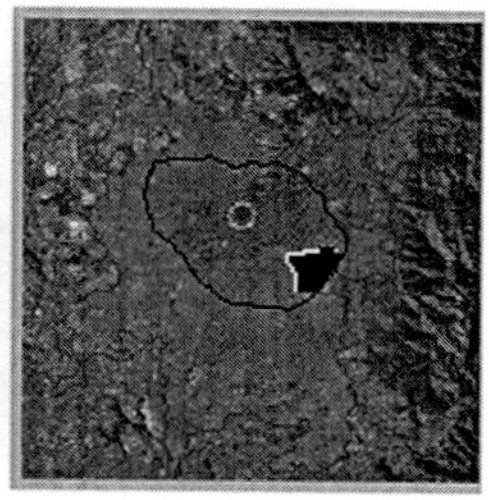
Type of District	- Low-income -stigmatised district - Former rural area - Residential zones without industry and with little commerce - Low access to urban opportunities	- Middle low-income district - Former village - Segregated residential, industrial and commercial activities - **Regular** access to urban opportunities	- Middle income district - Consolidated district - Mixed district with commerce, residence and industry - High access to urban opportunities
Urban Tissue			
Type of *"Barrio"*	- Dense urbanised areas - **Type of buildings**: Single-family housing, and estates - **Surrounded** by vacant land and many *poblaciones* - Relatively close to communal centre	- Disperse urbanisation - **Type of buildings:** Sites -and-services and estates - **Surrounded** by hills, pits for gravel extraction and rural area - **Far** from communal centre	- Dense urbanisation - **Type of buildings:** Estates and diverse types of housing - **Surrounded** by industry, commerce and main avenues - Close to communal centres
Type of Estates		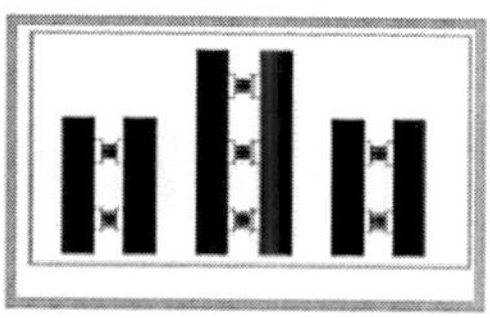	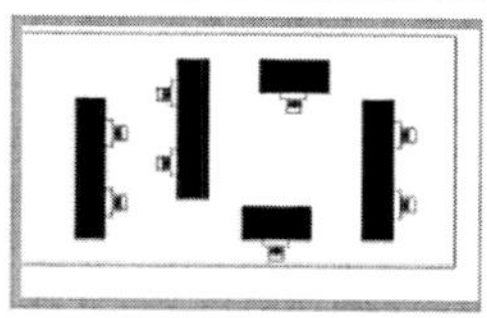
	- **Built in 1980**. Early stages of current housing policy - **Design** allows gradual transition from public to private space - **Density: 390 inh/ha** - **Flat dwellers: 2.030 - Flat Households: 330**	- **Built in 1993**. Typical model -"scissors"- applied in the 1990s - **Design** denies the composition of communitary areas - **Density: 1.296 inh/ha** - **Flat dwellers: 428 - Flat Households: 105**	- **Built in 1989**. Predecessor of "scissors" typology - **Design** aims to create communitary enclosed areas - **Density: 740 inh/ha** - **Flat dwellers: 3.450 - Flat Households: 520**

6.4 Comparative Summary of the Three Cases

	Villa San Ricardo	Villa Horizonte	Villa Las Cumbres
Spatial Configuration	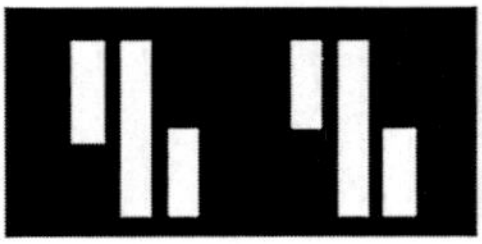		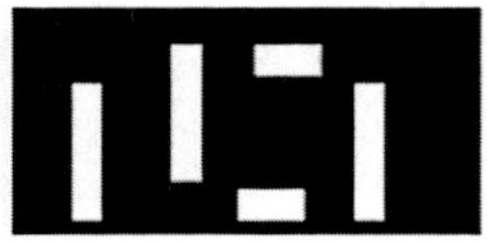
	- Estates made up of two *blocks* produce a "house" of 12 flats - Assembling of *blocks* results in a gradual transi tion from public to private spaces.	- Estates made up of two *blocks* produce compounds of 24 and 36 flats - Assembling of *blocks* resembles "barracks". - Common spaces are only the patios-passage	- Estates made up "independent" *blocks* with 6 flats - Assembling of *blocks* forms communitary squares and passages
Type of Façades and Configuration	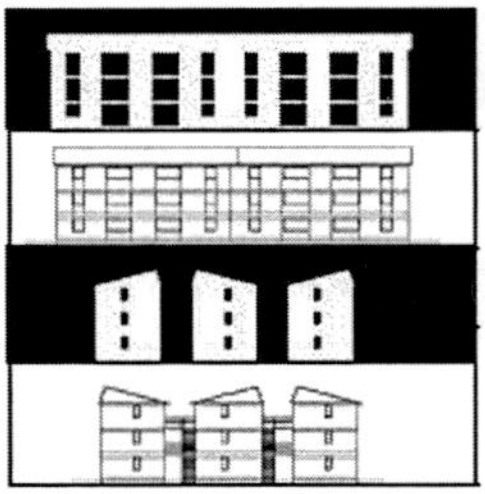	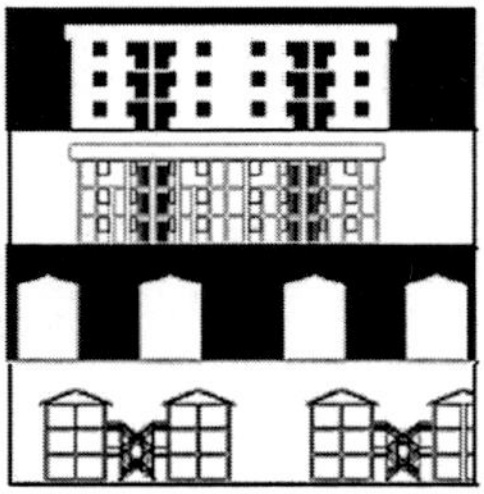	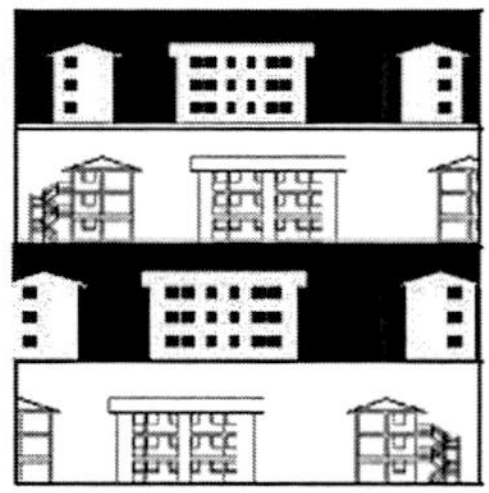
	- Design favours small communities - façades lessenes cumbersome apparence - Access to the flats through internal stair case	- Design does not favours small communities - façades without relation to the street. - Access to the flats through patio-passage	- Design favours small communities - façades relateto all sides - Access to theflats through external stair case
Residents' Interventions	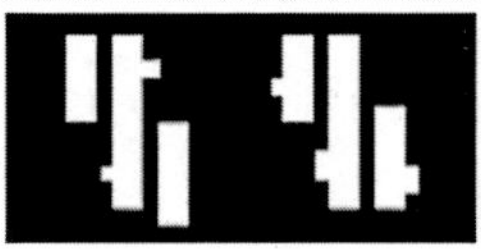		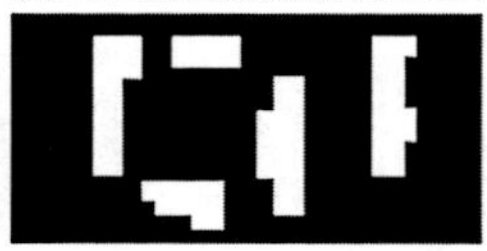
	- high level of interventions - most of first floors are used as extensions - extensions are for: shops, bedrooms and workshops - there are light extensions used as gardens or parking lots	- very high level of interventions - all backsides in first floor are occupied - there are extensions in second and third floors - there are light extensions used for storage	- low level of interventions - many first floors serve as extensions - extensions are used as hops, bedrooms and workshops. - some extensions are used as gardens or parking lots.
Type of Extensions			

6.4 Comparative Summary of the Three Cases

Residents' Perceptions

Villa San Ricardo

Villa Horizonte

Villa Las Cumbres

Community Bonds

Villa San Ricardo	Villa Horizonte	Villa Las Cumbres
- weak social bonds / lack of confidence/ fear / insecurity - dissatisfaction with flats and the environment / - the stay just because they are owners / no other alternative	- strong community bonds / familiar ties - reason expressed to continueliving in the compound - dissatisfaction with size and type of housing	- weak social bonds / lack of confidence / many tenants - discrimination from outsiders - not too long living in the compound - dissatisfaction with flats

Dwellings' Adequacy

Villa San Ricardo

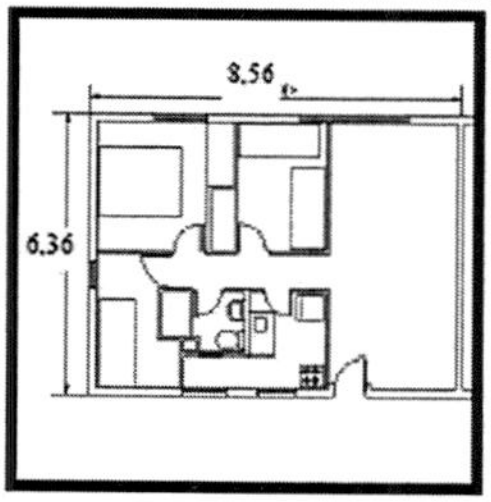

Villa Horizonte

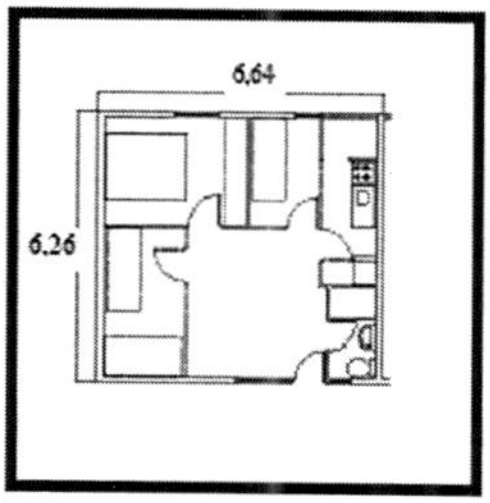

Villa Las Cumbres

Villa San Ricardo	Villa Horizonte	Villa Las Cumbres
- overcrowding / low quality flats - desire to improve structural and common spaces - aspirations to modify buildings appearance - No stark criticism of type of dwellings	- overcrowding is not an acute problem - desire to change common spaces and structural aspects - aspirations to modify buildings appearance - Criticism of type of dwellings	- high overcrowding - complains about privacy - many complains about the quality of the flats - desire to change buildings appearance - Criticism of type of dwellings and environment

Data

Villa San Ricardo

Unemployment	15,2 %
Poor	30,9%
Illiteracy	3,9%

Villa Horizonte

Unemployment	9,7 %
Poor	19,5%
Illiteracy	1,5%

Villa Las Cumbres

Unemployment	9,8 %
Poor	13,2%
Illiteracy	2,3%

Environment - Stigma

Villa San Ricardo	Villa Horizonte	Villa Las Cumbres
- People distrust their *comuna* and immediate surroundings - They believe there are too many drugs and delinquency - They believe they live in a bad neighbourhood - stigmatised by the type of neighbourhood and the *comuna*	- feelings of insecurity and lack of self-esteem - they believe their environment is "bad" - they believe that there is too much delinquency and drugs - stigmatised by the type of housing and the neighbourhood	- feelings of stigmatisation and insecurity - feelings of discrimination - they believe the whole compound is full of delinquents, drug-adicts and bad people - they believe their type of housing is a reason for discrimination

6.4.1 Classification of Findings: Upgrading and Integration Problems

Low quality of the dwellings

All three cases present constructive deficiencies that become apparent by the low standard of construction (almost no noise isolation, humid walls and defective water installations, corrosion in metal structures-stairs, among others).

Moreover, most of the interviewees expressed unconformity with the finishing of the dwellings and many of them have already made interventions such as replacement of sanitary devices, doors and windows.

Adequacy of the dwellings

Most of the people pointed out that the size of the dwellings is one of the main problems. In addition, overcrowding existing in all three *villas* clearly shows the inadequacy of the dwellings to fulfil family needs.

The reason why Villa Las Cumbres is the worst case in terms of overcrowding could be related to the fact that it is closer to urban facilities. On the other hand, the relatively lower level of overcrowding in Villa Horizonte could be related to the age of the compound .

Image of the estates

In spite of the fact that the three case studies are different in design and state of maintenance, most of the people expressed their desire of changing appearance.

As far as housing represents status, many residents believe that they are stigmatised just because they are living in this type of housing. Indeed, many of them expressed to have found prejudices from outsiders. Thus, they usually hide their address when applying for a job.

Integration to the city

The case of Macul shows that location and good connections to the rest of the city facilitate access to working places and services but do not assure that people feel integrated.

However, La Pintana and Puente Alto demonstrate that isolation and reduced accessibility to urban opportunities exacerbated stigma and feelings of exclusion. Feelings of stigmatisation appear when people compare their homes with other areas of the city.

Integration to neighbours

Reduced feelings of belonging: social networks and bonds with neighbours are weak; informal communitary actions are just some collective parties and organisation to make fences. However, some self-help is present in the cases where familiar or friends' ties are closer (Villa Horizonte) but this is not necessarily reflected in the improvement of the common spaces. Most of the people feel insecure in their neighbourhoods (drugs, youth gangs, and abandoned plots of land) and they do not feel protected by the police.

Integration to the dwelling

Most of the interviewees expressed dissatisfaction with their dwellings, which is related to problems of adequacy and quality. In addition, while owners expressed that they do not have another alternative but continuing living in the same place, tenants seem more inclined to move.

Integration to neighbourhood

Spatial discontinuities: estates typology are not integrated into the rest of the urban tissue due to the fact that they are mostly built in "super-blocks". They resemble "barracks" or isolated "warehouses" and usually show no relation with surrounding constructions.

Derelict environment: ownership of common spaces affects the levels of maintenance. Villa San Ricardo in La Pintana -whose estates are built in plots that belong to singular blocks- shows the highest level of communitary work done to improve the dwellings by introducing gardens, fences and painting the blocks. Villa Las Cumbres -which includes common squares and passages-has received almost no improvement but it does not look too deteriorated. Finally, Villa Horizonte presents the highest level of anarchic appropriation of common spaces.

6.5 Main Conclusions of the Case Studies

It becomes apparent that the priorities in the design of social estates have been the intensive use of land and the continuos reduction of construction costs. These facts are represented in measures such as the reduction in the size of common spaces, the increase in population densities per estate, and the internal design of flats that has become simpler.

In spite of the fact that location has an impact on the ability that individuals and communities have to access urban opportunities, it seems that the type of housing -and the symbolic values attached to it- seems to be the "common denominator" by which the dissatisfaction of the families can be measured. As a matter of fact, in a growing economy that has followed the "American way of life", image and appearance have become important factors in the measurement of self-esteem.

Nevertheless, the needs to upgrade standards seem evident as low quality and inadequacy of the dwellings make it impossible to cope with familiar needs. Besides particular differences, all the three cases show problems related to adequacy and quality of the dwellings. The resident's desire to take a part in future transformations seems also apparent in all three cases.

Whether the lack of feelings of belonging hampers or not social integration, and could therefore reduce the chances to organise compound improvements, seems unclear. On the one hand, Villa Horizonte illustrates that the presence of communitary bonds is not a sufficient precondition for a better maintenance or state of the estates. On the other hand, the Villas San Ricardo and Las Cumbres show many interventions by the residents to improve the environment (gardens, playgrounds, etc).

At this point, it comes into view that the design of public communitary spaces and clarity about ownership of these spaces are relevant factors for the analysis of the state of maintenance of the compounds. Therefore, any measure to improve physical aspects should consider not only the reconstruction of social networks which underpin sustainable and permanent improvements, but also the definition of legal aspects of the property, communitary rules and the incorporation of layouts that promote spatial integration.

PART III

Chapter 7: Conclusions, Interpretations and New Insights

7.1 Introduction

> *"...there never was a 'golden age' when life in the American ghetto and the French banlieu was sweet and social relations therein harmonious and fulfilling. Yet, it remains that the experience of urban relegation has changed in ways that make it distinctively more burdensome and alienating today."*
> Loïc Wacquant (2002:226)

Wacquant's statement can certainly be applied to the Chilean case where poverty also seems to have a new face: former widespread slums of informal housing have been replaced by low-standard social housing typologies that concentrated low-income families just in certain areas of the city.

Yet, the main hypothesis of this work stated that current housing policy has contributed to processes of social and spatial exclusion because it tends to "formalise" the relegation of the urban poor not only in the less attractive and poorly-served locations, but also in already stigmatised housing typologies that present restricted chances of upgrading.

The main aim of this work was indeed to explore the extent to which current Chilean housing policy affects urban spatial and social inequalities and, in particular, to find out whether the phenomenon of exclusion through housing has also taken place in the Chilean case. Hence, various theoretical assumptions, concepts and parameters were set out in order to analyse the role of the state and its housing policies in making an unequal city.

The principal assumption was that urban inequalities hamper social integration because they prevent equal access to urban opportunities for all citizens. In other words, part of the population is "excluded" from having equal access to economic, cultural or institutional privileges and benefits, goods and rights that are supposed to be recognised as "universal" in this society. This exclusion, on the other hand, is represented in the housing arena by the concept of "exclusion through housing".

Based on diverse research literature about the role of housing in urban inequalities, exclusion through housing was understood as a phenomenon that combines spatial and social aspects. It occurs when people are housed but in inadequate dwellings -overcrowded, with low standards- and they are involuntarily concentrated in locations that not only prevent access to goods and services, but also concentrate more people with the same problems -unskilled, unemployed, etc. Exclusion through housing also highlighted the role of housing and the neighbourhood in shaping outcomes such as health problems, low education attainment, and delinquency, as well as other "intangibles" such as depreciated identity, low self-esteem and lack of a sense of belonging.

As a result of this discussion, three main factors were identified as parameters to analyse the role of the government in the "production" of social and spatial exclusion: location, allocation and standards.

Location decisions may affect accessibility to main urban infrastructure, facilities and working opportunities, and therefore, may isolate or connect areas to the rest of the city. Allocation modalities may tend to concentrate or to spread low-income beneficiaries over the city, and therefore, to favour conditions of ghettoization or mixture respectively.

The level of standards used in compounds of social housing -both in terms of environments and dwellings- will also play a role in the levels of adequacy, maintenance and residential satisfaction. In addition, the main possible outcomes of social and spatial exclusion represented in negative aspects such as discrimination, low self-esteem and other social pathologies were also identified and used for the proposition of a theoretical model.

In the end, this conceptual framework and the model were researched through various approaches. A first approach was to conduct a review of the historical patterns of public interventions through housing policies in the city of Santiago which attempted to interpret the shifts in paradigms, particularly in terms of aims, location tendencies, allocation schemes and standards promoted. In other words, finding out which patterns of inequalities produce exclusion through housing could be viewed by reflecting on the past. The second approach was focused on the analysis of current housing policy and its implementation in the city of Santiago through the use of diverse indicators.

These indicators permitted the visualisation of current location tendencies and the levels of accessibility to urban opportunities as well as the general spatial distribution of poverty and physical assets. The third and final approach compared three cases studies that present different indicators at the city level.

Although all correspond to estates of *Vivienda Básica*, they were built in diverse locations, periods and using diverse typologies. The analysis of these cases studies aims at evaluating both the factors that create social and spatial exclusion as well as the possible main outcomes under diverse conditions.

7.2 The Historical Patterns of Housing Policy

The review of the historical development of Chilean housing policies particularly reveals how the state has reinforced some of the dynamics of social exclusion such as ghettoization. As a matter of fact, the revision of the *"long road"* of social housing in Chile permitted not only the identification of the main patterns of location, allocation and standards applied over time by different approaches, but also helped to trace the roots of spatial and social inequalities. Yet, the Chilean example goes to show how housing policies correspond to distinctive societal processes, as well as their political and technical representations. In other words, social housing is not merely the result of material processes, but also of a socio-historical order marked by class struggle over urban space, different political approaches to urban matters and particular patterns of economic development. Three main historical patterns were identified: early, universalistic and neo-liberal housing policies.

7.2.1 Early Housing Policies

In the late 1800s and early 1900s, initial social policies aimed to protect society from the *"menace of the poor and to redeem the proletarian classes"*. As the representative architecture for the upper classes and institutions, the model was imported from Europe: workers' housing -on a small scale- was supposed to introduce poor people to societal values.

As a result, the first *poblaciones* were provided not just with housing, but also with "complete" social and basic technical infrastructure which included healthcare, a post office and a church, among others. They were also located close to the city centre and to places of work in areas with accessible transportation means .

However, only a few of them were built directly by the government. The majority were made possible through the involvement of employers, unions and charity institutions. Neighbourhoods where not segregated by income but by the "type" of families allocated in most of these *poblaciones* which was usually restricted to formal workers and was not able to cope with the increasing demand coming from "informal" and other lower-income families.

In the end, overcrowded "*conventillos*" and the first land invasions set these low-income people outside of the formal system. Urban segregation slowly began as upper classes were already moving out of the city centre and locating themselves in new *comunas*.

7.2.2 Universalistic Policies

The1940s to the early 1970s was a period of "universalistic" policies -or a pro-welfare approach- when the government took an increasingly active role in the promotion of housing as a right. In this context, social policies were aimed at strengthening citizenship and advocating for social equity.

In addition, urban grassroots movements and political pressure marked a permanent tension in urban affairs. Social housing became a major societal subject, and every political sector made proposals. Thus, many strategies were attempted varying from the development of urbanised plots, sites and services projects or self-help construction to complete dwellings designed and constructed by governmental agencies.

Besides the efforts to solve infrastructural and shelter needs and to avoid evictions in existing slums, the government planned and built new *poblaciones*. In spite of the fact that the standards of these new *poblaciones* differed, they were increasingly matching the contemporary international debate about social housing design and quality and were completely regulated and defined by governmental agencies. In terms of the allocation system, the government implemented diverse systems.

The most important action was the promotion and creation of private and public savings and loans associations for housing which directly allocated their associates where new projects were developed. In the case of low income-families out of the system, the government was directly assigning subsidies according to visible needs and requirements.

The location of social housing also followed diverse patterns. On the one hand, the government and its agencies promoted the construction of social housing in diverse districts, including middle- and high-income areas. On the other hand, most of the slums were upgraded in the same place, and only those located in high-risk areas were displaced.

Nevertheless, a growing urbanisation process led by policies of industrialisation (import-substitution policies) as well as strong migration to the cities permanently challenged policies to cope with the demand, and none of these approaches was successful, and new illegal occupations of land continued even in well-off *comunas*.

7.2.3 Neo-liberal Policies

From 1973 to 1989, the so-called "neo-liberal revolution" changed the "paternalistic" state to a subsidiary one that only tended to the social needs of the poorest households and relied on market offer. Along with the withdrawal of the government from many social matters, full-scale privatisation was introduced, land was deregulated and a means-tested system for many social services -housing included- was developed. During the dictatorship era, land seizures were stopped, and many people were evicted from areas of high land value. Low-income families and grassroots movements lost their political right to exert pressure for solutions.

As a result, low-income families either crowded ("dropped-in") into the existing housing stock or assumed the rules of the game and followed the new subsidiary system. Social housing policies took a pragmatic approach whose main criteria were to reduce costs and to increase the quantity of units built. Housing was still accepted as "a right" but a right that could only be obtained through "one's own effort, sacrifice and time" (Gilbert, 2001:13).

In addition, housing standards were reduced to an acceptable minimum which was assumed as "maximal" by private developers. Moreover, social infrastructure requirements were eliminated, and even basic infrastructure was reduced to minimal levels (i.e.: unpaved roads). Housing location, on the other hand, became dependent on market offer and began to be strictly concentrated just in some areas of the city.

Fig. 103: Tendencies for social housing location, allocation and standards

Housing Policies	Years	Location	Allocation	Standards
Early Policies	Late 1800s early 1900s	• Close to city centre and working places	• Formal workers related to Unions, or employers	• "Imported" model from Europe • Social and basic infrastructure included
Universalistic Policies	1930 to 1973	• Diverse locations that include middle and high income districts	• Diverse mechanisms • Increasingly accepted "universal" right	• Diverse typologies • International standards • Governmental regulations
Neo-Liberal Policies	1974 to today	• Locations restricted by land prices and "unregulated" market	• Means-tested system • Allocation according to income	• Minimal standards according to market offer • No existing or minimal social and basic infrastructure

In addition, the allocation system that used a means-tested approach promoted the concentration of people with the same level of income and needs in just these areas. However, the system was not able to cope with the demand of the poorest families which were forced to drop-in on existing social housing in overcrowded conditions.

With the return to democracy in 1990, major emphasis was laid onto reaching the poorest and striving for "equality of opportunities". However, the approach did not change substantially, and the operation of the same type of programmes continues to this day. In an attempt to prevent expected pressures on the government and with the spectre of land seizures, the amount of subsidies was increased and new programmes (such as participative revival of the sites and services scheme) were launched in order to reach households with very low savings capacities.

Also the previous approach designed for low-income workers -with a slightly higher savings capacity- through the *Programa de Vivienda Básica*, was enhanced, and social estates eventually took over the largest share among the programmes focused on low-income families.

The above review and summary table show that in spite of the fact that former schemes were unable to cope with chronic deficits, social housing policies were increasingly embedded in paradigms that aimed at integrating low-income families into the cities. In contrast, the "unintended" result of the neo-liberal approach has been the consolidation of a partitioned city where low-income families are mainly confined in certain areas of the city.

7.3 Social and Spatial Exclusion in the City of Santiago

The analysis of the city of Santiago through social, demographic, physical and location indicators permitted the evaluation of the extent unto which governmental decisions about the location of social housing, their standards and the system of allocation represent relevant factors in the partition of the city of Santiago according to social classes.

Social housing has been mainly concentrated just in some districts that indeed lack appropriate infrastructure and which, in addition, already concentrate low-income families and low social indicators. This urban disintegration reveals the relation between the implementation of current housing policy and social and spatial exclusion in the city of Santiago.

7.3.1 The Location Factor

Social housing tends to be spatially segregated and located in areas with poor access to urban opportunities. Indeed, the high concentration of social housing in some districts and distinctive areas of the city appears as the most visible aspect of the current housing policies that can be connected to spatial and social exclusion. As a matter of fact, 90% of the social housing built between 1978 and 2000 was concentrated in 15 out of the 34 districts existing in Santiago where the south and southeastern districts concentrate 65% of the total.

Moreover, the analysis by periods (1982-1991 and 1992-2000) shows that there is a clear tendency to build social housing in just a few peripheral districts and that some rural areas are also becoming increasingly urbanised through the construction of more social dwellings. In spite of the fact that there is no clear relation between social housing and urban growth, many districts have expanded only because of the massive construction of new *poblaciones*.

These locations are not only unattractive because they are in peripheral locations, but also because other indicators at the city level confirm the unbalanced land value and accessibility to urban opportunities between districts. Indeed, most of the districts with high percentages of social housing lack enough or adequate infrastructure, schools, health facilities and working places. People have to commute to work, to school and to reach various services although travel times are not only related to distance, but in particular, to the supply of public transport and road quality.

7.3.2 The Allocation Factor

The allocation system is segregative and produces social exclusion. As a matter of fact, current housing policy has been allocating their beneficiaries in districts that already contain important shares of low-income families -many of the evicted from better-off districts- as well as former social housing and/or slums. Therefore, there is a kind of correlation between the concentration of social housing and poverty: the districts that contain high shares of social housing also concentrate high shares of low-income families, unemployed people and lower literacy levels, among other social indicators.

In other words, social housing beneficiaries have being successively allocated in socially undesirable areas where mostly low-income people already live. Nevertheless, the analysis at the city level does not provide enough evidence to prove that most of the poor in these districts dwell in social housing built through current policy or if they correspond to families dwelling in former programmes.

7.3.3 The Standards Factor

The low level of standards of social housing is represented at the city level, and there are clear value contrasts in housing as a physical asset. For example, the average square meterage of a dwelling strongly differs between districts. While well-to-do *comunas* reach averages between 100 and 200 squares meters, districts with high shares of social housing do not reach more than 50 sqm on average.

This contrast affects not only the physical image of the city, but also relates to income revenues -through real estate taxes- that every municipality receives and, therefore, their available budget for investment in the district. As a result, many local governments are refusing to receive more compounds of social housing and are forcing the government and the people to look for alternative areas.

Nevertheless, morphological contrasts have also become apparent in the typologies of housing that have been under implementation. While in the past, social housing resembled the upper class way of living on a small scale, the "garden city ideal", nowadays, the picture is much more complex and fragmented. On the one hand, high- and middle-class families are increasingly moving into single-unit housing in gated communities or into high-rise buildings surrounded by parks and surveillance. On the other hand, 86% of the social housing built in Santiago in the last decade has been three- to four-storey flats.

Nowadays, this typology accounts for 45% of the social housing built between 1978 and the year 2000 which amounts to almost 10% of the total housing built in Santiago. Unfortunately, this typology now harbours more problems than any other. Estates are collective properties, and most of the people inhabiting them are not prepared for life in flats, so these estates show many of the problems related to social exclusion through housing.

7.4 The Cases Studies and Exclusion through Housing

The three case studies carried out for this work show patterns of exclusion quite similar to those widely studied in Europe and the United States where certain neighbourhoods concentrate not only physical problems, but also increasing social conflict. As a matter of fact, many of the outcomes presented in the model of exclusion through housing became apparent.

Adding to the inadequacy and decay of buildings and their surroundings, various social pathologies also became apparent such as the concentration of underprivileged households, stigmatisation, vandalism and crime. Nevertheless, every case represents a particular situation, and not all the factors proposed in the model are fully representative of the Chilean case.

7.4.1 The "Production"and Outcomes of Social and Spatial Exclusion

In terms of the three main parameters, namely location, allocation and standards, there are important differences among the three cases. In spite of the fact that access to urban opportunities is a relevant aspects at the city level, the case studies show that spatial and social exclusion can be independent from this indicator.

In spite of the fact that spatial and social exclusion may be evident by the lack of access to infrastructure and working places -like in the case of Villa Horizonte-, spatial exclusion may also occur when a compound is located within a "well-positioned" district such as Macul, but its estates are confined in a determined sector of this district and are not integrated into its surroundings. In other words, the location factor may also play a "symbolical" role: to designate areas of lower quality for the poor.

In terms of the allocation factor, with the exception of Villa Las Cumbres in Macul, most of the people living in the three case studies are the original low-income owners and came from diverse other districts. The fact that some of them are formal workers, renters and informal workers suggests that the levels of "social homogeneity" are far from clear and the "in situ" collected information proved to be insufficient in clarifying the current socio-economic composition of the residents.

Nevertheless, the interviews provided some signals of social conflict between residents which are -in theory- associated with deprived neighbourhoods. For example, most of the interviewees distrusted their neighbours and believed they live in the worst environment but they feel trapped because they cannot go. The low levels of self-esteem present in most of the interviews is yet another signal of what some authors like Wacquant call "*the shame of living in a sub-standard type of housing*".

The standards of the dwellings in terms of area proved to be inadequate in all the cases: most of the people have already built an extension or expressed their desire to do it, and there are also significant levels of overcrowding.

The slight variations in standards and design between the cases provided some elements to judge possible outcomes such as maintenance, sense of belonging, among others. These differences in terms of design suggest that distinct configurations can support or prevent people's feelings of belonging and, therefore, affect their abilities to actively implement changes and improvements. Estates that include a smaller number of flats per unit not only facilitate community organisation, but also reflect a better state of maintenance (i.e., San Ricardo).

Furthermore, the configurations of estates also influences the type of extensions that people build: when a clear definition of common spaces and property rights existed, only a few, very limited extensions were implemented. In contrast, when the layout included uncontrolled areas, people usually appropriated them through dwelling extensions (i.e., Villa Horizonte).

On the other hand, typology and the meaning associated with the reality of living in social housing appear to be the most important factors behind people's dissatisfaction and their feelings of stigmatisation. Indeed, although the three cases differ in terms of their location, design and inhabitants' social composition, residents mostly believe that they live in the worst type of housing.

Social ties also affect feelings of belonging but are not necessarily linked to the existence of constructive interventions or feelings of stigmatisation. While in San Ricardo, for example, social ties are weaker than in Villa Horizonte, people have still intervened in their environment in a much more organised way. Moreover, people mostly relate their feelings of stigma to their neighbourhoods and to the fact of living in "social housing" rather than to the inappropriateness of their dwellings. Nevertheless, the exploratory interviews suggest that, in all cases, people would prefer to improve their dwellings and their surroundings rather than to move elsewhere.

7.5 Summary of Conclusions

Current Chilean housing policy has certainly "formalised" social and spatial inequalities and facilitated the consolidation of a partitioned city. This policy has also contributed to reducing what was once an institusionalised right (housing) to an object of public utility that stands out against socially accepted values such as social integration and equality of opportunities [74]. The city analysis and the exploratory case studies suggest that although the poverty approach assumed by the current policy is solving key aspects of shelter, it has disregarded what -in the words of Turner (1976:51)- *"housing does to the people"*.

According to this study, the main characteristics of the current Chilean housing policy that affect social exclusion through housing are the following:

- A system that acts as a gatekeeper by giving restricted alternatives to the applicants. Every applicant, according his or her own savings capacity, receives a determined standard of housing in a determined -mostly segregated- location of the city.

- A technical procedure that induces peripheralisation and homogenisation of districts by social classes. Social housing has a cost-ceiling which pushes its construction into areas where land is cheaper. People can build on their own land, but they can only afford land in some districts.

- A policy that relies on the market and neither takes into consideration people's expectations, nor the housing process of low-income families. As the bids for tenders depend on private offers, construction firms determine which place and which products people can receive.

- A design that jeopardises basic standards and does not include upgrading or measures of progressive improvement. Minimal standards have been understood as a maximum, and certain types that have proven to be economically viable are widely replicated.

- A typology that is associated with a symbolical meaning: the house for those that have no other option. Using a sentence from Wacquant (2002:225): *"A stigma of* [type of housing which] *superimposes itself on the already pervasive stigmata of poverty*"

---

(74) The last three Chilean democratic governments insisted on their interest in "growing with equity", which is even the current government's main motto.

- A location usually in districts that already present deficits in infrastructure, social services and employment. Most of these districts either already concentrate social housing or are in rural areas

Insights and Suggestions

> "*... housing problems must be restated in terms that indicate burdens or barriers created by housing procedures*" (Turner, 1976:64)

In Europe, most of the literature (Lee and Murie, 1997; Marcuse & van Kempen, 2002; Häußermann, 2001) relate social exclusion through housing to a process of impoverishment which forces low-income families, migrants or ethnic minorities to live in depreciated or undesirable houses. Here, many intertwined aspects trigger what scholars have called "a spiral of decay" or "neighbourhood effects". In Europe, the role of governments seems to be much more related to the income position of households rather than to their type of dwelling[75].

In contrast, the role of the Chilean government is much more "integral". Indeed, current housing policies themselves are creating undesirable typologies of housing and neighbourhoods to "warehouse" low-income families. In Chile, social housing policy determines the type of dwellings supplied, their yearly allocations and their location. The case study suggests that, in Chile, receiving a flat in a social housing estate condemns its beneficiaries to living in a stigmatised and inflexible type of dwelling.

In spite of the differences existing between European cases and the Chilean experience, their consequences are quite similar: without the application of upgrading policies, deterioration seems inevitable.

The following model (page 157) presents most of the aspects intertwined within the process of social exclusion through housing, which apply (with different emphasis on problems, governmental responsibility and impacts) to both the Chilean and the European cases.

---

(75) It is important to take into consideration that, in Europe, most of the problems with social housing estates are related to the reduction of the welfare system, the type of tenure (mostly tenants) and to the outward migration of better-off people. Yet, currently deprived neighbourhoods in Europe are a consequence of several failures which also include design problems, but are not based on a typology created to concentrate low-income families.

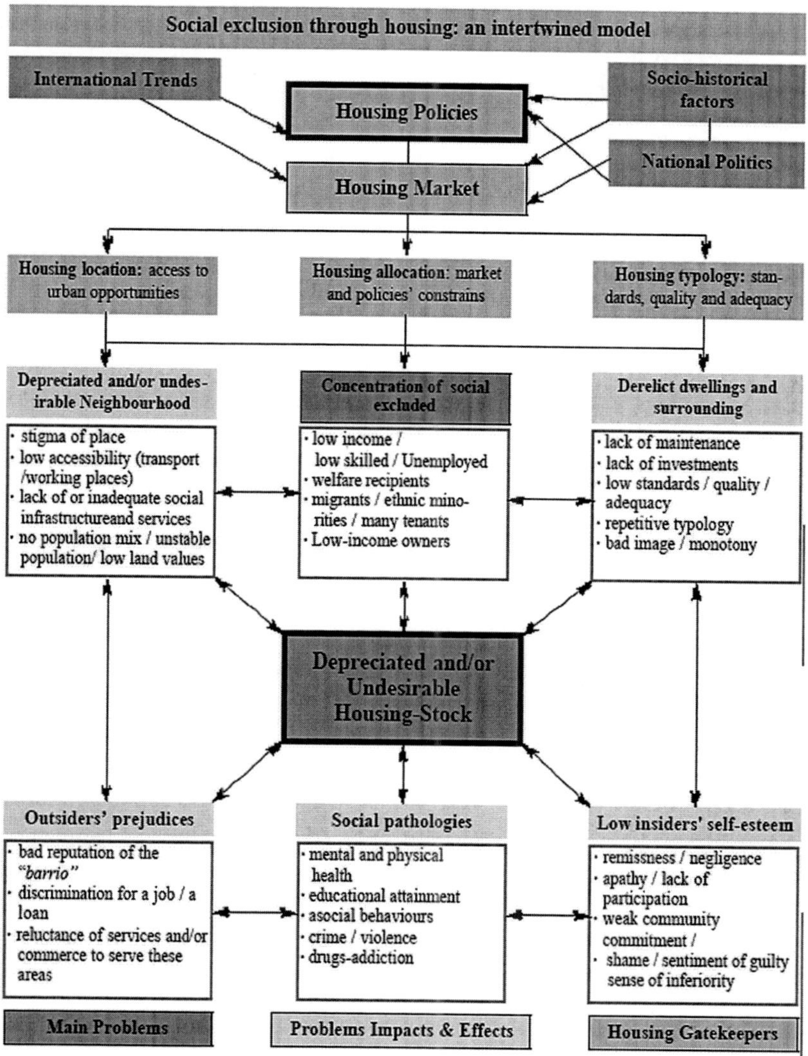
Social exclusion through housing: an intertwined model
International Trends
Housing Policies
Socio-historical factors
National Politics
Housing Market
Housing location: access to urban opportunities
Housing allocation: market and policies' constrains
Housing typology: standards, quality and adequacy
Depreciated and/or undesirable Neighbourhood
Concentration of social excluded
Derelict dwellings and surrounding
· stigma of place
· low accessibility (transport /working places)
· lack of or inadequate social infrastructureand services
· no population mix / unstable population/ low land values
· low income / low skilled / Unemployed
· welfare recipients
· migrants / ethnic minorities / many tenants
· Low-income owners
· lack of maintenance
· lack of investments
· low standards / quality / adequacy
· repetitive typology
· bad image / monotony
Depreciated and/or Undesirable Housing-Stock
Outsiders' prejudices
Social pathologies
Low insiders' self-esteem
· bad reputation of the "barrio"
· discrimination for a job / a loan
· reluctance of services and/or commerce to serve these areas
· mental and physical health
· educational attainment
· asocial behaviours
· crime / violence
· drugs-addiction
· remissness / negligence
· apathy / lack of participation
· weak community commitment /
· shame / sentiment of guilty sense of inferiority
Main Problems
Problems Impacts & Effects
Housing Gatekeepers

The main difference between this model of exclusion through housing and the theoretical model presented in chapter two lies in the fact that, as a conclusion, this proposal considers the undesirability and decay of a neighbourhood or type of housing at the core of the phenomenon. It also suggests that as long as the housing system continues with the same approach (quantitative, discriminatory), all intertwined aspects that cause exclusion will remain. Nevertheless, the model also highlights the need for more qualitative research in the Chilean case, especially in terms of the analysis of "outcomes of social and spatial exclusion".

In contrast to the historical emphasis on the supply of new housing, almost no efforts have been made to improve existing stocks. However, it seems evident that even without upgrading policies, people are increasingly making improvements and building extensions which suggest that upgrading programmes could include people's resources and their active participation. These improvements must be regulated not only for the sake of legality, but in particular, because of risks of dangerous and possibly unhealthy [(76)] constructions that compromise collective properties.

In addition, there are many other reasons and fundaments to promote and to support processes of upgrading. An upgrading process embodied in a long-run policy could meet people's expectations and changing needs, and in addition, it could help to regenerate the urban tissue in a more integrated way. By investing in neighbourhood improvement, the physical capital of the city would be balanced out, and the mixture of social classes become a possibility.

A participative process that involves most of the possible stakeholders would facilitate negotiated interventions that might even attract investment and would certainly have an impact on people's self-esteem. A professionally assisted process would not only prevent dangerous constructions, but might also produce aesthetically improved results. Building transformations could contribute to the efficiency of land use by, for example, increasing population densities which could have a positive impact on the urban economy.

In order to go beyond a merely discursive approach, policies for upgrading the existing stock of decaying estates should be related to a paradigmatic interest of the whole society in improving the redistribution of economic growth: more than enabling markets, housing policy should enable people.

[(76)] It refers not only to the fact that Chile is a seismically-active country, but also to the fact that people tend to make uncontrolled electric installations, to use polluting materials such as asbestos and to disregard basic architectural problems such as ventilation, natural lighthing, among others.

Yet, integration would not only mean inclusion in the market through employment or the right for housing "mobility", but it would also favour social inclusion as a participatory and common effort to improve life quality in the cities.

It is also necessary to change the understanding of housing as an object; a shift from providing "tangible" physical environments to the "non-tangible" provision of networks (skills, tools, instruments) and means instead of final products. Moreover, policies should prioritise sustainable pro-active and preventive measures and avoid reactive and ameliorative interventions.

Upgrading policies should be able to develop flexible structures for interactive social housing where professionals can play a role of mediators or guides. Still, upgrading policies should be part of a flexible iterative process which could change over time depending on societal transformations.

Upgrading and reintegrating existing social housing should mean much more than physical improvement. It should also contribute to the debate about new ways to face housing policies in Chile taking into consideration people's changing expectations and needs.

After decades of neglecting the relationship between housing policies and city development, a mental shift is necessary so that housing provision is no longer understood as a means to satisfy basic material needs, but also the rights of citizenship.

In the end, this work does not try to come up with detailed suggestions for the implementation of upgrading policies, but rather highlights the need to consider exclusion through housing a real problem that is increasingly affecting our society and its desire for democracy.

Appendix

Map 35: Working Map

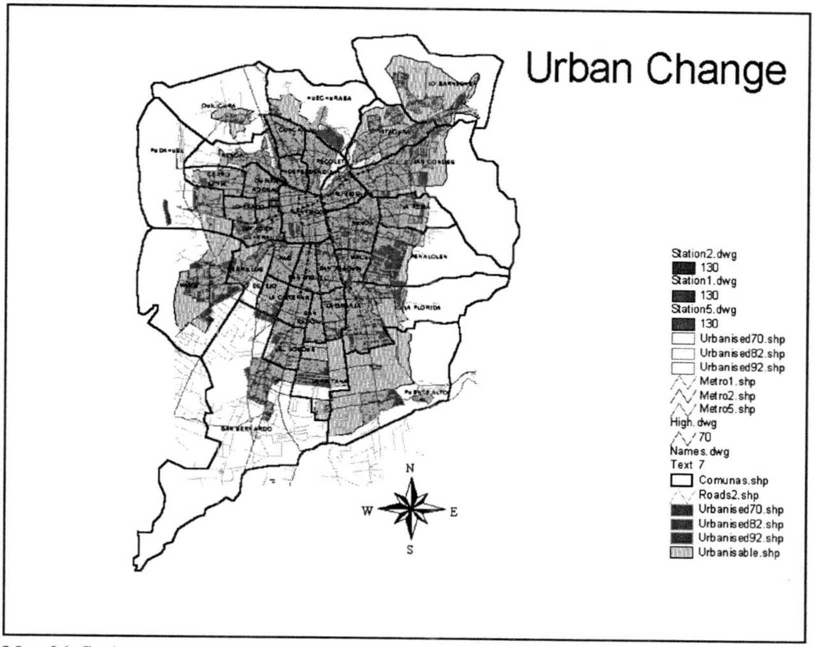

Map 36: Social Housing Location 1950 - 1985

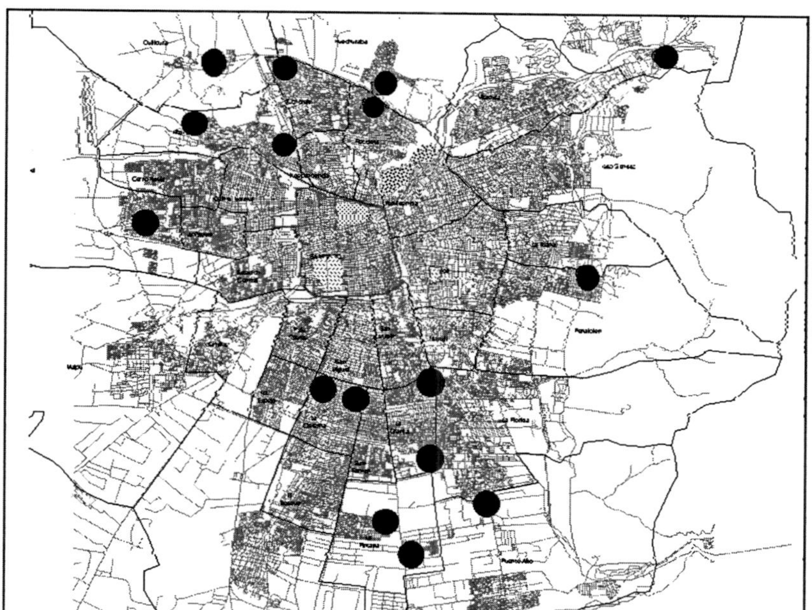

Map 37: Social Housing Location 1985 - 1989

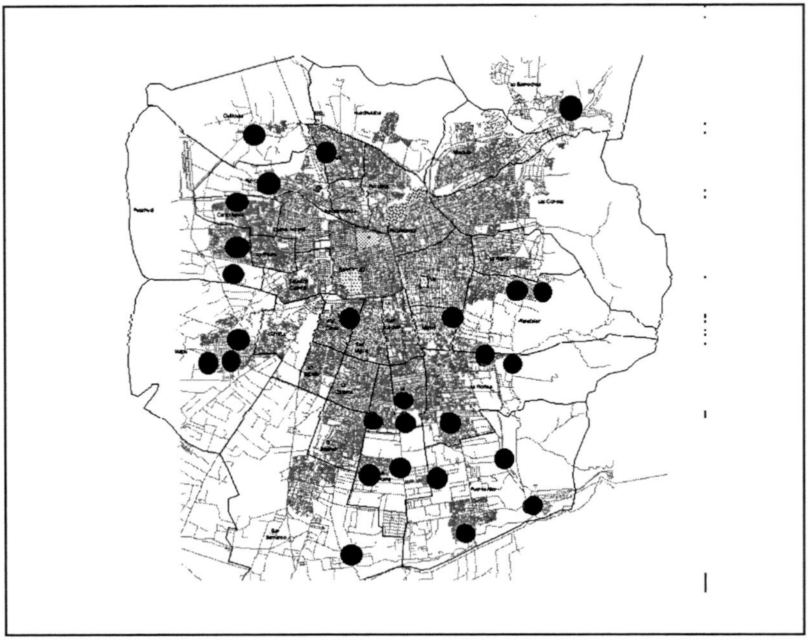

Map 38: Social Housing Location 1989 - 2000

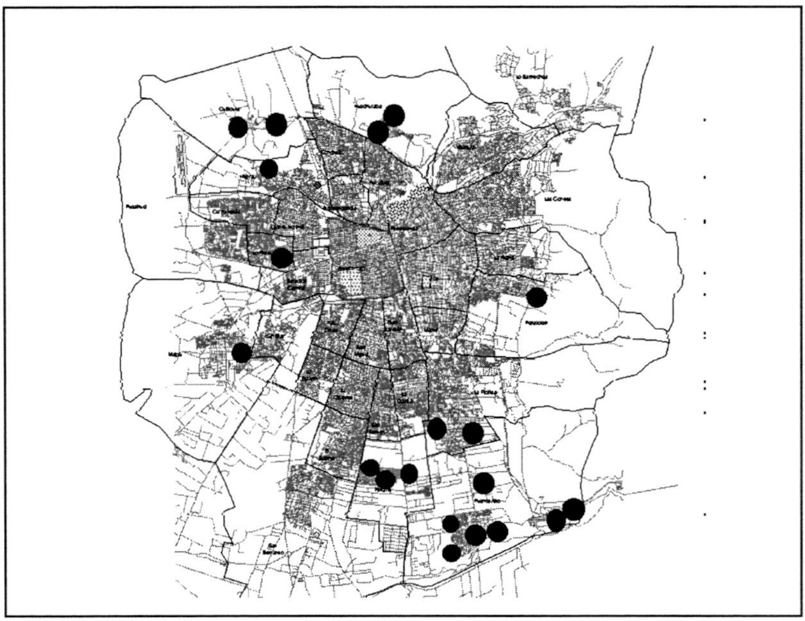

Box 6: Interview Sample: First Part

Identificación	Comuna:	*la pintana*	Persona Entrevistada	*Isidora Riquelme*	
Departamento	Población/Villa:	*San Ricardo*	Edad y Sexo Entrevistado	*45*	*F*
N°: Piso:	N° de hogares en la vivienda	1	Número de personas en el departamento	6	

Pregunta				
1. Dónde vivía Ud. antes?	Mismo barrio		Comuna vecina (o cercana)	
	Misma comuna otro barrio		Otra comuna lejana	*x*
	Otra ciudad		Otra región	
2. Hace cuántos años vive aquí?	Menos de un ano		Más de cinco años	*x*
	Más de uno menos de cinco años			
3. Es usted ?	Propietario	*x*	Pariente del propietario	
	Arrendatario			
4. Tiene amigos por aquí?	La mayoría viven aquí			
	La mayoría viven en otra comuna	*x*	La mayoría vive en otra ciudad	
5. Tiene Ud. Familiares aquí?	La mayoría de la familia vive aquí	*x*		
	La mayoría vive en otras comunas		La mayoría vive en otra ciudad	
6. Tiene planeado cambios	Mejorar su vivienda	x	Cambiarse de casa	
	En el conjunto (reja, otros)			
7. Que cambios quisiera hacer?	Superficie (más grande?)	x	Ventanas	x
	Color (pintura)	x	Puertas	x
8. Por qué quisiera cambiarse?	Problemas con los vecinos (convivencia)		Otros	
	El departamento es muy chico	x	Observaciones	
	El departamento tiene problemas estructurales (malos materiales, mala calidad) Especificar			
	Miedo, inseguridad	x		
9. Tipo de Contactos con los vecinos	Fiestas colectivas, celebraciones		Ayuda informal	x
	Trabajos comunes		Notas	
10. Formas de ayuda mutua entre los vecinos	Tiene confianza con sus vecinos	si	solo con algunosx	
11. Tipo de conflictos, problemas con los vecinos	Ruido		Falta de privacidad	x
	Problemas con los niños, adolescentes	x	Alcoholismo, drogas	x
	Falta de compromiso, o participación		Otros	
12. Por qué razones le interesa seguir viviendo aquí?	Vínculos familiares		Otros	
	Vínculos con los vecinos		V:no tngo a donde ir D:es mala leche la gente que vive aquí	
	Se siente parte del barrio			
	Su trabajo le queda cerca			
	Ventajas y desventajas (?)			

Box 6: Interview Sample: Second Part

1. *Espacios típicos para encontrarse con otros (1) familia, amigos. (2) Vecinos y otros conocidos, o desconocidos*	En el departamento	x	Otros
	Sede comunitaria u otro		
	En la calle, pasaje		
	La Plaza		
	El mercado		
	Centro deportivo Iglesia	x	
2. *Espacios típicos que evita o que le molestan*	La calle	x	Otros
	La plaza		
	El mercado La micro	x	
	Sitios eriazos	x	
3. *Rutina diaria*	Ir al trabajo, la escuela Ir de compras Juntarse con vecinos Juntarse con amigos Viaja a otros barrios		Otros
	Se queda en la casa	x	
	Hacer tramites		
4. *Lugares que le gustan y molestan*	Lugar preferido La casa Lugar más odiado la calle		Otros
5. *Cambios que le gustaría*	Apariencia si Estructura si		
	Espacios comunes si		
6. *Dónde se realizan las siguientes actividades*	Comuna trabajo		Otros
	Juegan los niños comuna		
	Compras comuna		
7. *Ha hecho transformaciones*	Ampliación si | M2 6 Otros cambios rejas, pintura		Uso dormitorio

Calificación de Problemas

Cuáles son los problemas principales de vivir aquí?	La mala calidad de los departamentos	x	Juventud conflictiva	x
	Mala infraestructura (plazas, transporte, agua, alcantarillado)	x	Delincuencia	x
	Malos servicios públicos		Vandalismo	x
	Niños abandonan la escuela	x	Alcoholismo	x
	Cesantia	x	Otros (indicar)	
	Vecinos "mala onda"			

Preguntas Adicionales	
Dónde trabaja Ud. U otro de la familia? Cuánto se demora en llegar al trabajo?	mi conviviente, trabaja en taxi, por lo tanto no hay horario
Qué otros barrios conoce? Cuántas veces por mes va a otro barrio o comuna?	pocos, casi nunca(solo cuando acompaña añ marido, que es rara vez)
Hay gente que la mira en menos por vivir aquí? Le	si

Box 7: Interview Questionnaire Sample: First Part

Identification	District:		Person Interwied	
	Conglomerate:		Age and Sex interviweneed	
	N° of households in the dwelling		Other	

Where do you live before?	Same neighbourhood		Neighbor district	
	Same district other neighbourhood		Another not neighbor district	
	Other city		Other region	
How many years are you living here?	Less than one year > one years and < five		More than five years	
Are you ?	Owner Renter		Relative	
Have you friends around?	Most of the friends live here Most of the friends live in other districts		Most of the friends live in other city	
Have you family here?	Most of the family live here Most of the friends live in other districts		Most of the friends live in other city.	
Any plan to make changes?	Dwelling improvements Dwellings		Move away	
Type of Modifications	Area Colour		Windows size Door quality	
Reasons to move away	Convivence problems Areal problems Structural problems		Others	
	Insecurity, fear			
Type of Bonds with neighbors.	Shared parties, celebrations		Informal social networks	
Patterns of reciprocal support between family and friends	Common works		Notes	
	Confidence relations? Trust			
Type of Tensions, problems, divisions with neighbors	Noise Kids or teenes troubles Lack of commitment		Lack of privacy Alcholism, drugs Others	
Reasons to stay here and not to moving away	Familiar bonds Communitary involvements		Others	
	Sense of belonging			
	Advantages & Disadvantages			
Typical spaces of encounter (1) relative, friends. (2) Neighbors, or other known or unknow people	Dwellings		Others	
	Communitary spaces Passages, streets			
	Squares			
	Market			
	Communitary centre Deportive centre			

Box 7: Interview Questionnaire Sample:Second Part

Pregunta	Opción		Otros
1. *Espacios típicos para encontrarse con otros (1) familia, amigos. (2) Vecinos y otros conocidos, o desconocidos*	En el departamento	x	Otros
	Sede comunitaria u otro		
	En la calle, pasaje		
	La Plaza		
	El mercado		
	Centro deportivo	x	
	Iglesia		
2. *Espacios típicos que evita o que le molestan*	La calle	x	Otros
	La plaza		
	El mercado		
	La micro	x	
	Sitios eriazos	x	
3. *Rutina diaria*	Ir al trabajo, la escuela		Otros
	Ir de compras		
	Juntarse con vecinos		
	Juntarse con amigos		
	Viaja a otros barrios		
	Se queda en la casa	x	
	Hacer tramites		
4. *Lugares que le gustan y molestan*	Lugar preferido	La casa	Otros
	Lugar más odiado	la calle	
5. *Cambios que le gustaría*	Apariencia si		
	Estructura si		
	Espacios comunes si		
6. *Dónde se realizan las siguientes actividades*	Comuna trabajo		Otros
	Juegan los niños	comuna	
	Compras	comuna	
7. *Ha hecho transformaciones*	Ampliación	si | M2 6	Uso dormitorio
	Otros cambios	rejas, pintura	

Calificación de Problemas

Cuáles son los problemas principales de vivir aquí?	La mala calidad de los departamentos	x	Juventud conflictiva	x
	Mala infraestructura (plazas, transporte, agua, alcantarillado)	x	Delincuencia	x
	Malos servicios públicos		Vandalismo	x
	Niños abandonan la escuela	x	Alcoholismo	x
	Cesantía	x	Otros (indicar)	
	Vecinos "mala onda"			

Preguntas Adicionales	
Dónde trabaja Ud. U otro de la familia? Cuánto se demora en llegar al trabajo?	mi conviviente, trabaja en taxi, por lo tanto no hay horario
Qué otros barrios conoce? Cuántas veces por mes va a otro barrio o comuna?	pocos, casi nunca(solo cuando acompaña aň marido, que es rara vez)
Hay gente que la mira en menos por vivir aquí? Le	si

Fig. 104: Number of social housing by Comuna and year (1978-1989)

Comuna	1978	1979	1980	1981	1982	1983	1984	1985	1986	1987	1988	1989
Cerrillos	0	294	0	160	0	0	0	0	0	0	0	0
Cerro Navia	0	0	0	0	0	0	0	1.029	0	775	796	0
Conchali	446	0	0	142	1.320	0	0	60	0	0	512	0
El Bosque	557	744	146	384	840	110	472	388	528	1.064	0	728
Estacion Central	0	0	0	0	0	0	0	192	0	806	512	0
Huechuraba	0	0	0	0	0	0	0	0	0	0	0	0
Independencia	0	0	0	0	0	0	0	0	0	0	0	0
La Cisterna	0	0	0	0	840	0	472	588	378	604	0	1.123
La Florida	576	892	472	236	717	0	328	1.504	2.647	2.311	1.508	3.281
La Grania	0	502	1.000	1.128	554	482	0	384	0	0	0	1.127
La Pintana	76	348	1.149	576	893	1.137	1.391	1.020	0	818	1.336	4.392
La Reina	170	164	0	0	0	0	0	0	0	0	263	0
Las Condes	0	0	360	36	0	0	0	0	0	324	120	0
Barnechea	148	0	0	0	0	0	0	0	0	0	300	1250
Lo Espejo		0	0	0	0	0	0	0	0	0	0	275
Lo Prado	574	156	0	504	576	0	0	156	0	119	472	890
Macul	700	96	534	1.458	264	0	0	0	300	0	495	572
Maipu	347	422	1.334	160	0	0	0	0	252	0	1.191	363
Nunoa	393	0	0	0	0	0	0	0	0	0	0	0
P.A.C.	0	0	0	0	0	0	0	0	0	0	0	0
Penalolen	1.546			0	264	420	1.314	0	0	363	0	134
Providencia	0	0	0	0	0	0	0	0	0	0	0	0
Pudahuel	348	280	382	0	630	540	1.540	0	1.884	1.198	0	740
Puente Alto	0	630	762	80	0	1.202	1.352	0	1.430	1.038	1.144	776
Quilicura	164	287	0	256	0	0	0	0	227	251	0	155
Quinta Normal	85	0	0	0	0	0	0	0	0	0	0	0
Recoleta	0	0	0	0	0	0	0	0	0	0	0	0
Renca	384	252	0	184	240	808	1.898	1.135	2.601	758	0	550
San Bernardo	30	0	0	476	139	110	962	2.407	592	901	686	470
San Joaquin	112	0	0	0	0	0	0	192	0	0	0	0
San Miguel	338	0	0	0	364	0	0	0	0	230	0	0
San Ramon	0	0	788	216	448	586	0	806	0	0	0	0
Santiago	268	126	0	0	0	0	0	0	0	0	0	0
Vitacura	0	0	0	0	0	0	0	0	0	0	0	0
Total	7.262	5.193	6.927	5.996	8.089	5.395	9.729	9.861	10.839	11.560	9.335	16.826
Percentage	3,84%	2,75%	3,66%	3,17%	4,28%	2,85%	5,14%	5,21%	5,73%	6,11%	4,94%	8,90%

Fig. 104: Number of social housing by Comuna and year (1978-1989)

Comuna	1990	1991	1992	1993	1994	1995	1996	1997	1998	1999	2000	Total
Cerrillos	0	0	0	0	0	0	0	0	767	0	1155	2.376
Cerro Navia	140	0	0	0	0	0	0	506	0	0	0	3.246
Conchali	0	285	144	0	0	0	0	0	60	0	0	2.969
El Bosque	0	1.168	708	0	570	288	171	0	172	0	120	9.158
Estacion Central	0	136	0	0	0	0	0	0	0	0	0	1.646
Huechuraba	0	285	144	0	0	0	0	0	0	0	279	708
Independencia	0	0	0	0	0	0	0	0	0	0	0	0
La Cisterna	0	1.080	360	0	0	0	0	0	0	0	0	5.445
La Florida	0	0	300	240	1.068	314	0	0	0	0	0	16.394
La Granja	292	237	0	498	0	0	0	111	0	45	0	6.360
La Pintana	1.577	2.400	488	959	663	1.016	1.130	0	0	688	0	22.057
La Reina	0	0	0	0	0	0	0	0	0	0	0	597
Las Condes	0	0	0	0	0	0	0	0	0	537	0	1.377
Barnechea	0	0	0	0	0	0	0	0	306		492	2.496
Lo Espejo	0	816	0	792	0	0	0	0	0	75	0	1.958
Lo Prado	150	0	114	108	204	384	243	588	178	0	0	5.416
Macul	144	0	0	0	0	0	0	0	0	0	0	4.563
Maipu	1.915	0	240	0	996	924	1.264	0	1.073	708	0	11.189
Nunoa	0	0	0	0	0	129	0	0	0	0	0	522
P.A.C.	0	588	264	0	0	0	0	0	0	0	0	852
Penalolen	550	1.489	1.416	276	0	0	0	0	0	270	846	8.888
Providencia	0	0	0	0	0	0	0	0	0	0	0	0
Pudahuel	0	1.830	2.918	0	0	0	0	0	422	0	0	12.712
Puente Alto	1.955	2.084	1.137	1.413	3.276	2.798	1.679	2.976	676	1.704	1.324	29.436
Quilicura	0	0	0	2.940	2.076	0	0	0	0	0	1.660	8.016
Quinta Normal	0	0	0	0	0	0	0	0	0	0	0	85
Recoleta	0	0	0	0	64	0	136	150	81	0	0	431
Renca	0	0	100	552	0	0	0	0	0	198	708	10.368
San Bernardo	52	682	740	864	336	0	2.391	2.076	0	750	0	14.664
San Joaquin	0	0	0	0	0	0	0	60	0	0	0	364
San Miguel	0	0	0	0	0	0	0	0	0	0	0	932
San Ramon	0	0	0	480	0	0	0	0	0	0	0	3.324
Santiago	0	0	178	0	0	0	0	0	0	0	0	572
Vitacura	0	0	0	0	0	0	0	0	0	0	0	0
Total	6.775	13.080	9.251	9.122	9.253	5.853	7.014	6.467	3.735	4.975	6.584	189.121
Percentage	3,58%	6,92%	4,89%	4,82%	4,89%	3,09%	3,71%	3,42%	1,97%	2,63%	3,48%	100,00%

Fig. 105: Accessibility Matrix, travel times in Minutes - First part

ID	Comuna	TO 1	TO 2	TO 3	TO 4	TO 5	TO 6	TO 7	TO 8	TO 9	TO 10	TO 11	TO 12	TO 13	TO 14	TO 15	TO 16	TO 17
1	Cerrillos	0.000	28.457	34.19	23.94	11.68	37.02	23.84	20.10	32.47	28.73	34.44	33.34	31.06	41.34	17.56	15.12	32.19
2	Cerro Navia	28.07	0.000	34.88	36.82	17.60	35.00	24.56	32.751	30.80	43.58	48.32	36.44	34.17	46.35	31.44	19.28	35.29
3	Conchalí	34.19	34.80	0.000	36.98	23.11	37.53	12.44	29.98	36.65	40.751	45.48	33.27	31.00	41.18	28.60	27.28	32.12
4	El Bosque	23.94	36.82	36.98	0.000	25.67	41.011	26.86	21.38	23.28	18.48	23.19	33.78	34.45	44.65	14.80	29.84	33.76
5	Estación Central	11.98	17.60	23.11	25.67	0.000	28.57	12.79	18.58	25.85	29.45	34.17	22.28	20.02	30.30	17.29	7.62	21.14
6	Huechuraba	37.62	35.03	37.53	41.011	28.57	0.000	27.22	33.94	36.44	44.77	48.51	24.00	19.03	20.42	32.61	30.74	31.89
7	Independencia	23.84	24.56	12.44	26.86	12.78	27.22	0.000	19.58	26.31	30.48	35.16	22.96	20.06	30.80	18.29	16.96	21.81
8	La Cisterna	20.10	32.75	29.9	21.38	18.59	33.94	19.59	0.000	23.28	23.08	26.80	29.68	27.38	37.35	12.92	22.79	25.67
9	La Florida	32.47	30.80	36.65	23.28	25.65	36.44	26.31	23.28	0.000	17.58	22.71	19.96	23.53	38.25	23.36	29.82	19.851
10	La Granja	28.73	43.58	40.75	18.48	29.43	44.77	30.43	25.08	17.58	0.000	17.88	28.45	34.02	46.74	18.56	33.80	28.44
11	La Pintana	34.44	48.32	45.48	23.19	34.17	48.51	35.16	29.80	22.71	17.88	0.000	33.18	38.75	51.48	23.30	38.34	33.17
12	La Reina	33.34	36.44	33.27	33.78	22.28	24.00	22.96	29.68	19.96	28.45	33.18	0.000	11.12	25.86	28.34	26.46	14.52
13	Las Condes	31.06	34.17	31.00	34.45	20.02	19.03	20.69	27.38	23.53	34.02	38.75	11.12	0.000	20.85	26.07	24.18	20.09
14	Barnechea	41.34	46.35	41.18	44.65	30.30	20.42	30.86	37.35	38.25	46.74	51.48	25.86	20.85	0.000	36.25	34.37	33.75
15	Lo Espejo	17.56	31.44	28.60	14.80	17.28	32.61	18.29	12.92	23.36	18.56	23.30	28.34	26.07	36.25	0.000	21.46	26.34
16	Lo Prado	15.12	19.28	27.28	29.84	7.62	30.74	16.96	22.78	29.82	33.80	38.34	26.46	24.18	34.37	21.48	0.000	25.31
17	Macul	32.19	35.29	32.12	33.74	21.14	31.89	21.81	23.67	19.85	28.44	33.17	14.52	20.09	33.75	26.34	25.31	0.000
18	Maipu	31.68	38.26	45.78	28.32	24.31	47.23	33.45	31.25	37.82	33.08	37.80	42.9	40.67	50.85	24.79	24.40	41.79
19	Ñuñoa	26.48	20.52	26.39	29.80	15.38	23.78	16.05	22.73	10.35	27.841	32.57	8.30	13.87	27.60	21.42	19.53	9.30
20	Pac	15.48	28.30	25.34	16.65	14.05	28.59	15.05	10.85	23.84	20.57	25.11	25.11	22.80	33.08	8.23	18.25	23.11
21	Peñalolén	32.98	36.06	32.84	30.47	21.80	26.50	22.53	29.25	16.08	25.17	28.90	8.06	13.60	28.33	27.9	26.05	11.24
22	Providencia	34.45	27.59	24.38	27.84	13.47	18.53	14.07	22.78	21.49	28.95	34.08	12.53	7.50	20.35	18.46	17.57	14.08
23	Pudahuel	24.08	28.21	36.21	38.77	16.55	36.07	25.89	31.08	38.75	42.53	47.27	35.39	33.12	45.30	30.38	10.23	34.34
24	Puente Alto	52.99	60.28	57.11	43.79	48.13	58.02	46.80	43.53	20.48	38.46	43.19	40.44	46.01	58.79	43.87	50.30	40.43
25	Quilicura	33.45	27.80	30.34	36.25	22.38	17.61	20.05	29.18	35.90	40.02	44.75	32.55	30.27	39.28	27.38	26.55	31.40
26	Quinta Normal	20.73	8.80	26.07	31.92	9.73	27.08	16.86	24.08	31.80	35.68	40.42	28.54	28.27	36.45	23.54	11.38	27.30
27	Recoleta	30.48	33.99	30.42	33.87	19.43	7.85	20.30	20.80	30.48	37.64	42.57	26.60	21.93	29.31	25.48	23.60	25.09
28	Renca	24.48	15.30	29.80	35.57	13.38	18.94	19.38	28.50	35.46	39.34	44.07	32.30	28.08	40.01	27.19	15.48	30.97
29	San Bernardo	29.98	43.87	41.08	22.45	29.72	45.06	30.72	25.35	32.06	27.23	34.96	40.77	38.50	48.09	38.85	33.89	38.77
30	San Joaquín	21.08	30.30	27.28	23.32	15.99	38.29	16.94	14.27	15.26	23.75	28.48	21.38	23.17	33.38	14.94	20.21	15.04
31	San Miguel	16.08	27.09	24.34	17.19	12.65	28.27	13.85	6.60	18.85	20.96	23.69	23.08	21.71	31.88	8.82	17.30	20.01
32	San Ramon	26.28	38.78	35.94	27.32	24.62	39.98	25.82	16.78	21.88	30.13	34.86	31.79	33.41	45.94	18.95	28.79	26.82
33	Santiago	17.28	21.34	17.40	19.51	6.98	22.46	7.85	12.44	20.56	23.28	28.01	17.20	14.93	25.11	11.14	11.86	16.09
34	Vitacura	32.78	35.84	32.87	36.12	21.08	17.90	22.36	24.05	20.79	33.28	42.97	17.33	12.56	15.58	27.74	25.86	25.24

Fig. 105: Accessibility Matrix, travel times in Minutes - Second part

ID	Comuna	TO 18	TO 19	TO 20	TO 21	TO 22	TO 23	TO 24	TO 25	TO 26	TO 27	TO 28	TO 29	TO 30	TO 31	TO 32	TO 33	TO 34
1	Cerrillos	38.643	26.412	15.408	32.926	34.454	24.08	32.987	33.454	20.736	30.488	24.437	29.896	21.086	16.067	26.217	17.281	32.740
2	Cerro Navia	38.264	20.52	28.306	36.014	27.599	28.211	60.28	27.808	8.800	33.98	15.309	43.874	30.301	27.096	38.786	21.140	35.845
3	Conchalí	45.786	26.39	25.367	32.844	24.389	36.21	57.114	30.347	26.079	30.421	29.808	41.085	27.280	24.347	35.946	17.402	32.875
4	El Bosque	28.324	29.803	16.650	30.479	27.843	38.77	43.798	36.258	31.921	33.87	35.572	22.455	23.32	17.194	27.323	19.508	36.126
5	Estación Central	24.112	15.398	14.054	21.802	13.47	16.559	48.132	22.387	9.730	19.43	13.38	29.722	15.998	12.654	24.623	6.98	21.08
6	Huechuraba	47.232	23.730	28.598	26.503	18.537	36.073	58.022	17.614	27.089	7.85	19.69	45.063	31.2	28.275	30.69	21.46	17.904
7	Independencia	33.452	16.05	15.083	22.53	14.075	25.89	46.08	20.053	16.865	20.30	19.38	30.721	16.94	13.855	25.82	7.851	22.36
8	La Cisterna	31.258	22.73	10.854	29.254	22.789	31.08	43.532	28.807	24.080	20.80	28.501	25.352	14.27	6.603	16.78	12.447	24.05
9	La Florida	37.822	10.351	23.842	16.08	21.494	38.75	20.481	35.908	31.802	30.48	35.464	32.062	15.264	18.851	21.88	20.56	20.790
10	La Granja	33.082	27.841	20.578	25.17	28.954	42.53	38.461	40.02	35.680	37.64	39.34	27.234	23.754	20.967	30.13	23.28	33.283
11	La Pintana	37.824	32.573	25.110	28.902	34.080	47.27	43.189	44.758	40.421	42.57	44.072	31.905	28.486	25.809	34.86	28.010	42.972
12	La Reina	42.940	8.307	25.110	8.064	12.534	35.39	40.44	32.558	28.344	26.605	32.30	40.738	21.358	23.060	31.79	17.220	17.335
13	Las Condes	40.670	13.877	22.809	13.604	7.501	33.12	46.01	30.278	26.273	21.936	28.085	38.507	23.171	21.719	33.412	14.937	12.342
14	Barnechea	50.858	27.60	33.088	28.33	20.354	45.30	58.79	38.207	36.452	29.312	40.014	48.095	33.38	31.868	45.94	25.118	15.584
15	Lo Espejo	24.798	21.423	8.232	27.917	18.462	30.38	43.87	27.882	23.543	25.48	27.194	38.852	14.940	8.821	18.955	11.14	27.748
16	Lo Prado	24.408	19.538	18.254	26.05	17.577	10.25	50.30	26.557	11.380	23.60	15.051	33.862	20.116	17.304	28.79	11.86	25.863
17	Macul	41.798	9.30	23.111	11.249	14.087	34.34	40.43	31.402	27.306	25.09	30.958	38.779	15.043	20.093	26.825	16.08	25.244
18	Maipu	0.000	36.02	30.530	42.51	34.084	33.38	58.404	33.517	30.363	40.69	34.084	31.750	33.23	27.309	37.238	27.09	42.347
19	Ñuñoa	36.022	0.000	18.285	9.817	7.40	28.49	39.85	25.625	21.689	20.23	25.181	33.853	14.480	17.088	28.228	10.28	19.092
20	Pac	30.528	18.285	0.000	24.67	18.224	27.15	43.622	24.680	20.306	22.25	23.95	20.862	11.730	6.753	10.380	7.902	24.580
21	Peñalolén	42.518	9.817	24.679	0.000	15.804	34.09	37.348	32.118	28.113	26.704	31.675	36.252	20.202	23.559	28.508	16.777	19.812
22	Providencia	34.088	7.402	18.224	15.031	0.000	28.39	41.945	23.854	19.058	18.246	23.22	31.862	10.998	15.304	20.708	8.522	11.846
23	Pudahuel	33.336	28.459	27.154	34.092	26.507	0.000	59.23	35.40	20.320	32.53	23.981	42.822	28.08	28.264	33.723	20.40	34.78
24	Puente Alto	58.408	39.850	43.623	37.361	41.945	59.23	0.000	56.388	52.383	50.971	55.948	32.543	35.740	39.402	42.12	41.047	50.231
25	Quilicura	33.517	25.625	24.842	32.118	23.854	35.40	56.38	0.000	19.907	20.31	12.748	40.310	26.537	23.522	35.214	16.74	30.759
26	Quinta Normal	30.363	21.68	20.306	28.113	19.058	20.318	52.380	19.907	0.000	25.68	7.605	35.975	22.22	19.285	30.867	13.247	27.944
27	Recoleta	40.695	20.237	22.256	26.701	18.246	32.53	50.971	20.517	25.680	0.000	22.840	37.054	24.151	21.336	32.89	14.354	22.804
28	Renca	34.084	25.181	23.950	31.675	23.220	23.98	55.94	12.748	7.605	22.840	0.000	38.624	25.851	22.836	34.53	16.284	31.505
29	San Bernardo	34.758	33.850	20.862	36.252	31.862	42.82	32.542	40.310	35.975	37.05	38.624	0.000	27.378	21.251	34.388	23.57	40.178
30	San Joaquín	33.238	14.480	11.730	20.202	10.998	28.08	35.74	26.537	22.280	24.15	25.851	27.378	0.000	8.608	18.67	9.797	24.842
31	San Miguel	27.308	17.088	6.753	23.556	15.304	28.26	39.40	23.522	19.185	21.336	22.836	21.251	8.608	0.000	12.69	6.782	23.303
32	San Ramon	37.238	28.228	10.380	28.508	20.708	33.72	42.12	35.214	30.879	32.89	34.53	31.388	18.67	12.69	0.000	18.47	35.084
33	Santiago	27.098	10.280	7.902	16.777	8.522	20.40	41.047	16.748	13.247	14.35	16.284	23.570	9.797	6.782	18.473	0.000	16.408
34	Vitacura	42.347	19.090	24.580	16.082	11.846	34.78	50.231	30.759	27.944	22.809	31.505	40.178	24.842	23.303	35.028	16.408	0.000

Box 8: Social Exclusion through housing: matrix of problems
Typical Problems of exclusion through housing and its possible consequences

Typical spaces of encounter (1) relative, friends. (2) Neighbors, or other known or unknow people	Dwellings Communitary spaces Passages, streets	Others
	Squares Market Communitary centre Deportive centre	
Typical disgussting or avoided public spaces	Street Passages	Others
	Square	
	Market Transport	
Typical daily routine	Going to work / to school	Others
	Going to shopping Meeting the community Meeting friends Going to other neighbourhoods Staying at home Making aarons around	
Beloved and hated places	Favourite place Most hated place	Others
Prioritary changes	Appearance	
	Structure	
	Shared spaces	

Additional questions

Where do you work? Where do you take your transport? How long it takes? Where do your Children go to school? Where they play?	Which other neighbourhoods do you know? How many times per month, year are you going to other places? Any feeling of discrimination or stigmatisation?
It is important where they live at the moment to apply for a job? Do they have access to credit or services?	What they speculate outsiders would think about them? Are they well protected or menace by the police?

Making a Ranking of problems Which are the predominate problems for you?	Physical decay	Youth anti-social behaviour	
	Poor infrastructure Poor service's quality	Delinquency Vandalism	
	School abandonment / achievements Unemployment	Alcoholism, Drugs Others	

Fig. 106: Sample of performed indicators and average

ID	*Comuna*	Unem-ployed	Food Subsidies	Social Housing	Time To Cbd	Sqm. Built	Distance Health	Average
1	Cerrillos	0,37	0,44	0,07	0,53	0,00	0,24	0,28
2	Cerro Navia	0,17	0,00	0,13	0,58	0,00	0,65	0,25
3	Conchali	0,39	0,18	0,09	0,69	0,01	0,52	0,31
4	El Bosque	0,28	0,45	0,32	0,41	0,01	0,66	0,35
5	Estacion Central	0,53	0,40	0,06	0,81	0,01	0,48	0,38
6	Huechuraba	0,49	0,30	0,03	0,46	0,02	0,43	0,29
7	Independencia	0,56	0,59	0,00	0,88	0,02	0,38	0,41
8	La Cisterna	0,69	0,58	0,19	0,64	0,04	0,46	0,43
9	La Florida	0,50	0,58	0,51	0,29	0,04	0,50	0,40
10	La Granja	0,06	0,30	0,17	0,42	0,05	0,54	0,26
11	La Pintana	0,25	0,03	0,69	0,19	0,05	0,48	0,28
12	La Reina	0,75	0,46	0,01	0,50	0,05	0,12	0,32
13	Las Condes	0,77	0,75	0,04	0,65	0,05	0,23	0,41
14	Lo Barnechea	1,00	0,83	0,09	0,35	0,09	1,00	0,56
15	Lo Espejo	0,22	0,09	0,07	0,58	0,10	0,52	0,26
16	Lo Prado	0,34	0,22	0,15	0,74	0,11	0,67	0,37
17	Macul	0,51	0,25	0,06	0,55	0,11	0,42	0,32
18	Maipu	0,67	0,58	0,34	0,47	0,14	0,00	0,37
19	Ñuñoa	0,72	0,61	0,00	0,74	0,15	0,35	0,43
20	Pedro A.Cerda	0,59	0,27	0,03	0,63	0,15	0,82	0,42
21	Peñalolen	0,57	0,15	0,26	0,46	0,15	0,67	0,38
22	Providencia	1,00	1,00	0,00	0,88	0,20	1,00	0,68
23	Pudahuel	0,51	0,23	0,42	0,61	0,21	0,55	0,42
24	Puente Alto	0,52	0,43	1,00	0,00	0,23	0,22	0,40
25	Quilicura	0,42	0,53	0,26	0,49	0,24	0,61	0,42
26	Quinta Normal	0,51	0,46	0,00	0,72	0,24	0,51	0,41
27	Recoleta	0,44	0,36	0,02	0,68	0,27	0,51	0,38
28	Renca	0,00	0,14	0,34	0,70	0,27	0,32	0,30
29	San Bernardo	0,44	0,41	0,55	0,37	0,29	0,40	0,41
30	San Joaquin	0,48	0,35	0,01	0,67	0,38	0,51	0,40
31	San Miguel	0,52	0,52	0,02	0,75	0,48	0,37	0,44
32	San Ramon	0,35	0,08	0,08	0,41	0,70	0,68	0,38
33	Santiago	0,66	0,34	0,01	1,00	1,00	0,57	0,60
34	Vitacura	1,00	1	1,00	0,55	1,00	1,00	0,93

Fig. 107: General Data Case Studies and Interviews / checklists results (1st part)

Data Comuna	Puente Alto	Macul	La Pintana
Population	492.915	112.535	190.085
Households	97.907	39.794	30.794
Average peop/house	5	3	6
Area	2.983	1.238	1.545
Density (Inh./area)	165	91	123
Social H 78-81	1.472	2.788	2.149
Social H 82-91	10.981	1.775	14.964
Social H 92-00	16.983	0	10.981
Total Dwellings	124.059	28.005	41.398
Nr. Housing Social	29.436	4.563	22.057
Apartments/blocks	13.894	1.511	4.982
Unemployment	9,74 %	9,8 %	15,20 %
Budget/ Inhabitants	62,58	61,34	77,2
Poor	19,59%	13,21%	30,91%
No Poor	80,41%	86,79%	69,09%
Public Transport CBD	71 Minutes	45 Minutes	62 Minutes
Average cost land '92	15,95 US$/m2	63,31 US$/m2	8,03 US$/m2
Illiteracy rate	1,5	2,3	3,9
Average years studies	10,3	11	8,7
Child mortality	9,5	9,6	12,6
Early pregnancy	12,2	10,4	20,6
Low income	47%	16%	82%
Middle-income	53%	73%	18%
High-income	1%	11%	0%
Owner	80,15%	66,27	74,26%
Renter	15,04%	18,23	14,83%
Data Compounds	**Villa Horizonte**	**Las Cumbres**	**San Ricardo**
Population	2113	2300	4296
Households	500	492	998
Housing number	296		337
Apartments/ blocks	84	330	324
Total Social Housing	374		661
Households in blocks	108	492	519
Population in blocks	428	2300	2100
Area flats	36=41,18 ; 42=40,78	222=45,54; 108=44,88	53,86 m2
Pred-material walls	Red-bricks	Red-bricks	Red-bricks

Fig. 107: General Data Case Studies and Interviews / checklists results (2nd part)

Data Compounds	Villa Horizonte	Las Cumbres	San Ricardo
Year of construction	1993	1989	1980
Interviews / Basic questions	Villa Horizonte	Las Cumbres	San Ricardo
Average age of interviewees	40	38	42
Sex interviewees	6 women- 2 men	4 women - 4 men	4 women -4 men
Average persons per house	5,75	7,25	6,5
Average households per house	1,4	1,5	1,6
People coming from far away	87,5 %	87,5 %	62,5 %
People living more than 5 years	87,5 %	62,5 %	62,5 %
Owners	87,5 %	50 %	87,5 %
Tenants	(relatives)	25%	(relatives)
Average extensions	75%	50%	75%
Average m2 increase	7,8	6	6
Predominant use of extension	Dormitory	Dormitory	Dormitory
Reasons to live or move	Villa Horizonte	Las Cumbres	San Ricardo
Bad quality dwellings	62,5	100	100
Bad Infrastructure	12,5	50	75
Bad services	12,5	12,5	50
Not moving due to lack of alternative	25	12	50
Not moving due to they are owners	62,5	62,5	50
Important familiar ties	37,5	25	37,5
Neighbours ties	0	12,5	25
Belonging to neighbourhood	25	37,5	25
Close to work	0	25	12,5
Meeting point : dwelling	100	100	62,5
Communitary centre	12,5	25	50
Street	37,5	62,5	50
Passage	62,5	62,5	50

Fig. 107: General Data Case Studies and Interviews / checklists results (3rd part)

Data Compounds	Villa Horizonte	Las Cumbres	San Ricardo
Market	25	25	12,5
Sport centre	62,5	62,5	87,5
Church	50	62,5	37,5
Interviews /social relations	Villa Horizonte	Las Cumbres	San Ricardo
Friends living here	37,5	25	25
Friends other districts	25	37	62
Family living here	75	25	50
Family other districts	25	37,5	37,5
Social contact - parties	12,5	50	37,5
Mutual help	87,5	50	75
Communitary works	12,5	50	12,5
Confidence in neighbours	Regular	Regular	Regular to good
Interviews /Problems neighbours	Villa Horizonte	Las Cumbres	San Ricardo
Noise	87,5	37,5	62,5
Kids / teens behaviour	37,5	87,5	50
Lack of privacy	50	87,5	62,5
Lack of commitment	12,5	25	25
Alcohol or drugs	87,5	75	87,5
Hated places: home	12,5	25	25
Kitchen	12,5	12,5	0
Square	25	0	12,5
Empty land	62,5	75	87,5
Street	12,5 or 25	25	50 or 87,5
Bus	25	62,5	50
market	12,5	12,5	0
Loved spaces: home	62,5	50	50
Yard	12,5	12,5	12,5
Interviews /social problems	Villa Horizonte	Las Cumbres	San Ricardo

Fig. 107: General Data Case Studies and Interviews / checklists results (4 th part)

School abandonment	0	75	50
Unemployment	75	50	75
Social relations (problematic)	25	25	37,5
Conflictive youth	75	75	62,5
Delinquency	62,5	87,5	87,5
Vandalism	75	62,5	62,5
Alcoholism	50	75	87,5
Drugs	37,5	25,0	50
Unprotected by the police	75	87,5	62,5
Interviews /Plans to change	Villa Horizonte	Las Cumbres	San Ricardo
Appearance	75	87,5	87,5
Structure	62,5	87,5	75
Common spaces	50	87,5	75
Dwelling	100	100	87,5
Blocks (compound)	50	0	37,5
Area dwelling	100	100	100
Painting	75	100	87,5
Windows	75	62,5	50
Doors	62,5	62,5	50
To move	0	0	12,5
MAIN Problems	Bad quality	Bad neighbours	Dealers here
	Overcrowding	No confidence	Bad people
	Drug dealers	Bad materials	
Interviews /routines and stigma	Villa Horizonte	Las Cumbres	San Ricardo
Going to work	37,5	50	62,5
Going to shopping	25	12,5	25
Meeting neighbours	0	37,5	25
Meeting friends	12,5	25	25
Others	12,5	12,5	0
Stay at home	87,5 women	62,5 W+men	62,5 W+men
Paper-works	12,5	12,5	12,5
Travel times minutes	58	50	45
Visit other districts: Oft	25	25	37,5
Rarely	50	50	62,5
Always	12,5	12,5	0
Never	37,5	25	0

References

References

ALTERMANN, R., and CARS, G. (1991). *"Neighbourhood regeneration and evaluation"*. Mansel, 1991

ARTHURSON, K., and JACOBS, K. (2003). *"A Critique of the Concept of Social Exclusion and its Utility for Australian Social Housing Policy"*. Australian Housing and Urban Research Institute, Southern Research Centre. Paper presented at the UK Housing Studies Association Conference, Bristol, September 2003.

ASSAEL, H. (1998). *"La Búsqueda de la equidad"*. In: Revista de la Cepal N° 50, 1998. www.eclac.org/espanol/Revistacepal/rvcincuenta/Assael.htm

ATKINSON, R., and KINTREA, K. (2001) *"Neighbourhoods and social exclusion: The research and policy implications of neighbourhood effects"*. Department of Urban Studies University of Glasgow. Discussion Paper, September 2001

BAKER, J. (2001). *"Urban Poverty and Social Exclusion in Uruguay"*. World Bank, Urban Development. http://wbln0018.worldbank.org/UrbanCalendar/urban.nsf/0/ 8dbac70e4c0382f685256b1e0076 dd63?OpenDocument

BALCHIN P., and RHODEN, M. (1998) (Eds.). Housing: The Essential Foundations. Routledge, London and New York.

BASSET, K. and SHORT, J.R. (1980). *"Housing and Residential Structure. Alternative Approaches"*. Routledge & Kegan Paul, 1980

BECK, U. (2000). *"Mundo feliz: La precariedad del trabajo en la era de la globalización"*. Paídos, Barcelona, 2000

BECKER, H., ET AL. (2002). *"Socially Integrative City Programme:An Encouraging Three Year Appraisal"*. www.difu.de/english/occasional/socially-integrated-city-appraisal.shtml

BORJA, J., and CASTELLS, M. (1997). *"Local y Global: la gestión de las ciudades en la era de la información"*. United Nations for Human Settlements (UNCHS) (Madrid: Taurus)

BOYNE, G.A. (1996). Constrains, Choices and Public Policies. University of Wales, Cardiff. Research in urban policy, Volume 6. Jai Press.

BROUDEHOUX, A.M. (1994). *"Neighbourhood regeneration in Beijing: an overview of projects implemented in the inner city since 1990"*. Chapter 1, definition of concepts. In: http://www.mchg.mcgill.ca/mchg/amb/ambch1.htm

BURGER, T. (1987). *Max Weber's Theory of Concept Formation. History, Laws and Ideal Types*. Expanded Edition, Duke University Press, Durham 1987

BURTON, E. (2000). *"The Potential of the Compact City for Promoting Social Equity"*. In Williams, K. et al (Eds.): Achieving Sustainable Urban Form, pp. 19-29. E & FN SPON, London and New York, 2000

CAMBRIDGE INTERNATIONAL DICTIONARY ONLINE (2001), http://dictionary.cambridge.org

CARMONA, M., and KOLTSEE, T. (1998) *"Neoliberalismo y Estrategias Urbanas"*. Flacso, Sede Costa Rica, 1998.

CASTAÑEDA, J. (1996) *Métodos de Investigación*. Mc Graw Hill, Mexico 1996

CED (1990). *"Santiago Dos Ciudades: análisis de la estructura socio-espacial de la región metropolitana de Santiago"*. Centro de Estudios para el Desarrollo, Santiago 1990.

C.A. (1998). Documento: Reseña de la Vivienda Social en Chile: Separata Revista CA (Ciudad y Arquitectura), pp. 12-17. Enero, 1988

COLEGIO DE.ARQUITECTOS (2003). Colegio de Arquitectos de Chile, in: www.arqchile.cl/colegio_de_arquit.htm

COLLADOS, A. (1996). *"Compatibilizar vivienda y urbanismo"*. In Revista CA, Ciudad y A Aquitectura N°86, octubre-diciembre 1996.

CUMMINGS, J., and DI PASQUALE, D. (1997). *"The Spatial Implications of Housing Policy in Chile"*. www.cityresearch.com

DAVIS, S. (1995). *The Architecture of Affordable Housing*. University of California Press, June 1995

DAVIS, M. (1992). *City of Quartz: Excavating the Future in Los Angeles*. Vintage Books USA, March 1992

DE MATTOS, C. (1999). *"Santiago de Chile, globalización y expansion metropolitana: lo que existía sigue existiendo"*. In EURE, Revista Latinoamericana de Estudios Urbano Regionales, Vol. XXV, N° 76, Diciembre 1999, pp. 29-56

DE RAMON, A. (2000). *Santiago de Chile: (1541-1991) historia de una sociedad urbana*. Editorial Sudamericana, Buenos Aires, 2000.

DIFU (2000). *" Programmgrundlagen"*. Deutsche Institut für Urbanistik, DIFU, Arbeitspapiere zum Programm Soziale Stadt, Band 3, Februar 2000

DREIER, P., ET AL. (2001). *"Place Matters. Metropolitics for the twenty-first century"*. University Press of Kansas, 2001.

DUCCI, M.E. (1997). *"El lado obcuro de una política de vivienda existosa"*. In EURE, Revista Latinoamericana de Estudios Urbano Regionales, Vol. XXIII, N° 69, Julio 1997, pp. 99-115.

-------- (1997). *"Santiago, ¿una mancha de aceite sin fin? ¿Qué pasa con la población cuando la ciudad crece indiscriminadamente?"*. In EURE, Revista Latinoamericana de Estudios Urbano Regionales, Vol. XXIV, N° 72, Septiembre 1998.

-------- (1998): *"Urban Health in Chile"*. Instituto de Estudios Urbanos, P. Universidad Católica de Chile in: www.mrc.ac.za/UHDbulletin/june98/chile.htm

ECLAC (1995) *The Equity Gap*. Economic Commission for Latin American and Caribbean Countries in: http:/www.eclac.org/english/basictexts/gab.html

ENGELS, F. (2000). *"The Great Towns"*. In R, T. Le Gates, and F. Stout (Eds.), The City Reader ,pp.46-55. Second Edition (2000)

FARIA, V. (1994). *"Social Exclusion in Latin America: An Annotated Bibliography"*. International Institute for Labour Studies, IILS, in: www.ilo.org/public/english/bureau/inst/papers/1994/dp70/

FAUSET, P. G. (2000). *"The Hulme State and the 'Homes for Change' Development: Britain's First Major Sustainable Housing Project"*. In Williams, K. et al (Eds.): Achieving Sustainable Urban Form, pp. 303-309. E & FN SPON, London and New York, 2000

FERRAZ, A.R. (1999). *"Economic Adjustment and Housing Policy : General Trends and the Chilean Case"*. Primer Congreso Virtual de Arquitectura. Diciembre 1999 - Enero 2000.

FORREST, R., ET AL. (1999). *Home Ownership in Crisis? The British experience of negative equity economic*. Ashgate Publishing Ltd.

FISCHER, K., ET AL. (2003). *"Transformación económica, políticas y producción de la segregación social en chile y méxico"*. in Scripta Nova, revista electrónica de geografía y ciencias sociales, Universidad de Barcelona, Agosto 2003.

FOSIS (2002). *"Proyecto Piloto :'Formación para la vida en comunidad'"*. Convenio entre el Fondo de Solidaridad e Inversion Social (Fosis) y el Ministerio de la Vivienda y Urbanismo (MINVU). Resumen preliminar de la experiencia, Marzo, 2002

FRANKE, T., ET AL. (2001) . *"Neighbourhood Management - A Key Instrument in Integrative Urban District Development"*. Paper delivered at the EURA- Conference, *"Area-based initiatives in contemporary urban policy - innovations in city governance"*, Copenhagen, 17-19 MAy 2001

GIBALDI, J. (2001). *MLA Handbook for Writers of Research Papers*. Fourth Edition. The Modern Language Association of America, New York, 1995.

GILBERT, A. (1998). *The Latin American City*. Revised edition. Printed by Russell Press, Notthingham NG7 §HJ.

-------- (1996) (Ed.). *The Mega City in Latin America*. United Nations University Press, In: www.unu.edu/unupress/unubooks/uu23me/uu23me00.thm

-------- (1999). *"The diffusion of Housing Subsidiary Programmes: informed adoption or forced feeding"*. University College London, DPU, in: http://www.hull.ac.uk/futgov/housesub.htm

-------- (2001). *"Power, ideology and the Washington consensus: The development and spread of Chilean Housing Policy"*. Future Governance Papers, in: http://www.hull.ac.uk/futgov/papers/Pubpapers/Gilbert4.pdf

GOUGH, I., and OLOFSSON, G. (1999). *Capitalism and Social Cohesion*. MacMillan Press Ltd., 1999

GROSS, P. (1988). *"La vivienda social hasta 1950"*. In Documento: Reseña de la Vivienda Social en Chile:Separata Revista CA (Ciudad y Arquitectura), pp. 12-17. Enero 1988

GUROVICH, A. (1988). *"Las Articulaciones Urbanas"*. In Documento: Reseña de la Vivienda Social en Chile:Separata Revista CA (Ciudad y Arquitectura), pp. 62-65. Enero1988

HALL, P., and PFEIFFER, U. (2000). *Urban Future 21: A global agenda for twenty-first century cities*. The Federal Ministry of Transport, Building and Housing of the Republic of Germany .E & FN SPON 2000

HARAMOTO, E. (1983). *"Políticas de vivienda social: Experiencia Chilena de las últimas tres décadas"*. In Mac Donald, J. "Vivienda Social", Santiago. Corporación de Promoción Universitaria, 1983.

-------- (1988). *"La Vivienda Social Chilena. 1950/85"*. In Documento: Reseña de la Vivienda Social en Chile:Separata Revista CA (Ciudad y Arquitectura), pp. 57-61. Enero 1988

-------- (2000) *"El Diseño de la vivienda y de su entorno barrial y urbano"* . In Sugranyes, A., et al.: Consulta sobre la política habitacional en Chile, pp. 129-135. Oficina de desarrollo urbano para Sur América, RUDO, USAID Santiago de Chile, enero 2000.

HARBERGER, A. (1979). *"Notas sobre los problemas de vivienda y planificación de la ciudad"*. In Revista AUCA N° 37, 1979. pp 39-41.

HARVEY, D. (1979). Urbanismo y desigualdad social. Siglo Veintiuno Editores, Impreso en Mexico, 1979.

-------- (1989). *The Condition of Postmodernity: an inquiry into the Origin of Cultural Change*. Blackwell, Oxford.

-------- (2000) *"Social Justice, Postmodernism, and the City"*. In R, T. Le Gates, and F. tout (Eds.), The City Reader ,pp.199-207. Second Edition (2000)

HÄUSSERMANN, H., ET AL. (2001). *"Berlin: innovative policies for social integration"*. In Keskloot, O. "The Spatial Dimensions of Urban Social Exclusion and Integration". In Urbex Series No. 21. http://gp.fmg.uva.nl/urbex/

HIDALGO, R. (1999). *"La vivienda social en chile: la accion del estado en un siglo de planes y programas"*. in www.ub.es/geocrit/sn-45-1.htm

-------- (2002). *"Vivienda social y espacio urbano en Santiago de Chile: una mirada retrospectiva a la acción del Estado en las primeras décadas del siglo XX"*. In EURE, Revista Latinoamericana de Estudios Urbano Regionales, Vol. XXVIII, N° 83, Mayo 2002, pp. 83-106.

IDB (2003). *"Social Exclusion in Latin America"*.Inter-American Development Bank In: http://www.iadb.org/sds/SOC/publication_1740_e.htmInter

INE (1983), Instituto Nacional de Estadísticas. Censos 1970-1982 Cifras Comparativas, Tomo II.

-------- (1992) *Censo Nacional de Poblacion y Vivienda 1992.* Instituto Nacional de Estadísticas

-------- (2003). *Resultados Censo 2002.* Instituto Nacional de Estadísticas. www.ine.cl

INTENDECIA REGIONAL METROPOLITANA, (2001), Estadísticas Regionales. In http:/www.gorerm.cl/estadist2.html

JENKS, M. (2000). *"The Acceptability of Urban Intensification".* In Williams, K. et al (Eds.): Achieving Sustainable Urban Form, pp. 242-250. E & FN SPON, London and New York, 2000

JIMENEZ, F. (1999). *"Reporting Social Well-being through Urban Infrastructure Indicators".* Master's Thesis, Centre for Infrastructure Planning, Stuttgart Universität.

KATZMAN, R. (2001). *"Seducidos y abandonados: el aislamiento social de los pobres urbanos".* In revista de la Cepal, N° 75, Diciembre 2001, pp. 171-189.

KEMENY, J. (1992). *"Housing and Social Theory".* Routledge, London 1992

KNORR-SIEDOW, T.(1999): *"Present and future Outlook for large Housing Estates".* Europäische Akademie für Städtische Umwelt, 1999, in www.eaue.org/hausfut.htm

KUSNETZOFF, F. (1990) (Ed.). *"The State and Housing in Chile -regime types and policy choices".* In Shidlo G. (Ed.) "Housing Policy in Developing Countries", pp. 48-66. Routledge , London 1990

LE GATES, R.T. and STOUT, F. (2000) *The City Reader.* Second Edition, Routledge, Taylor and Francis Group.

LEE P., and MURIE, A. (1999). *Spatial and Social divisions within British Cities. Beyond Residualisation.* Housing Studies, Volume 14, Number 5 / September 1, 1999 Carfax Publishing Company, part of the Taylor & Francis Group.

LEVITAS, R. (1998). *"The inclusive society?: Social exclusion and new Labour".* MacMillan Press Ltd. Hampshire and London, 1998.

LUONGO, M., and BAIRES, S. (2001).*"Socio-spatial Segregation and Urban Land Regulation in Latin American Cities".* Lincoln Institute of Land Policy, Conference Paper, in: www.lincolninst.edu/pubs/dl/603_luongo_baires.pdf

MAC DONALD, J. (1994). *"¿Cuantas casas faltan? El déficit a nivel nacional y regional".* Documento de Trabajo N o 16-94, Corporación de Promoción Universitaria, Santiago, Chile.

MADANIPOUR, A., ET AL (1998).*"Social Exclusion in European Cities, processes, experiences and responses".* London, The Stationary Office.

MARCUSE, P., and VAN KEMPEN, R. (eds.) *Of States and Cities: The partitioning of urban space.* Oxford University Press 2002

MARTINEZ, U. (1999). *Pobreza, segregación y exclusion espacial. La vivienda de los inmigrantes extranjeros en España.* Icaria, Institut Català d'Antropologia.

MASSEY, D., and DENTON, N. (1988). *The dimensions of residential segregation.* Social Forces, 67 , pp. 281-315

-------- (1993). *American Apartheid: Segregation and the Making of the Underclass.* Cambridge, MA: Harvard University Press.

MIDEPLAN (1999). *"Resultados de la VII encuesta de caracterización socio-económica nacional"* (CASEN 1998). Documento N°6, situación habitacional en chile 1990-1998. Santiago de Chile, julio 1999. www.mideplan.cl

MINEDUC (2001) *Déficit de escuelas en la Región Metropolitana*. Ministerio de Educación.

MINVU (1979). *Política Nacional de Desarrollo Urbano*. Ministerion de la vivienda y urbansimo. Santiago.

-------- (1984) *Decreto Supremo N°62*. Programa Vivienda Básica

------- (1989). *Ley y Ordenanza General de Urbanismo y Construcciones.*

-------- (1994) *Plan Regulador Metropolitano de Santiago*. E&C Editora y Catalogos S.A., Santiago de Chile, 1995.

-------- (2000) *Informativo Estadistico N° 247*. Noviembre- Diciembre 2000

-------- (2001) *Diagnóstico de Patologías en la edificación de viviendas sociales*. División Técnica de Estudio y Fomento Habitacional. Santiago de Chile, 2001

-------- (2002) *"Satisfacción residencial en la vivienda básica serviu: la perspectiva del capital social"*. División Técnica de Estudio y Fomento Habitacional. Santiago de Chile, 2002

MOFFAT, S. (2000) *"Vivienda social e institucionalidad"*. In Sugranyes, A., et al.: Consulta sobre la política habitacional en Chile. pp. 188-198. Oficina de desarrollo urbano para Sur América, RUDO, USAID Santiago de Chile, enero 2000.

MORRIS, J. and WINN, M. (1990). *"Housing and Social Inequality"*. London, Shipman 1990

MOULIAN, T. (1997). *"Chile actual: anatomía de un mito"*. LOM Editores, Universidad Arcis, 1997

MURIE, A. (2001). *"The Dynamics of Social Exclusion and Neighbourhood Decline: Housing Welfare Regimes and the Underclass"*.In Eurex, Lecture 4, University of Birmingham.

MUSTERD, S. (2000). *"Social Exclusion adn Segregation: Neighbourhoods effects"*. In Eurex, Lecture 5, University von Amsterdam (Draft).

-------- (2001): *"The Spatial Dimensions of Social Exclusion and Integration"*. Urbex Series No. 20. A Comparative report on social exclusion and integration in neighbourhoods. European Union Fourth RTD Framework Programme 2001

NIETO, L.M. (2000). *"Recuento y diagnóstico de 15 años de la política habitacional. Produccion de Vivienda y equipamiento"*. In SUGRANYES, A., ET AL.: Consulta sobre la política habitacional en Chile. pp. 34-59. Oficina de desarrollo urbano para Sur América, RUDO, USAID Santiago de Chile, enero 2000.

NOVOMERC (2001) *"Descripcion de los grupos socioeconomicos en chile: grupos socio-economicos en Santiago de chile"*. In www.novomerc.cl/poblacion.html

OLIVARES, G. (2002). *"Estudio de las ventajas y desventajas de desarrollar soluciones habitacionales para estratos medio-bajo y bajo en comunas interiores de la ciudad de Santiago"*. Informe de Práctica Profesional. Instituto de Geografía de la Pontificia Universidad Católica de Chile. Marzo, 2002

O'LEARY J. (1998). *"Town Planning and Housing Development"*. Balchin P., and Rhoden, M. (1998)(Eds.). Housing: The Essential Foundations, pp. 122-153. Routledge, London and New York.

PAQUETTE-VASALLI, C. (1998). *"Le logemont locatif dans les quartiers populaires de Santiago du Chili: Les Raissons de essor limite"* .Doctorate's Thesis in Urbanism, Ecolé Nationale des Ponts et Chauseés, July 1998.

PARDO, C. (2000). *" Housing Finance in Chile: The Experience in Primary and Secondary Mortgage Financing"*. Inter-American Development Bank, Washington, D. C. Sustainable Development Department Best Practices Series. http:www.iadb.org/sds/ifm

PORTES, A. (1989). *"Latin American Urbanization in The years of the Crisis"*. Working paper N°1, Program In Comparative International Development. Department of Sociology Johns Hopkins University Baltimore. Latin American Research Review. Vol.24. n°3.

POWER, A., and WILSON, J. (2000). *"Social Exclusion and the Future of Cities"*. CASE paper 35, February, London.

RICHARDS, B. (1995). *"Poverty and Housing in Chile: the Development of a Neo-liberal Welfare State"*. In Habitat International, Vol. 19. N°4. pp. 515-527. Elsevier Science Ltd. Printed in Great Britain.

RODRIGUEZ, A. and ICAZA, A.M. (1989): *"Evictions and the right to housing"*. in www.idrc.ca/books/focus/861/bibliog.html

--------- and WINCHESTER, L. (2001). *"Santiago de Chile. Metropolización, globalización, desigualdad"*. In EURE, Revista Latinoamericana de Estudios Urbano Regionales, Vol. XXVII, N° 80, Mayo 2001. pp. 121-139

ROJAS, E. (1999). *"The Long Road to Housing Reform. Lessons from the Chilean Experience"*. Inter-American Development Bank Washington, D. C. Sustainable Development Department Best Practices Series. www.iadb.org/sds/soc

-------- and GREENE, M. (1995). *"Reaching the poor: lessons from the Chilean housing experience"*. Environment & Urbanisation, 7-2, pp 31-49 quoted by Rojas, E. in: www.iadb.org/sds/utility.cfm/173/english/pub/1080

ROMAN, O. (2000). *Estrategia de Desarrollo Santiago Región 2000-2005*. Ordenamiento Territorial e Infraestructura. Diagnóstico estratégico, 2000

ROMERO, L.A. (1997). *"¿Qué hacer con los pobres? Elite y sectores populares en Santiago de Chile, 1840-1895"*. Editorial Sudamericana, Buenos Aires, 1997

SABATINI, F. (1999). *"Segregación Social en Santiago de Chile: conceptos, métodos y efectos urbanos"*. Lincoln Institute Research Report. Lincoln Institute of Land Policy, 1999

-------- (2000). *"Reforma de los mercados de suelo en Santiago, Chile: efectos sobre los precios de la tierra y la segregacion residencial"*. In EURE, Revista Latinoamericana de Estudios Urbano Regionales, Vol. XXVI, N° 77, Marzo, 2000.

-------- ET AL. (2001). *"Segregación residencial en las principales ciudades chilenas: Tendencias de las tres últimas decadas y posibles cursos de acción"*. In EURE, Revista Latinoamericana de Estudios Urbano Regionales, Vol. XXVII, N° 82, Diciembre 2001. pp. 21-42

SAITH, R. (2001). *"Social Exclusion: the Concept and Application to Developing Countries"*. QEH Working Paper Series Working Paper Number 72. Queen Elizabeth House, University of Oxford

SASSEN, S. (1991). *The Global City: New York, London, Tokyio*. Princeton: Princeton University Press.

-------- (1994). *Cities in a World Economy*. Thousand Oaks, Pine Forge Press, 1994

SAUNDERS, P. (1993). *Social Theory and the Social Question*. Second Edition, Routledge, London, 1993

SAVAGE, M., and WARDE, A. (1993). *Urban Sociology Capitalism and Modernity*. Sociology for a Changing World.

SCHTEINGART, M. (2000): *"Pobreza y Alternativas de Equidad Social"*. El Colegio de Mexico 2000.

SCOTT, J.C. (1998). *Seeing like a state: how certain schemes to improve the human condition have failed*. Yale University Press, New Haven and London, 1998.

SECTRA (1997) *Plan de Desarrollo del Sistema de Transporte del Gran Santiago 1995-2010*. 1997. Ministerio de Transportes y Telecomunicaciones, Chile, 1997

SEN, A. (1999). *"Sustainable Human Development: Concepts and Priorities"*. In: htpp:/www.undp.org/hdro/oc8b.html.

-------- (2000). *"Social Exclusion: Concept, Application, and Scrutiny"*. Asian Development Bank, Office of Environment and Social Development: June 2000.

SENNETT, R. (2002). *Carne y Piedra. El cuerpo y la ciudad en la civilización occidental.* Alianza Editorial, Madrid,

SILVA, S. (1997). *"Análisis de la evolución de la política habitacional"*. Informe final. Ministerio de la vivienda y urbanismo, Santiago. Estudios de la vivienda social. pp. 263-280.

SHIDLO, G. (1990) (Ed.). *"Housing Policy in Developing Countries"*. Routledge , London 1990

SKIFTER, H. (2001). *"Excluded places. On the Interaction between Segregation, Urban Decay and Deprived Neighbourhoods"*. Article for Journal of Housing and the Built Environment. www.by-cg-byg.dk/eura/workshops/papers/workshop2/skifter.pdf

SMITH, A. (2001) Regeneration Paper. Presented to the session *"Beyond the social construction of nature: re-thinking political economy and environment"*, at the AAG Meeting New York City 2001. www.aag.org

SMOLKA, M., and SABATINI, F. (2000). *"Land Market Deregulation Debate in Chile"*. Lincoln Institute of Land Policy, Landlines. www.lincolninst.edu/landlines/2000/January/January2.htm

SOJA, E. (2000). *Postmetropolis, Critical Studies of Cities and Regions.* Blackwell Publishers 2000

STREN, R. (ed.) (1995) *Urban Research in the Developing World.* Volume 3: Latin America. Centre for Urban and Community Studies, University of Toronto.

-------- (1998). *Urban Research in the Developing World: From Governance to Security.* Comparative Urban Studies Project, Occasional Paper No. 16. Woodrow Wilson International Center for Scholars, 1998.

SUGRANYES, A., ET AL. (2000). *Consulta sobre la política habitacional en Chile.* Informe final. Oficina de desarrollo urbano para Sur América, RUDO, USAID Santiago de Chile, enero 2000.

TURNER, J. (1976). *Housing by People.* Towards Autonomy in Buildings Environments. Marion Boyars, London- New York. Reprinted 1991.

UNCHS (2001) *Cities in a Globalizing World: Global Report on Human Settlements, 2001* United Nations Centre for Human Settlements (Habitat)

UNCRD (1994) *Enhancing the management of metropolitan living environments in Latin America* . United Nations Centre for Regional Development, Research Report Series No. 1, 1994

UNDP (1998). *"Desarrollo humano en Chile 1998:Las Paradojas de la modernización"*. Programa de Naciones Unidas para el desarrollo, PNUD Marzo 1998.

-------- (2000). *Desarrollo humano en las comunas de Chile.* Programa de Naciones Unidas para el desarrollo, PNUD. Temas del desarrollo sustentable, 2000.

UNITED NATIONS (1995): *"The future of human settlements: Good Policy can make a difference"*. Preparatory Committee for the UN Conference on Human Settlements, Habitat II. A/Conf.165/PC.3/CRP.2. 15 November 1995.

UNESCO (2000). *"Urban Research in Latin America"* - Discussion Paper Series - No 4. in: http:/www.unesco.org/most/valleng.html.

UNRISD (1994). *"Social Integration: Approaches and Issues"*. Briefing paper N°1, World Summit for Social Development, March 1994.

U.S. CENSUS BUREAU (2002). *"Residential Segregation: definitions"*. In: http://www.census.gov/hhes/www/housing/def.html

VALLADARES, L. and PRATES, M. (1994). *"Urban Research in Latin America: Towards a*

Research Agenda". In: http://www.unesco.org/most/valleng.htm

VAN KEMPEN, R. (1998): *"Divided Cities in the Netherlands: Ethnic Segregation, Urban Problems and the Policy Agenda"*. Paper presented at the International Conference on Divided Cities and Strategies for Undivided Cities, Göteborg, Sweden - May 25-26 1998. In: www.international.metropolis.net/events/goth/dividedcities.html

VAN VLIET, W. (1998). *"The Encyclopaedia of Housing"*. Sage, Thousand Oaks, CA, 1998

VRANKEN, J. (2000): *"Social differentiation, social fragmentation, social inequality and social exclusion"*. In Eurex, Lecture 4, University von Antwerpen (Draft)

WACQUANT, L. (1991). *'What makes a ghetto? Notes toward a comparative analysis of modes of social exclusion'*. Paper presented at: Conference on Poverty, Immigration, and Urban Marginality in Advanced Societies, Maison Surger, Paris, May 1991.

------- (2002). *'The Rise of Advanced Marginality'*, in P. Marcuse and R. van Kempen (eds.), Of States and Cities: The partitioning of urban space, 221-239. Oxford University Press 2002

WHITE, P. (1998). *"Ideologies, social exclusion and spatial segregation"*. In Musterd, S and Ostendorf, W (eds.), Urban Segregation and the Welfare State, Londres, Routledge.

WHITEHEAD, C.M. (2003). *"Restructuring Social Housing Systems"*. In Forrest, R., and Lee, J.(Eds.): Housing and Social Change, East-West Perspectives. Housing and Society Series. London.

WILLIAMS, K. (2000). *"Does Intensifying Cities make them More Sustainable"*. In Williams, K. et al (Eds.): Achieving Sustainable Urban Form. pp. 30- 45. E & FN SPON, London and New York, 2000

WORLD BANK (1992) *The housing indicators program. Volume II: Indicator tables*. Washington D.C. - (1993) Housing: Enabling markets to work. A World Bank Policy Paper.

------- (1997). *Chile. Poverty and Income Distribution in a High-Growth Economy 1987-1995*, Washington DC (Report 16377-CH)

------ - HABITAT. (1994). *Housing Indicators, 1994 edition*, Washington DC quoted by Rojas, E. in : www.iadb.org/sds/utility.cfm/173/english/pub/1080

YOUNG, I.M. (1990). *Justice and the Politics of difference*. Princeton University Press, 1990

-------- (2000). *Inclusion and Democracy*. Oxford University Press, Oxford political theory, 2000

ZEGRAS, C., and GAKENHEIMER, R. (2000). *"Urban Growth Management for Mobility: The Case of the Santiago, Chile Metropolitan Region"*. MIT. Department of Urban Studies and Planning

ZEYLMANS, M. (2002). *" 'Welfare Capitalism and Social Capitalism' - Comparing the ideals of Welfare States"*. Comparison of Welfare States in the United States, Germany and Chile. In: http://tis.zdv.uni-tuebingen.de/webroot/sp/spsba01_W98_1/comparison.htm

ZICCARDI, A. (2000). *"Las ciudades y la cuestión social"*. In Revista de la Escuela de Económia y Negocios, Año II, No. 4, abril 2000. In: www.unsam.edu.ar/unsam/Ediciones/articulos4/Ziccardi.pdf